**Calderdale College Library**
Tel: 01422 399350

You may renew this item for a further period by post, telephone or personal visit, provided it is not required by another reader. Please quote your ID no. and the seven digit number on the barcode label.
**No more than three renewals are permitted.**

**NB** Overdue books are charged at 5 pence per item per day.

# ASPECTS *of* LEEDS

## Discovering Local History

# 3

Edited by
## Lynne Stevenson Tate

*Series Editor*
Brian Elliott

**Wharncliffe Books**

**First Published in 2001 by**
**Wharncliffe Publishing**
**an imprint of**
**Pen and Sword Books Limited,**
**47 Church Street, Barnsley,**
**South Yorkshire. S70 2AS**

Copyright © Wharncliffe Books 2001

*For up-to-date information on other titles produced under the*
*Wharncliffe imprint, please telephone or write to:*

**Wharncliffe Books**
**FREEPOST**
**47 Church Street**
**Barnsley**
**South Yorkshire S70 2BR**
**Telephone (24 hours): 01226 - 734555**

**ISBN: 1-903425-05-0**

A CIP catalogue record of this book is available from the
British Library

**Cover illustration:** *Rothwell's Parade, New Briggate (demolished 1960s)*

Printed in Great Britain by CPI UK

# CONTENTS

# INTRODUCTION

## *by Lynne Stevenson Tate*

CURIOSITY IS A TRAIT COMMON to most people. We are curious about what will happen to us in the future; curious about what is happening around us now and curious about what has happened in the past. Walking through the streets of our cities, towns and villages, particular buildings and features impose themselves on our conscious and questions begin to form in our minds. Why was that building built like that? What was here before the ring road? Why is there a tunnel in the middle of this lane?

It is questions like these that fuel the drive of local history and the *Aspects* series, from Wharncliffe Publishing; and are the ideal vehicle to carry the articles which are the result of the research undertaken in response to these questions by someone who was interested enough to carry it out.

*Aspects of Leeds 3* has proved an interesting volume to work on. For the first time we have widened our geographical area to include all the areas which now have a Leeds postcode, even though historically, the ties to Leeds may never have been too strong. This has meant that articles on Aberford, Lotherton and Burley-in-Wharfedale could now be included.

Once again our authors are many and varied. Some are first timers who have never had anything published before. Some have been published before but are first timers in the Aspect series. You may be all familiar with the phrase 'like father, like son', but the Saffer's have turned this around. David Saffer is the co-author of an article on Leeds United, which appeared in *Aspects of Leeds 2*. He encouraged his father Dr Harold Saffer to write an article for this current volume. I am sure that this is a first. David has written more about Leeds united in this volume; this time between the years 1919 and 1939.

Isadore Pear has produced an article on boxing in Leeds based on the recollections of some who actually fought at that time.

Tony Shelton has been researching those dream builders, the Thompson family for many years, and has produced an article for this volume based around their involvement in the Golden Acre estate. Margaret Ratcliffe reminds us that the famous author of *Swallow's and Amazons*, Arthur Ransome (and his family) had strong links with Leeds and the University here. The University also played a large part in the life of Arthur Greenhow Lupton. This eminent businessman and patron of good causes in the late nineteenth and early twentieth centuries is the subject of Joan Newiss' article.

Burley-in-Wharfedale is the setting for Pam Shaw's article and she charts the rise and fall of industrialization through the influence of Foster and Fison's mill. Maisie Morton's family had strong roots in an area of Armley known as 'the hill'. This area was originally the site of some old tenter's fields and a small, mixed community grew up there. It has all gone now. Roundhay Hall is now the site of a BUPA hospital but the house and grounds have gone through a number of owners and change of use over time and Margaret Plows links all of these together.

Christine Nolan and Harold Saffer give overviews of two very dissimilar Institutes. Christine's article is on the short lived National Institute of House Workers which, in the years immediately after the war, aimed at improving the lot of the cleaning lady by setting minimum standards of pay and conditions. Harold Saffer took up a career in dentistry and provides insight into the training and practices of a profession, which has changed so dramatically in the second half of the twentieth century.

Villages may grow or contract over time as industries, occupations or situations exert influences on the indigenous communities. Some villages are swallowed up into the encroaching cities and some may disappear all together. One of these was the village of Lotherton whose history is charted by Dave Weldrake from its pre-history to the present day. Near to Lotherton is Aberford and during a visit to some friends who live there we were taken on a walk around the village. During this walk we came across a tunnel, the remains of some sort of a raised platform and some buildings at the end of a type of hard surfaced lane leading apparently nowhere. Graham Hudson's article enlightened me to its purpose. It is the site of the old, unusual railway called the Aberford Fly Line.

It is always a challenge to put together twelve disparate articles and turn them into a book. The stars are of course the authors, who have been very patient while waiting to see their work in print. My thanks go to them and I hope they are satisfied with the end result.

Thanks are due as always to the Wharncliffe team. Brian Elliott, the series editor for his steady hand on the tiller, and finally to the production team for the unique *Aspects* look to the finished book.

This book is dedicated to all those local historians past and present whose work is so important to us, so if you have an article we may be interested in, do let me know.

# 1. THE ABERFORD FLY LINE

## *by Graham Hudson*

THE FOOTPATH KNOWN AS THE FLY LINE runs from Garforth to Aberford through the old Parlington estate. Once this was the route of a standard-gauge railway, carrying coal, passengers and goods to the Great North Road, but so largely has the site now returned to nature that, walking the Fly Line today, one may doubt trains ever ran this way at all. Thus the appearance of a tunnel on the route, known as the Dark Arch, is a reassurance to the rambler. But trains did not go through this tunnel – they went round it.

Garforth and Parlington lie on the northern outcrops of the West Yorkshire coalfield, where the Beeston, the Middleton Main, the Middleton Little and other seams crop out.[1] Prominent among those with an interest in the coal were the Gascoignes, who were mining hereabouts as early as the seventeenth century. With the death of the last baronet, Sir Thomas Gascoigne, in 1810, the family's lands and coalmines passed to his step-son-in-law Richard Oliver, who added the old family name to his own.[2] It was he, Richard Oliver Gascoigne, who in the 1830s was to build the Fly Line as the essential rail link for his coal trade to the north (Figure 1). Within a few years of its inception however, as the network of main lines rapidly extended throughout the county, the need for the railway was to be much reduced, and the Fly Line's role thereafter would be that of local branch-line, the communications link between Aberford and the outside world, until the railway's closure through road competition in the twentieth century.

Although the town was less than nine miles to the west, and accessible mostly over turnpike roads, Mr Gascoigne's collieries had no trade with Leeds, nor was there trade southwards into the Aire valley, both districts being well served by collieries closer to hand. But his pits were ideally situated to supply districts off the coal measures. Thus, coal from Garforth and Parlington went north up the Great

**Figure 1.** Richard Oliver Gascoigne, 1763 - 1843, owner of the Parlington and Garforth collieries and builder of the Aberford Railway. *Leeds Museums & Galleries (Lotherton Hall)*

North Road to Wetherby, Knaresborough and Boroughbridge; north-east to Tadcaster and into the Ainsty (but not to York which could be more cheaply supplied from the collieries in the Aire valley via the Aire & Calder and Ouse navigations), and east towards Selby (though as that town itself was on the Ouse, its trade too was outside Gascoigne's trading area).

Coal was sold only at the pit bank – it was not delivered. It was the coal merchants themselves who made the long journeys to Garforth from Wetherby and elsewhere. In 1758 Charles Brandling laid a waggonway from his Middleton Colliery to Leeds to supply a depot for coal sales on the edge of town, and in 1774 Sir Thomas Gascoigne had planned a sixteen mile canal and waggonway system to link Garforth with the Wharfe below Tadcaster, which would have enabled him to establish a coal depot with river links to Selby and York.[3] But this ambitious scheme was taken no further.

The collieries had always been worked as part of the estate and managed by local men. Gascoigne chose to continue mining as a family concern also but, possibly in the capacity of a new broom, and lacking that familiarity with coal mining that his predecessors had accrued over the generations, went elsewhere for his expertise, in 1813 appointing Thomas Fenwick of County Durham as his coal viewer. On taking up the post Fenwick found several pits working the Beeston coal at the Parlington Colliery, which Sir Thomas Gascoigne had opened in 1801, and a single coal pit over towards Barnbow.[4] He recommended that the latter be finished as soon as possible and, foreseeing Parlington also working out within a few years, advised it was time for Gascoigne to establish a new colliery. Initially Fenwick considered making the new winning at Hawks Nest on the south of Parlington, thus to access further Beeston, but problems with water when Parlington was abandoned were foreseen, and in the event the colliery was sited even further south, in the Firth Field, to work the Middleton Main and Middleton Little seams. Opened in 1815, this was Garforth Colliery.

In 1819 another Durham man, John Watson, replaced Fenwick as coal viewer. Taking stock of the collieries' trade, Watson noted that incursions into their market area were now being made by collieries in the Aire valley and others near Barnsley – pits with access to the Ouse, Wharfe and Ure via the Aire & Calder. Also the coal now being raised from Garforth Colliery was proving to be of inferior quality, and Watson feared there would be serious loss of trade when Parlington closed and Gascoigne's pits could no longer supply Beeston.[5]

In 1820 the combined sales from Gascoigne's two collieries was close on 40,000 tons but when in 1822 Parlington finally worked out, leaving only Garforth in work, sales fell to less than 26,000.[6] A new source of Beeston coal was now essential and Watson revived Fenwick's earlier idea of sinking at Hawks Nest. To facilitate future drainage (for apart from the proximity of the now flooded Parlington workings the sandstone beneath Hawks Nest was known to be deeply saturated) Watson ordered the extension northwards of an existing drainage tunnel or 'driftway' serving Garforth Colliery. This was already close on a mile and a half in length, discharging into Kippax Beck on the parish boundary, and would have to be driven most of the further 1550 yards between the Firth Field and Hawks Nest before sinking could commence (Figure 2).

Slightly over two miles west of Garforth, and serving much the same market area, was Samuel Waud's Manston Colliery. Waud's pits also worked the Beeston, but Gascoigne's closer proximity to the Great North Road had so far given him the trade advantage. Then, in either 1827 or 1828, Waud opened another pit to the Beeston at Crossgates a mile or so further west, coincidentally with the opening of a new turnpike between Leeds and Collingham.[7] This turnpike afforded a more direct route from Wetherby, and the trade advantage now passed to Waud. The distances to both Garforth and Crossgates were an even ten miles, but as yet Gascoigne could supply only the less favoured Middleton coals. In 1828 Garforth's sales fell to a new low of less than 23,000 tons.

With his existing trade confined largely to the north, and that trade now seriously affected, Gascoigne was not the only West Riding industrialist feeling the need for better communications. Proposals for a Leeds-Hull railway surveyed by George Stephenson, which would have passed through Garforth, had been published in 1825. Gascoigne is known to have obtained estimates of the costs of iron rails from the Tindale Fell colliery in Cumberland at about this time, probably in connection with a prospective branch line from Hawks Nest to the proposed railway.[8] Nationwide economic depression however brought postponement of the Leeds-Hull scheme, and when the idea was revived in 1829 it was for a Leeds-Selby line (with steam packets plying thence to Hull) based on a new survey by James Walker. Gascoigne was a member of the railway committee, and was subsequently to be made a director when a company was formed.[9]

Over the intervening seven years work on extending the driftway had continued, but only intermittently, and the drift was still 600 yards short of Hawks Nest when the Leeds & Selby Railway received its Act

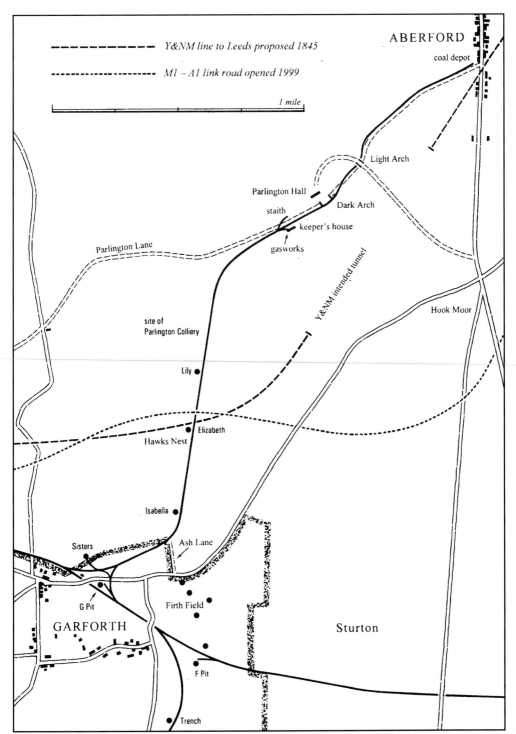

**Figure 2.** General location map showing the pits of Garforth Colliery and the route of the Aberford Railway. Built-up areas in Garforth are indicated as c.1850; the line of tone shows the approximate boundary of urban Garforth today.

of Parliament at the end of May 1830. Construction began in October.

Early in 1831 William Wharton was appointed colliery auditor. Also a Durham man, it was Wharton who was to see the solution to the problem of Gascoigne's dwindling north trade which, as he quickly came to acknowledge, was 'all flown to Manston'.[10] On the evening of 12 February 1831, Wharton wrote to Watson describing how progress in the drift was currently much hampered by old workings encountered in the Middleton Main, and suggesting that borings be made at the point then reached to ascertain whether there was much water in the sandstone below, and if there proved not to be:

> *. . . why not sink close by, to the Lower seam & lay a railway by way of Parlington to Aberford which will bring there best coals much nearer to the Tadcaster & Wetherby markets than Mr Waud's Coals, which seem to me to be driving ours out of this market – It strikes me also that this new Railway will be of much service in forming a direct communication for heavy goods, Corn, etc between Aberford and Leeds, by way of the new Railway & the carts coming from Tadcaster could bring goods from Tadcaster to Aberford to be forwarded from there by the Railway at trifling cost.*[11]

Wharton added that these musings had been 'all off work &... occurred to me this morning – on looking into the map & considering how easily a Railway might be laid...'[12] Thus, the Aberford Fly Line enjoys the distinction, perhaps unique in railway history, that for this line we have not only the day on which it was first thought of, but almost the very hour.

Both proposals were accepted, shaft sinking commencing in June 1831. But whatever was concluded from any trial borings made, considerable difficulties with underground water *were* to be experienced, resulting in the tubbing of the shaft – its lining with cast iron – where it passed

**Figure 3.** Isabella pit c.1920. The building on the left is the colliery engine house built in the early 1830s.

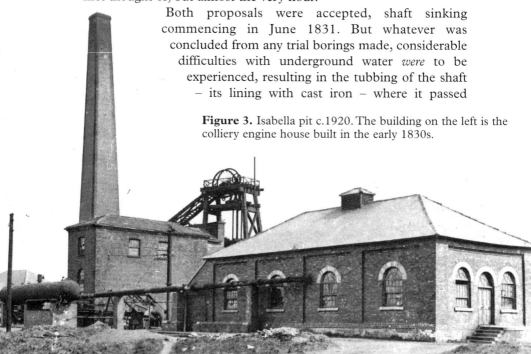

**Figure 4.** Aberford Depot, coal yard and coal staiths in the 1880s.

through the waterlogged sandstone. This perforce also sealed off the intended offtake to the driftway. Thus, when the pumping engine was subsequently installed, water from the shaft sump had to be lifted all the way to the surface instead of being discharged into the drift as originally intended. The drift was to remain of value throughout the working life of the colliery however, keeping the water-table in the sandstone well below the top of the tubbing. Named the Isabella in honour of Mr Gascoigne's elder daughter, the new pit went into production in 1833 (Figure 3). By this date construction of the Leeds & Selby was well advanced.

Inspired by the Leeds & Selby enterprise a committee had also been formed in York for linking York and Leeds by railway. Choosing from three possible routes, the committee, among them George Hudson the future Railway King, opted for a line to join the Leeds & Selby at Garforth, thus to enjoy running rights to Leeds over Leeds & Selby metals. The York & Leeds would inevitably have come through Parlington, very likely passing within 400 yards of Parlington Hall, and to secure Gascoigne's concurrence Hudson is said to have promised to build a new residence for the family well away from the railway.[13] The siting of the existing Parlington Hall was not without its drawbacks already, and with the added incentive of direct rail communication to York for his colliery Gascoigne was probably more than willing to agree. Representatives from the York & Leeds discussed future arrangements with the Leeds & Selby directors in February 1834.

The survey for Wharton's other brain-child, the Aberford Railway, was prepared in 1833 by William Harker and William Walker, the contract in due course being let to Robert Kirkup, who in another capacity was in charge of the locomotive department of the Leeds & Selby.[14]

The Leeds & Selby Railway opened to passengers on 22 September 1834, goods traffic commencing in December. Through 1835 Gascoigne was to send 13,991 tons of coal over the railway; Waud, 13,212. It is also clear from Leeds & Selby records that Gascoigne's sales to Leeds, the market previously closed to him, proved to be greater than those to Selby – 8,876 tons compared with 1,771. The remaining 3,344 tons were consigned to intermediate points along the line. Some of the Selby coal went on up the Ouse to York, and also down river as part of the coasting trade to the south of England, the first cargo of seaborne coals leaving Selby by schooner bound for Rochester, Kent, early in March 1835.[15] This initial cargo originated in Waud's pits, but no doubt Garforth coal was soon to follow.

Bearing in mind earlier sales figures, and that to the continuing output from Garforth colliery was to be added that of the new Isabella pit, the coal carried by the L&S can represent but a portion of the whole. Apart from some coal sold at the pit-head, the balance – presumably a considerable tonnage – can only have been sold via the new railway coal depot at Aberford, thus fulfilling Wharton's expectations of a return of the colliery's north trade (Figure 4). That the Aberford Railway was certainly in operation by late 1834 is indicated by the Leeds & Selby directors' minutes for 31 October 1834, when Gascoigne's land agent:

> . . . applied for Mr Gascoigne to have sidings provided for him at the following places agreeably to the Act viz at Brown Moor, Crawshaw Cover, Aberford Railway, Two Coal Pits, Sturton Lime Kiln and the Depot at Milford for the Sale of Coal, which were all agreed to.[16]

By this time the possibility of Gascoigne running a passenger service on the Aberford Railway was also in the air, the directors' minutes for their 28 November meeting stating:

> Mr Gascoigne enquires if any coach he may establish on the Aberford Railway in conjunction with the Company's Line will be forwarded attached to the general Train, or the Passengers and Goods taken into the Company's Carriages and on what terms?[17]

As no response to this enquiry was noted in the minutes the directors were presumably non-committal, and it was to be rather more than another two years – February 1837 – before Gascoigne's passenger service actually came into operation.

The reasons for the introduction of the service are not wholly clear. Aberford in the 1830s still had the status of a small market town on the Great North Road, with good communications north and south. To Leeds there were three carriers in the week and, according to Pigot & Co's *National Commercial Directory* of 1834, there was also the Nettle coach, which ran between the *Fox* in Aberford and the *White Hart* in Briggate, Leeds, on Tuesdays, Thursdays and Saturdays (8am from the *Fox*; 4pm from the *White Hart*). However, there is no reference to this conveyance, nor to any other Aberford-Leeds coach, in Baines & Newsome's *General & Commercial Directory of the Borough of Leeds* published five years later, so perhaps by this time the Nettle had been discontinued, leaving Gascoigne's tenantry with no easy access to the Leeds markets. As will be shown, the passenger service was never regarded as a source of profit by Richard Oliver Gascoigne, and that it was to operate on Tuesdays only (one of the Leeds market days) rather than the Nettle's three days, suggests that Gascoigne saw both a social need for the service and little likelihood of competition for its passengers.

The *Leeds Intelligencer* of 25 February 1837 gives an early account of the passenger service, and of a mode of operation that to modern ears will sound somewhat unusual:

> *A carriage has been recently placed by Mr. Gascoigne, upon his railway between Aberford and Garforth, for the accommodation of persons frequenting the Leeds markets from the former town and neighbourhood. The carriage will contain sixteen persons, and is drawn with great ease by an active horse at the rate of ten miles per hour from Aberford, to meet the Selby railway train proceeding to Leeds in the morning. It returns immediately after the arrival of the evening train with increased speed to Aberford. Mr. Gascoigne's railway being laid (with some short intervals) as a continued inclination from Garforth to Aberford, carriages of proper construction and weight will run with great rapidity from one extremity of the railway to the other without any other propelling force than that of gravity, an advantage of immense economical importance to a railway where the traffic upon it is (as upon the Aberford railway) in the direction from its higher to its lower termination.*

The railway descended one hundred feet in just under three miles. The carriage was manned by a breaksman and, on the gravity-driven runs down to Aberford, the horse that was to pull the carriage back up to Garforth rode in its own 'dandy cart' coupled behind. The initial descent from Garforth station down to the Isabella was on a steep gradient of 1:72, ensuring a good start for the train on its freewheeling journey (working in the reverse direction, a stationery engine was necessary for drawing full coal chaldrons up from the Isabella to the main line).

After passing under the coal-screens of the Isabella, the railway continued northwards alongside Hawks Nest Wood to the Elizabeth pit, named after Gascoigne's younger daughter (Hawks Nest was the site originally intended by Watson for the new winning and, located so far from the Leeds & Selby, it is probable that Elizabeth pit was opened, circa 1835, primarily to supply the north trade via the Aberford depot). Six hundred yards further the railway passed the abandoned Parlington Colliery site. The line then swung north-east through woodland to join Parlington Lane, where there were a siding and coal staith for the hall and, in later years, a private gasworks adjacent to the gamekeeper's house. The railway was level here but soon began to descend again, bringing into view the 'Dark Arch' – the tunnel referred to in the opening paragraph (Figure 5).

Parlington Lane was a long-established coal road, the conduit for Parlington Colliery and the earlier pits over by Barnbow. Inconveniently, the lane passed between Parlington Hall and its deer park, and it may have been Sir Thomas Gascoigne who first hid the passing coal traffic from sight of his hall windows by cutting the lane deeper here, at the same time raising the nearer ground behind a massive retaining wall. Around 1814 his son-in-law took this a stage further, enclosing the deepest section of the lane in a tunnel – the Dark Arch – and extending the lawn of the hall over it.[18] A 'ha ha' or sunken fence was made alongside the tunnel to prevent deer from straying over. Coal traffic along the lane would have ceased in 1822 with the closure of Parlington Colliery, then recommenced in 1834

**Figure 5.** The Fly Line at the Dark Arch, clearly showing how the railway went round the tunnel not through it. Parlington Lane, running at a lower level than the railway, is hidden by the low wall on the left.

**Figure 6.** Manning Wardle *Empress* c.1920 at the Light Arch on Parlington Lane – a hazardous blind spot on the railway. Cart ruts show how horse-drawn and rail traffic converged at this point.

with the coming of the railway.

Still today, the Dark Arch comes as a surprise to the walker along Parlington Lane, seemingly bespeaking a railway tunnel, but to have taken track through the arch would have denied the lane to all other traffic. Fortuitously, the ha-ha formed virtually a ready-made cutting, so it was simply deepened and widened and the railway taken that way.

The next feature for passengers to note as the carriage rolled along was the Light Arch, a bridge carrying the private carriageway from Hook Moor to the hall over the old coal road. This had to be rebuilt and the arch raised some twenty inches to enable railway traffic to pass under (Figure 6). The Light Arch created a hazardous blind corner, and here estate regulations must have given the freewheeling carriage right of way over all other traffic. The breaksman would be clanging his bell long before the arch was reached. After passing the bridge it was then but another half mile to the Aberford depot where, with wooden brake blocks screeching on iron wheels, the breaksman brought the carriage to a halt just short of the terminus buffers.

The Leeds & Selby directors saw the Aberford Railway as a wholly legitimate branch of their own enterprise, though privately owned, and once it was in operation ensured that their own train timings should cause no delay to its passengers. The minutes of 3 March 1837 record:

*Mr Wharton stated the detention of the Abberford train on Tuesday. It appears the delay was starting late from Selby. In future the Selby Train is to arrive at Abberford at ¼ past 9.AM to meet the Aberford Train.*[19] (Clearly, the second 'Abberford' should have been *Garforth*.)

But the Aberford passenger service was destined to operate for little more than three years. In 1835 the promoters of the York & Leeds Railway decided against joining the Leeds & Selby, opting instead to pass under the line well to the east of Garforth and link with the North Midland (Leeds-Derby) near Methley. Renamed the York & North Midland, with George Hudson now as its chairman, in May 1839 the line was completed as far as Milford on the Leeds & Selby, where a junction was put in for exchange of traffic. By this both Gascoigne and Waud got rail access to York, upwards of 45 chaldrons of Garforth and Manston coal being sent to the city on the opening day.[20] Junction with the North Midland was achieved in 1840, and in the same year the York & North Midland took a lease on the Leeds & Selby (which had been experiencing financial difficulties). Following this, traffic between Leeds and York was re-routed via Methley and passenger services between Milford Junction and Leeds were drastically cut, the trains convenient for the Aberford connection being among those cancelled. Thus, with its service no longer viable, the Aberford passenger carriage ceased to run.

**Figure 7.** Sisters pit in the early 1900s. The footbridge over the colliery sidings gave access from Garforth station to the Fly Line platform. Today, the foreground area is largely covered by Safeway's car-park.

Then in 1845 the York & North Midland's growing fiefdom was threatened by two rival proposals for direct Leeds-York railways, and to combat them Hudson found himself obliged to revive virtually the old York & Leeds scheme of 1834. Again the line would have gone via Parlington (passing under the deer park in a 1500-yard tunnel) and was welcomed by the Gascoignes. Yet it was not to be. Work began – as witness the viaduct still standing today over the Wharfe at Tadcaster – but ceased with the Railway King's fall from power in 1849.

Richard Oliver Gascoigne died in 1843, in the same year that Sisters pit, named after his two co-heiresses, was opened adjacent to Garforth station (Figure 7).[21] It was probably around this time also that the last of the colliery's pits in the Firth Field worked out. In 1850 Isabella Gascoigne married Captain, later Colonel, Frederick Charles Trench, who adopted the family name, and in 1852 Elizabeth married his cousin, Frederick Mason Trench, the second Baron Ashtown. The families owned the colliery jointly.

Before Hudson's overthrow the York & North Midland had expanded considerably, and with it the trade of the colliery. In 1850 Garforth and Manston coal was carried to virtually every station on the system from Whitby in the north to Hull on the east, Garforth's tonnage amounting to 74,864 - Manston's, 110,048.[22] The usefulness of the Aberford Railway as a mineral line was diminished perhaps as early as 1848, stations at Tadcaster and Wetherby on the York & North Midland Harrogate branch rendering the coal merchants' journeys down the Great North Road no longer necessary. Aberford depot thereafter was to service essentially a local market of around 5000 tons per year.

In 1852, following representations from Aberford, the passenger service was reinstated, trains now running on both Tuesdays and Saturdays, the two Leeds market days. Passengers travelled in a primitive van lit by three small windows either side (Figure 8).

**Figure 8.** The horse-drawn High Flyer passenger van standing in retirement by the platform at Sisters Pit .

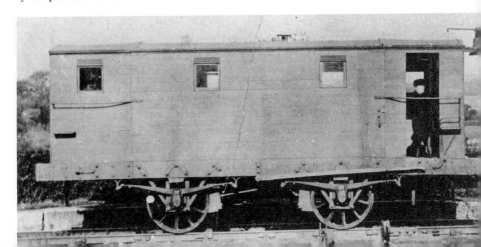

Whether this was the original carriage of 1837 or a replacement is
unclear, but the one surviving photograph suggests space for more
than the sixteen passengers mentioned by the *Leeds Intelligencer*. The
van was known – ironically one supposes – as the *High Flyer*, local
usage shortening this to 'the *Fly*', from which derives the colloquial
name for the railway itself – the Aberford Fly Line. As with the earlier
service, the *High Flyer* was gravity- and horse-operated, and on at
least one occasion passengers were severely bruised when the
brakesman was tardy in his duties and the vehicle slammed into the
Aberford buffers.

In 1870 and 1871 the colliery purchased two 0-4-0 class H saddle-
tank locomotives from Manning Wardle & Co of Leeds. Respectively,
these were given the names *Mulciber*, synonymous with Vulcan, the
blacksmith god, and *Ignifer*, 'the bringer of fire'. By 1872 at the latest
one or other of these was working on the Fly Line, but as in the days
of horse-operation, in the Garforth direction only. Gravity still held
sway from Garforth to Aberford.

Through the 1870s Aberford's need for communication with
Leeds increased. By 1878 two omnibuses were plying to Leeds via
Barwick-in-Elmet on market days with an additional trip on
Thursdays, and in 1881 Colonel Gascoigne was approached with a
request that the colliery run a daily service on the Fly Line.
Conferring with his lawyer, the colonel was dismayed to discover that
the two families might already be liable to a penalty of £2 per day in
respect of the existing service, leviable on them by the Board of Trade
as operators of an unauthorised railway. Recourse to a London
barrister better versed in railway law, brought reassurance that as the
line was a wholly private concern the regulations in question did not
apply, nor was there anything to hinder the more frequent service.
With the introduction of daily trains the High Flyer was replaced
with a proper second-hand four-wheel railway coach. This had four
compartments, one 1st class, the others 3rd, one of the latter a
'smoker'. Distinctions of class were maintained, a higher fare being
charged for 1st-class travel. Having no brake, the advent of the
carriage ended the gravity runs down to Aberford, trains thenceforth
being steam-hauled in both directions.

From its inception, the passenger service had been run as a public
benefit, not as a source of profit. When application was made to the
Treasury on Richard Oliver Gascoigne's behalf in 1837 regarding
stage-carriage duty, it was stated that the amount payable would be
very little 'especially as the greater proportions of the persons who
are expected to travel will be conveyed gratis'; whilst in 1839 it was

reported that 'On this Railway his tenants and the neighbouring farmers frequenting the Leeds Market are carried on one day in the Week, some without payments of any fares and others for the sum of 6d.'[23] One wonders on what basis liability to payment was determined.

Details of fares in the Fly Line's later years have been given by M B Wray:

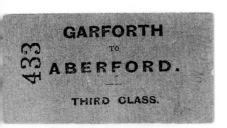

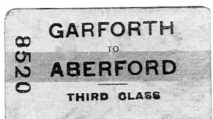

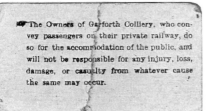

**Figure 9.** Aberford Railway third-class single and return tickets, and ticket back printed with the colliery's disclaimer. Ticket 433 (collection of Michael Stewart) is faintly date-stamped for 14 July 1910. No first-class tickets are known to have survived.

*Fares were originally 3d single and 6d return third class and 9d return first class, at this period the singles were coloured brown and returns blue but at a later date when the third fare was 5d single and 10d return, with the firsts proportionately higher, the tickets were white with a red stripe on the return half.*[24]

Printed on the backs of tickets (Figure 9) was the disclaimer:

*The Owners of Garforth Colliery, who convey passengers on their private railway, do so for the accommodation of the public, and will not be responsible for any injury, loss, damage or casualty, from whatever cause the same may occur.*

The Gascoignes were taking no chances.

It is a great pity that nothing comparable to the Watson papers is extant for the later history of the Fly Line. The railway was part of the life of Aberford, Parlington and Garforth, and already seen as quaint around the turn of the century, but neither Speight nor Bogg makes the briefest reference to it. 'Rightaway', rambling along Parlington Lane in 1907, indicates a 'waggon road' on his sketch map but notices nothing of the Fly Line in his text.[25] Even the *Garforth Observer*, started by the Garforth Elocution & Literary Society in 1884, its contributors greatly charmed by aspects of local character, had nothing to say. Thus the

**Figure 10.** Manning Wardle loco, believed to be *Ignifer*, at Aberford Depot c.1893 with driver Tom Roberts on the footplate. The man in the bowler is the Depot Agent, Thomas Townend, who in 1905 William Flockton was to describe as 'stationmaster, platform superintendent, and booking clerk, a composite unit like the crew of the 'Nancy Bell'.

one description we do have, written in 1905 by a William Flockton of Oulton, illuminates its moment like a colour slide but briefly seen:

> While preparing to walk back to Garforth we learnt that the Garforth Colliery Company run a passenger service on their coal line between Garforth and Aberford occasionally (it may be daily), and better still that the carriage would be leaving in about half an hour. My companion who is prone to become enervated by prolonged siestas, hailed the information with delight, and in due course we went to the starting place, and ran about like two superannuated footballers in search of the ticket office, which we found in a lane at the end of a foot road between gardens. Booking and 'bolting', we climbed a small 'earthwork' (used as the platform) as the train, an ancient second-class [sic] carriage of four compartments, backed up. The stationmaster, platform superintendent, and booking clerk, a composite unit like the crew of the 'Nancy Bell,' gave the signal, we climbed into a 'smoker,' the whistle sounded – and we were 'agon.' (Figure 10) We never touched high motor car speed, nor did we want to, for the track runs through or alongside the park amid charming scenery. We 'unloaded' at another earthwork, and in three minutes we were at the railway station en route for Leeds.[26]

The passing scenery Flockton enjoyed through the carriage window would have been little different from that seen in the 1830s, except for Lily pit. Following serious flooding caused by a breach in the Sisters pit tubbing in 1872, Lily was sunk in 1875 as a reserve pit beyond the outcrop of the troublesome sandstone. The pit was given up in the 1880s. In 1900 the far more important Trench pit was sunk close to the North Eastern Railway's Castleford branch to mine a large area of the two Middleton seams inaccessible from the old pits in the Firth Field. It was probably with Trench in mind that the colliery purchased a more powerful Manning Wardle class-I saddle-tank in 1897, the year of the Diamond Jubilee. The new loco was named *Empress* in the queen's honour. This was the only loco of the three that the North Eastern Railway – successors to the York & North Midland – would permit to travel over its metals to the Trench sidings.

Before the First World War the annual output from Isabella, Sisters and Trench reached 440,000 tons. But things everywhere were different afterwards, and in December 1920 Colonel F R T T Gascoigne, the old colonel's son, sold the collieries. The new company, Garforth Collieries Ltd, also signed a sixty-year lease on the Aberford Railway, undertaking to afford 'reasonable facilities' for public travel. Colonel Gascoigne paid £2000 for repairs to *Empress*. She was then the only loco still working at Garforth. *Ignifer* was no longer in service whilst *Mulciber* had been sold some time before 1912 to Low Laithes Colliery near Wakefield (and possibly there renamed *Tiger* (Figure 11).

Created in the early railway age, the Aberford Railway had from 1834 to 1848 played its essential role as an outlet for Garforth Colliery. That role had then been much diminished as the pattern of railway

**Figure 11.** Manning Wardle loco, believed to be *Mulciber*, ready to leave Sisters Pit platform with Aberfordians returning from Leeds. The four-compartment passenger coach replaced the old *High Flyer* when a daily service was introduced in 1881

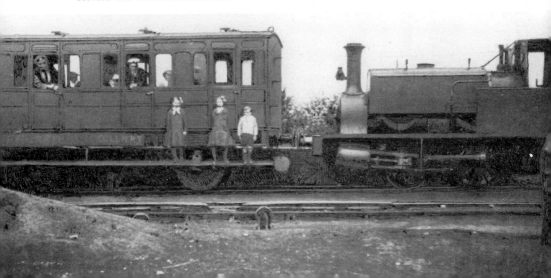

communications spread, but for the people of its locality the Fly Line had continued to serve as a link into that pattern. Now with the advent of motor transport after the war, the Fly Line had outlived its time.

Garforth Collieries did not prosper and in 1922 ownership of the company passed to the Old Silkstone Collieries of Dodworth near Barnsley, who saw the Fly Line as more an encumbrance than an asset. Soon the passenger service was cut back to two days per week. In 1919 James McHamish & Co of the Pioneer Garage at Garforth had begun operating a bus service on Tuesdays, Fridays and Saturdays between Aberford and Leeds, this venture folding in 1922 when one of the partners pulled out. Then in December 1923 Messrs Mouncey & Wilson of Aberford instituted their daily Red & White bus service to the city, which enterprise was itself soon challenged by the Blue bus service operated by Gillatt of the Aberford Motor Co (in due course the two were to combine as the Red, White & Blue Services.) With its track long ill-maintained owing to the war, and now faced with road competition, there was no future for the railway. In March 1924, eighty-seven years after the first passengers had come freewheeling down from the main line, *Empress* drew the last train back up the Fly Line to Garforth (Figure 12).

**Figure** 12. Manning Wardle *Empress* c.1920; photograph believed to have been taken in the proximity of the Parlington Hall gasworks.

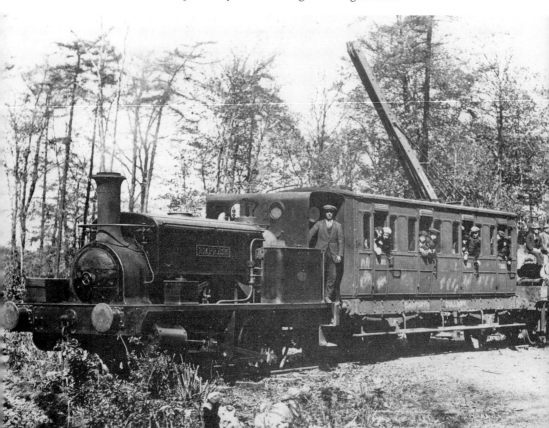

The end of the story is soon told. *Sisters* worked out in 1922, Isabella in 1926. In 1925 the company opened the new Barnbow Colliery near Manston, but neither this nor *Trench* pit survived the company's bankruptcy in 1930.

Patterns of communication continue to change. In 1988, after a long period of dispute, the Fly Line was confirmed as a public footpath, and in 1999 the Ml-Al link road was opened, its bold embankment crossing the Fly Line at Hawks Nest. Today what were once the Sisters Pit sidings are occupied by Safeways car-park and the initial section of the old railway is lost under an industrial estate but, walking on down Aberford Road, then turning left on Ash Lane, one soon comes to the concrete works which has long occupied the Isabella site and from there the Fly Line is clear to follow.[27] It makes a pleasant walk to Aberford. En route most of the features mentioned in this paper will be easily identified, careful searching at the terminus even disclosing the narrow ginnel up which Flockton and his companion 'booked and bolted' in 1905. And from Aberford it is then less than a mile and a half further to Lotherton Hall, where one may see portraits of Sir Thomas Gascoigne, who planned but never achieved the extension of his colliery's trade, and of his son-in-law, Richard Oliver Gascoigne, who did.

## Notes and References

This article is largely based on research originally carried out by the author for his book *The Aberford Railway & the History of the Garforth Collieries*, (David & Charles, 1971), the chief sources for which are:

Gascoigne Collection, West Yorkshire Archive Service, Leeds District Archives.

Watson MSS, Northumberland Record Office, Newcastle Upon Tyne.

Leeds & Selby Railway and York & North Midland Railway archives, Public Record Office, Kew. Extracts from the Leeds & Selby minute book are published by permission of the British Railways Board Records Centre. Readers may also be interested to look up 'Garforth Collieries & the Aberford Railway', *Annual Report & Bulletin* 10, National Register of Archives, West Riding Northern Section, 1967, which the author wrote whilst engaged on the original research. The elusive 'Rightaway' article mentioned therein, when it did turn up, proved to be Flockton's of 1905.

1. The coal seams have been known by a variety of names but for consistency the names employed by the Geological Survey are used here. Some old variations were: Beeston – *Low Main*; Middleton Main – *High Main, Bright Coal, Silkstone*; Middleton Little – *Hard Band, Flockton*.

2. Richard Oliver married Sir Thomas's step-daughter Mary Turner, daughter of Sir Charles Turner of Kirkleatham, in 1804.

3. Sir Thomas had two collieries at this time, one at Sturton on the east of Garforth and another adjacent to the site of the present Garforth golf course. The latter, though actually sited within the manor of Barwick in Elmet, was known as Garforth Colliery. The canal-and-waggonway system would have served both. The sole evidence for the scheme is the hand-drawn *Plan of a Line for a Canal & Waggonway from Garforth Colliery to the River Wharfe belonging to Sir Thos. Gascoigne Bart, 1774*, now at Lotherton Hall. The survey was made by George Dixon, of Cockfield, Co Durham, and the plan executed

by J. Bailey. The style of drawing suggests that the intention was to publish an engraving, but none are known. There is a photocopy in the Leeds District Archives.

4. Owing to the difficulty and expense of moving coal underground in the eighteenth and early nineteenth centuries, the practice was to extend a colliery by sinking fresh pits rather than by pushing the workings further and further from a single shaft.

5. Fenwick appears to have been unlucky in his siting of the colliery. On taking up his post Watson noted that the Middleton Main to the west of the Firth Field under Garforth Moor was known to be better coal, though difficult of access owing to water problems; and south of the Firthfield was the site of what at the turn of the century would be Trench Pit, where both Middleton seams were to prove of good quality.

6. It is evident that Parlington had been kept working longer than Fenwick in 1813 had expected, presumably to maintain output of Beeston coal as long as possible.

7. The site of the pit is now occupied by the Crossgates Centre. Waud's customers left the turnpike near Shadwell, crossing Winn Moor on the lane that is still known today as the Coal Road.

8. Hill, Thomas, *A Treatise Upon the Utility of a Rail-way from Leeds to Selby & Hull,* 1827.

9. Gascoigne's attendance at directors' meetings was infrequent and in December 1830 his son Thomas took his place on the board.

10. Letter 15.2.1831. Watson MSS (Wat/3/35/22), Northumberland Record Office, Newcastle Upon Tyne, hereafter WMSS.

11. Letter 12.2.1831. WMSS.

12. *Ibid.*

13. Colman, F.S., *History of the Parish of Barwick in Elmet,* Thoresby Society XVII, 1908. Curiously, whilst quoting Richard Oliver Gascoigne, who died in 1843, as the man to whom Hudson's offer was made, Colman links the story with the viaduct at Tadcaster, an outcome of the later 1845-9 York-Leeds scheme. Colman very likely had the story as an old family anecdote from the elder Colonel Gascoigne during the time he was working on the Gascoigne archives at Parlington. Fifty and more years after the events, a conflation of the two railway schemes in the colonel's mind would not be surprising.

14. Interview with ninety-three-year-old Billy Varley, *Yorkshire Weekly Post,* 25 June 1910. In 1834 Varley witnessed Kirkup effecting running repairs at Micklefield on the first locomotive to travel between Leeds and Selby, and stated that 'Afterwards Kirkup made the colliery railway from Garforth to Aberford.' There can be little doubt however that the railway per se was in being by this date, but traffic may not yet have commenced.

15. *Leeds Mercury,* 7 March 1835.

16. Leeds & Selby minute book, RAIL 351/1, Public Record Office, Kew, hereafter, L&S. With the exception of Brown Moor and Crawshaw Cover, sidings were subsequently installed at each of the places mentioned. The 'Two Coal Pits' were Garforth Colliery's F Pit and G Pit, both adjacent to the main line.

17. *Ibid.*

18. West Yorkshire Archive Service, Leeds District Archives, GC MA 53, building specification: *Plan & Section of the Bridge over the Coal Road front of the House,* 1813. Interestingly, on this plan the intended tunnel is indicated as no more than 76ft in length whereas the tunnel as it exists today is approximately 350ft. Examination of the masonry shows that the structure is built in three sections, suggesting progressive extension over a number of years.

19. L&S.

20. *Yorkshire Gazette,* 1 June 1839.

21. Gascoigne's two sons Thomas and Richard had died in the April and December of the previous year. In 1844 the sisters erected Aberford's fine gothic-revival almshouses as a memorial to their father and brothers.

22. York & North Midland coal ledger, RAIL 770/95, Public Record Office, Kew. Manston Colliery, its scattered pits at various times working at Brown Moor, Whitkirk, Crossgates and Seacroft, was now owned by Samuel Waud's son Edward, who was to be declared bankrupt in 1866.

23. T/1/4145, Public Record Office, Kew.

24. Wray, M.B. 'The Aberford Railway', *Stephenson Locomotive Society Journal,* November 1961.

25. 'Rightaway', 'For Riders and Ramblers', *Yorkshire Evening Post,* 20 April 1907.

26. Flockton, W., 'A Look Round Aberford', *Yorkshire Weekly Post,* 28 October 1905.

27. Ordnance Survey Explorer map 289 *Leeds* shows the route clearly, but is not essential.

# 2. ROUNDHAY HALL: A PERSONAL HISTORY

*by Margaret Plows*

THE SUBURBS OF LEEDS HAVE MANY EXAMPLES of large Georgian mansions built by wealthy merchants escaping the smoke and grime of the nineteenth century city centre. Unlike the great country houses, held by one family and developed over hundreds of years on the same site, these were occupied by the original owner for relatively short periods. By the middle of the twentieth century most were in institutional use or divided for multiple occupation. One of these is Roundhay Hall now part of a modern hospital. My father lived and worked here as a gardener from 1946 to 1972 when the Hall was owned by Leeds General Infirmary (LGI). We lived in the South Lodge at the entrance to the grounds. I knew of one previous owner, Lord Brotherton, as my father had worked as a young gardener here in 1930 under the instruction of the then head gardener Rolf Gatecliffe. The Brotherton name is well known, appearing as a benefactor for both Leeds University Library and a wing of the LGI. This evoked a personal interest and I set about tracing the complete history of Roundhay Hall.

## Pre-history

The land in this area had been farm and park land from the time of the Doomsday book. Later, two Granges from Kirkstall Abbey in Leeds were set up here: Roundhay and Allerton, both names still in use today.[1] The enclosure map of 1810 (Figure 1) for Chapel Allerton reveals that little appears to have changed with the area still sparsely populated.[2]

Only Chapel Allerton itself shows any sign of development, Allerton Grange being merely a farm and with the large estate of

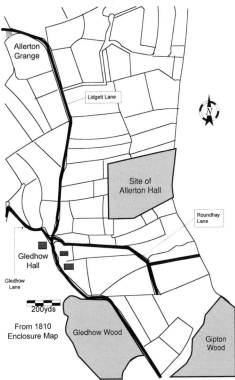

**Figure 1.** Extract from 1810 Enclosure Map for Chapel Allerton. *Redrawn by Trevor Plows*

Gledhow Hall built in 1764. This latter stood at the junction of four lanes: Gledow Lane (now Gledhow Lane), Lidget Lane (now Lidgett Lane), a lane (now Gledhow Wood Road) and Roundhay Lane (now an extension of Gledhow Lane). Allerton Hall, (now Roundhay Hall), was soon to be built on the land marked to the north of Roundhay Lane. Whilst we are now used to large scale suburban development on the edge of a town these houses were grand development each standing in grounds of many acres. Roundhay Hall is a typical example.

## First Owner, John Goodman 1822-1842

John Goodman was part of a new trend when, like other wealthy merchants in the area, he moved from Burley to Roundhay during the 1830s. Owners of the early manufacturing processes had lived on site as did their workforce. This was now changing. The wealthy merchants of Leeds were seeking to move out from the higher taxed, dirty and quickly developing unplanned city centre, to the new suburbs in the north of the city. Around 1810 the break up of once large estates due to the deaths of Samuel Elam (Roundhay Estate) Wade Browne (Chapel Allerton) and others, meant land now became available in this area.[3] Roads had improved with the turnpikes radiating out to the northern townships and villages, the Leeds and Collingham Turnpike opened in 1824.[4] These roads made it possible for the merchants with their private carriages to now live in new mansions in the cheap, healthy suburbs and be the first generation of commuters.

Derek Linstrum's *West Yorkshire Architects and Architecture* gives the date of the construction of Allerton Hall as the 1820s by the architect John Clark. Clark was also the designer of Mansion House at Roundhay Park for the Nicholson family. The archives hold two sets of deeds concerning Allerton Hall relating to either the purchase of the land or the building of the house. The first dates from March 1822 and was made between John Hebblethwaite and Robert Elam to Benjamin Goodman, George Banks (whose wife's maiden name was Goodman) and John Goodman concerning land at Roundhay.[5]

The second set of Deeds dated May 1822 made between Wade Browne, John Hebblethwaite and Robert Elam to various people which included John Goodman, George Goodman and George Banks concerned land at Chapel Allerton.[6] These refer to the site of what became known as Roundhay Hall but the house was originally named Allerton Hall. At this time there were two Allerton Halls, this one and another at Chapel Allerton.

The 1841 census gives a reference to John Goodman aged fifty years and his son Benjamin aged fifteen years as resident in Roundhay.[7] In addition, *Whites* trade directories for 1839, 1842 and 1843 show that John Goodman, a Stuff merchant, as living at Roundhay not Gledhow. Those of 1845 and 1847 have his house listed as Balks House, Wortley, apparently indicating that he had moved from the Gledhow/Roundhay area between the 1843 and 1845 directory compilations. This, allowing for slight chronological errors, ties in with the information below on William Smith at Gledhow. There has to be some doubt whether John Goodman actually lived at Allerton Hall, but he was party in the purchase of the land and commissioned the hall to be built.

### Second Owner, William Smith (of Gledhow) 1842-1872

William Smith like John Goodman was a stuff merchant of Leeds. The census returns for 1851, 1861 and 1871 all show some members of the Smith family living at *Allerton Hall*, Gledhow.[8,9,10] He was Mayor for Leeds in 1840 between the times when George Goodman, John Goodman's brother, was Mayor in 1836 and again in 1850-51. It seems likely that the families would have known each other through business and civic life.

William Smith intended to write his own autobiography but failing health prevented this. He did write an account while wintering in Biarritz in March 1867.[11] From this very interesting account read out at his memorial service at Brunswick Chapel, we get a picture of a self-made man of integrity and a leading light in the strong Methodist community of Leeds. He held annual breakfasts at Allerton Hall for over a hundred guests to raise money for the Methodist missionary cause. He was married with six children, his wife had died bearing the last in 1834. William Smith died at Allerton Hall on the 21 December 1868 having lived there twenty-six years. After his father's death, George Smith and his family lived on at Allerton Hall until he sold the property in 1872.

The table below shows William Smith's payments in lieu of tithes:

| Landowners | Occupier | Nos. referring to plan | Name and description of lands and premises | State of cultivation | Quantities in statute measure | | | Payable to Vicar of Leeds | | | Payable to Appropriators | | |
|---|---|---|---|---|---|---|---|---|---|---|---|---|---|
| | | | | | A | R | P | £ | s | d | £ | s | d |
| Smith William Esq. | Himself | 230 | House, Outbuildings, Garden, Pleasure Grounds | | 9 | 1 | 30 | | | | | | |
| | | 229 | House, close | Arable | 1 | 1 | 32 | | | 6 | | | 5 |
| | | 231 | Park | Grass | 9 | 18 | | | 3 | 2 | 1 | 9 | 2 |
| | | | | | 20 | - | - | | 3 | 8 | 1 | 14 | 2 |

(extract from Tithe Map and Documents, Chapel Allerton 1846)[12]

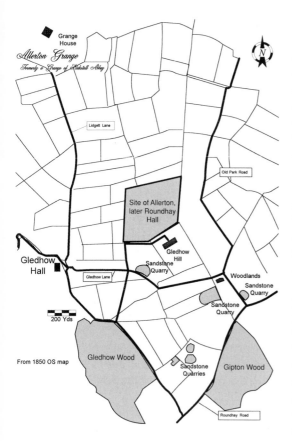

**Figure 2.** Extract from 1850 6″ Ordnance Survey Map. *Redrawn by Trevor Plows*

Even after he had paid a rate of one shilling in the pound on the Hall coming to around £20 per year, his total tithe and rates would be under £22. This would compare very favourably with the amounts being paid in rates in the centre of Leeds. These had greatly increased since the Corporation had exercised its power, under the *Courts House Acts*, to raise money for public improvements. This made it even more attractive for those with the mobility and money to move away.[13]

In the 1840s it would have proved difficult for working people to live in Gledhow and travel to Leeds using the current transport system. This consisted of a few horse-drawn omnibuses, travelling from Leeds to Chapeltown and Oakwood. They were infrequent and easily affected by changes in the economy. However by 1870 horse-drawn trams followed by steam trams travelled as far as Moortown, although even catching one of these meant walking some distance through muddy lanes.[14]

The 1850 Ordnance Survey Map shows Allerton Hall, Gledhow outlined (Figure 2). If this is compared to the earlier Enclosure Map of 1810 the main differences are the two new estates of Allerton Hall and Gledhow Hill now Roundhay School. The road network has increased to include these properties and other smaller ones, but the scene is still a rural one. Industrial activity is represented by the several sand stone quarries, stone from these would have been used locally.

## Third Owner, Henry Price Bowring 1872-1913

The new owner of Allerton Hall has little recorded of his life in Leeds. Deeds were exchanged in February 1872 between George Smith and his sister to Henry Price Bowring, Edward Bowring and John Bowring. There are two additions to the estate one in January 1874 and another in July 1875 these lots are shown on the site plan (Figure 3), partly situated in Roundhay. These brought the estate to about twenty six acres.[15,16,17]

From his wife's obituary notice printed in the *Yorkshire Post* of May 1908 Bowring moved to Leeds after working for C T Bowring, a shipping firm in Liverpool. This move was on his retirement after his marriage in 1865 to the daughter of William Illingworth of Illingworth, Ingham of Leeds (Timber Merchants). Henry Bowring died in 1893. His wife and two children continued to live at Allerton Hall, where his wife was appreciated for her charitable works in the neighbourhood. Before her death and after the marriages of her children she had rented a house at Meanwood and put the Hall up for sale. The property and estate must have taken some time to settle or sell. It was not until 1913 that her son Henry Illingworth Bowring, who lived at Highfield in the south east corner of the estate, finally disposed of it.[18]

**Figure 3.** Site plan showing the changes to the estate. *Compiled by the Author from various deeds of Roundhay Hall.*

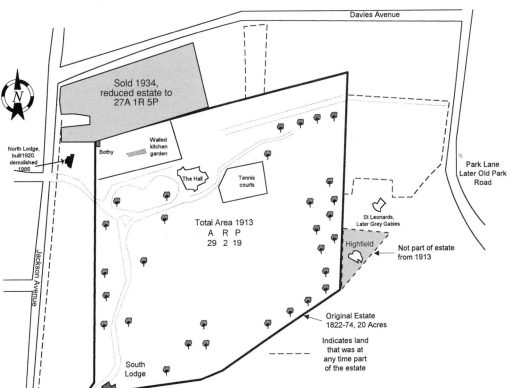

Miss Jessie Beverley, who at the time was in her nineties, wrote to the *Yorkshire Evening News* stating that her maternal grandfather was Mr William Smith formerly owner of Allerton Hall. She recalled Mrs Bowring holding 'Hay Partys' when local children played in the grounds of the Hall. The best party she remembered was in 1897 when each child received strawberries in an enamelled 'Jubilee' beaker.[19]

By 1900 the growth of the community at Gledhow is large enough to warrant its own Post Office being built. The Ordnance Survey map for 1901 shows Oakwood with a Post Office and Tramway terminus. This was the first electrified tram route and carried the people of Leeds to within walking distance of Roundhay Park. At Oakwood a parade of shops was built in 1898 that supplied more services to Gledhow.  Roundhay at last became part of the Leeds district in 1912.

### Fourth Owner, Lord Brotherton 1913-1930
Lord Edward Allen Brotherton, the next owner of the Hall was the most well known. He purchased Allerton Hall on the 20 October 1913 and renamed it Roundhay Hall. Above the front door he placed his coat of arms, with the motto *Studeo Esse Utilis* (I study to be useful). The purchase price was £13,477.10s. The deeds reconciled parcels of land making the total size of the estate over twenty-nine acres (Figure 3).[20] By the time he bought Roundhay Hall Lord Brotherton, had already made a fortune from his chemical works at Wakefield.  He had developed unique processes and exploited niches in the market.

He was born in Manchester, on 1 April 1856, the son of Theophilus Brotherton, a cotton manufacturer. The eldest of seven children, he ran away to sea for a short time at fourteen. Leaving school at fifteen he then attended evening classes at Owens College where he laid the foundations of his knowledge about the chemical industry. He had a strong spirit of adventure and was an individualist.  He married an artist Mary Brookes in 1883, but she died in childbirth during the first year of their marriage and he never remarried.[21]

In 1913-14 when he was Lord Mayor of Leeds, his Lady Mayoress was his niece by marriage Mrs Dorothy Una Ratcliffe. She was an author, traveller and aviator whom he treated as a daughter ultimately bequeathing her Roundhay Hall. Her authorship brought her recognition for its use and preservation of Yorkshire dialect. During 1914 he personally funded the Leeds Pals Battalion and offered the services of his chemical works to the country for the war effort. A holder of many civic and national offices in both Wakefield and Leeds, he was also a great benefactor to many charities and institutions taking a personal interest in them all.

From 1922 onwards Lord Brotherton developed an interest in manuscripts and first editions and had the study extended at Roundhay Hall to house these works. He endowed the University of Leeds with a library which still bears his name and his collections are now kept there.[22] It was his wish that literature should be accessible to all and that his collection and others should stay in this country.[23] On his death in October 1930 he was given full civic honours at Leeds Parish Church followed by burial at Lawnswood Cemetery.

Lord Brotherton's nephew and managing director Charles Frederick Ratcliffe (subsequently adopted the name Brotherton), was a benefactor of the Brotherton Wing at the Leeds General Infirmary in 1942. His son David Brotherton, still lives on a farm near Kirkham Abbey, Lord Brotherton's summer residence near Malton.

During this time the area started to be built up, and the purely rural occupations were changing. Ordinary people commuted, using the now circular tram service, to work in factories and offices in and around Leeds. A bus service linking the trams at Moortown and Oakwood for the residents of Gledhow started to run from Shadwell to Oakwood around 1926.

### Fifth Owner, Dorothy Una Ratcliffe 1930-1936

She inherited Roundhay Hall with Lord Brotherton's hope that she and her husband, Charles Frederick Ratcliffe, would live there. Instead they divorced in 1932 and she soon remarried and went to live at Acorn Bank, Temple Sowerby in Westmoreland.[24] She offered Roundhay Hall to the Leeds Corporation but they turned it down. Roundhay Hall was sold in January 1936, to The Finsbury Estates Company whose director was Edward Warwick Broadbent.

### Sixth Owner, Edward Warwick Broadbent 1936-45

When he purchased Roundhay Hall the deeds show consolidation of land to the west adjacent to Jackson Avenue. Planning permission for the building of houses and a road had been granted for this land but was never used. Land to the north, abutting Davies Avenue, was sold for the building of detached or semi-detached houses (Figure 3).25

During the war the Leeds General Infirmary used the Hall as a sixty-two bed annexe to the infirmary and it was sold to them in 1945 with twenty-six acres of land for £25,000.[26] At this time

**Figure 4.** This aerial photograph of 1985 shows how the area surrounding Roundhay Hall has developed. *Photograph courtesy of Granville Harries, Dorchester Ledbetter photographers*

Edward Broadbent was living at Highfield in the grounds. His obituary notice in August 1960, stated he lived at Shadwell, was a chartered accountant and Secretary and Director of Price Tailors Limited, with a life long interest in the Christian Science Church. There is no record that he lived at the Hall and may have bought it only as an investment.

As can be seen from the aerial photograph (Figure 4) the area has become built up since 1900. Large numbers of houses were built before the war, leaving small plots of land for infill building. Only the large estate of Brackenwood on the site of Allerton Grange was yet to be built in the late 1950s. By then purpose built shopping parades had appeared in addition to the corner shops that had been constructed among the developments. By 1956 transport had further improved with a direct bus service to Leeds. The trams stopped running in this area around 1960.

**Seventh Owner, Leeds General Infirmary 1945-1986**

Initially the Hall continued as a convalescent hospital, during which time in 1946 my father returned as gardener living in the renovated south lodge. The Preliminary Training School (PTS) for nurses at the LGI moved to Roundhay Hall in 1951 with a purpose built nurses' home constructed in the south east corner of the kitchen garden (Figure 5). In 1969 the PTS moved back to the LGI and the Hall remained empty with my father, until his retirement, as a gardener and caretaker. In March 1974 the Hospital for Women moved temporarily to Roundhay Hall while a new hospital was built in Leeds. This involved the addition of some new buildings next to the old hall, in all there was accommodation for ninety patients. After the new hospital was completed in the early 1980s the Hall stood empty until it was finally sold to BUPA private hospitals in 1986. Not all the land was sold, the LGI retained ten acres with access to Old Park Road which was subsequently sold for housing.

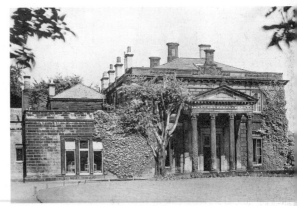

**Figure 5.** Roundhay Hall in 1951. *Author's Collection*

**Eighth and Current Owner, BUPA Hospitals from 1986.**

The site opened as a seventy eight bed hospital in September 1989 after a £6m project to add the new buildings to the renovated Hall. This Georgian hall with its portico supported on Corinthian columns is now a Grade II listed building which has been beautifully restored. The new low rise buildings of the hospital seeming insignificant alongside it. The derelict kitchen garden is a car park and the gravel drives the gardeners once had to rake are now tarmac (Figure 6).[27]

**Figure 6.** Side view of Roundhay Hall, 1994. *Author's Collection*

**The South Lodge**

My family's connection with Roundhay Hall started in 1930

when my father, Joseph (Joe) Thirsk, went to work there as a gardener. Born at Pontefract in 1908, the youngest of thirteen children, his mother died when he was two years old. He left school at thirteen and went to work for Morley's Boot and Shoe repairers in the town. At the age of eighteen he moved on to work for a solicitor called Bentley working as under-gardener and chauffeur but had to leave after two years due to cut backs in staff. It was whilst in his next job in 1929 that he met his future wife Constance (Connie) who was the same age. Connie, whose family home was a farm at Burringham near Scunthorpe had worked for a solicitor called Blackmore at Hamphall Stubbs near Doncaster since going into service at the age of fourteen.

This is an extract from Joe's reference written by Mr Blackmore dated January 1930:

> *Joseph Thirsk has been employed here for the past six months as under gardener. He has assisted with two hunters and driven a Morris car. I have found him a good clean and tidy worker, always willing and obliging, neat and methodical in his work and in his person. I am very sorry to part with him as I think he is a very useful youth, but I am going to manage with one servant less in future.*

Joe first worked at Roundhay Hall towards the end of Lord Brotherton's life. At that time, as a single man of twenty-two, he lived on the job with other gardeners in an old building known as the bothy situated in the north west corner of the walled kitchen garden. In April 1931, after working at Roundhay Hall for just over a year he 'moved to better himself' and went to work as a gardener at Hazelwood Castle near Tadcaster, then a monastery, now a hotel, until December 1933.

After courting for four and half years, my parents were finally able to marry on 12 February 1934. My mother's employers, the Blackmores, found work for both Connie and Joe with friends of theirs, a Mr and Mrs David Steel, a steel works owner in Sheffield, with residences at Wilsick Hall near Doncaster and Spring Grove, Wharncliffe Side, near Sheffield. Their first home was a remote tiny rented cottage, on top of a hill with no running water, at Birkfield Green, Thurgoland, also near Sheffield. Eight months later they moved to Belmont Crescent down in the village. Joe was enlisted in October 1940 and spent the next five years serving in Burma. During this time my mother returned home to look after an aunt and then spent the rest of the war back at Wilsick Hall as a companion to Mrs Francis Steel and as nanny to her young son David.

When my father was 'demobbed' my parents came to Leeds

looking for work, staying with his brother Tom in Oakwood. In December 1945 my father applied for a job as gardener at Roundhay Hall. He was appointed by the Infirmary Board of Governors and started work at the end of February 1946, soon after going to live in the South Lodge on the estate (Figure 7). He continued living and working there until his retirement in 1972 at the age of sixty five. I was born at Hyde Terrace Maternity Hospital in January 1951, a much longed for baby, their only child.

**Figure 7.** Lodge whilst I was living there.
*Author's Collection*

My memories of the Hall are of a childhood in the 1950s spent freely roaming the grounds as if they were an extension to the Lodge garden. I watched the seasons change, enjoying the carpet of purple and white crocuses in the spinney (opposite the Lodge) which had been planted by my father in Lord Brotherton's time. There were giant rhododendrons lining the driveways and a clump of scented yellow azaleas in front of the Lodge window. In the summer months, at weekends and in the evenings, while my father tended the greenhouses I would follow him around. I remember one greenhouse in particular with a wall covered in bright red geraniums. The kitchen garden was used to provide produce for the Hall and every Friday cut flowers were sent down to the Infirmary by ambulance. Bedding plants were grown to supply both sites, and my father even in his sixties would prick out thousands of wallflower seedling in the summer heat. October was the conker season and this, along with the autumn colours and smells, made this my favourite time of year. I would be given rides in the large wooden wheelbarrows whose sides could be raised with extra boards to help transport more leaves to the mounds of leaf mould that resembled hay stacks. In winter I would accompany my father when he went to stoke the boilers that heated the greenhouses. It always seemed to snow for my birthday in January followed closely by the appearance of the first snowdrops. After the age of eight or nine I still enjoyed the freedom of the grounds alone or with friends, but my interest in gardening waned. It was only when I started to create my own garden in 1971 that I

**Figure 8.** My father at work in 1966. The photograph shows where Lord Brotherton's Camellia walk was sited. *Author's Collection*

realised how much I had absorbed from watching my father (Figure 8).

Up to starting school I spent little time outside the Hall's entrance with its green iron gates that were closed every evening. My mother would sometimes take me into Leeds on a Monday morning when it was quiet. The Co-operative at Oakwood was where we did our weekly shop until a friend took over a local corner shop in 1959 and a newly built parade of shops opened nearby in 1957. A baker's van would call and milk and coal were delivered. We had an allotment on the estate and my mother kept chickens in the Lodge garden. My father's tied job meant we got little opportunity for outings but we did go by bus to visit friends and relatives and on day trips to the East Coast. A visit to the Canal Gardens at Roundhay Park to feed the ducks is something I enjoyed like many young children in the area have over the last century (Figure 9).

It was the gardens and grounds of Roundhay Hall that were my world, not the Hall itself. When I was born the Hall was still in use as a hospital but later that year it changed to become a Preliminary Training School (PTS). It was somewhere I only entered occasionally. Some members of staff were close friends of my parents; in fact I was named after the sister-in-charge one

**Figure 9.** Author and Parents on a visit to Mary Darley's house, at Headingley, previously she had 'lived in'. *Photograph courtesy of Mary Darley*

**Figure 10.** Nursing staff in 1950. Nurses Julie Marsh (far left), Annie Naylor (third left), Mary Darley, who still lives nearby, (far right) and Sister Margaret Fox (front). *Photograph courtesy of Mary Darley*

Margaret Fox who, with her fiancée Bert Parker and Nurse Julie Marsh were my God Parents (Figure 10). Margaret had a difficult decision to make between Bert and her career, as nurses at that time had to resign when they got married, but they did eventually marry. My mother enjoyed visitors to our home who were always made very welcome. When guests arrived my quieter father would be dispatched to make a cup of tea for everyone. I would sit on the floor, forgotten for a time, listening to these grown ups talking. In the fifties, 'the war' and 'whether there would be another' was an important topic of conversation, but a lot of the time it was gossip about the nursing staff and speculation about when Matron would next descend on the Hall. The 'live-in' staff probably felt the Lodge offered somewhere to relax away from their working environment. These visitors to the Lodge all spoilt me, they would bring me presents often made by the patients on the rehabilitation wards at the Ada Hospital.

Within a few years of the National Health Service being set up the Infirmary employed four people in the grounds of the Hall. These were Eric Bradbury who ran the administration side of the gardens, my father, a man called Bob and a youth.

**Figure 11.** Staircase at Roundhay Hall after refurbishment 1986. Statues of Venus and the Shepherd Boy, from Lord Brotherton's Collection, can be seen in the alcoves. *Photograph courtesy of Granville Harris, Dorchester Ledbetter photographers*

When I was a little older I went with my father as he checked the Hall out of term time. What stayed with me from these visits was: the unusual smells in the kitchens, the feel of the cold marble floor; and the statues, in alcoves, on the staircase and in the entrance hall that contrasted with the damp tropical atmosphere of the conservatory where I liked to sit in the big wicker chairs (Figure 11). The Hall was not a place I felt comfortable in and it was always a relief to go back outside into the fresh air of the grounds. In contrast my mother thought the Hall was wonderful and she could explain to me what the dumb waiter was, why the main staircase divided half way up and how a set of panels in a ground floor room could be folded back to make one large room to hold a dance in.

The PTS School was run by two tutors, Sister Bird and Sister Morley who lived in the North Lodge, now demolished, which was adjacent to the BUPA entrance. They would tell my parents about the things the young nurses got up to. I would see these same trainees looking smart in their crisp uniforms and pretend I was a nurse like them.

Our life was not all idyllic, as my father worked very hard in all weathers and for many years suffered recurrent bouts of malaria, a legacy of his time spent in Burma. The Lodge, though very attractive from the outside, was damp and difficult to heat. The bathroom had been installed in what had been a cold store and was freezing all year round. The lounge was cosy round the fire in winter and a cool haven in summer. But as this central area, with its high ceiling, gave access to the two bedrooms, kitchen and the porch, it was very draughty. The Lodge was a tied property that had been renovated in 1946 for my parents to live in and at that time of housing shortages they felt lucky to find both employment and somewhere to live. My mother always felt proud to live at the Lodge. It was not until I started work in central Leeds that I came to appreciate how privileged I was to have been brought up in such beautiful surroundings. Perhaps the merchants who had purchased Roundhay Hall also felt they were capturing the countryside within the town boundary.

I was married from the South Lodge on a sunny day in October, 1971. My parents moved out in the following January in preparation for my father's retirement on his sixty-fifth birthday that September. After his retirement my father had the time to make my mother a lovely garden at their new home, a council house at Moortown. My parents enjoyed six years of retirement before my father died in December 1978. Soon after this my mother moved back to Gledhow to be near us where she died in December 1987.

I am pleased for myself and my parent's memory to think that both the Hall and the South Lodge have been renovated and appear to have a useful future rather than falling into decay.

## Notes and References

1 Lee, J, *Leeds a Guide and History*, p75.
2 Ref DB/M 145 West Yorkshire Archive Service, Leeds.
3 Wilson, R G, *Gentleman Merchants.*
4 Gilleghan, J, Roundhay Hall, BUPA Brochure.
5 Deeds HN 665 655  1882 West Yorkshire Archives Service, Wakefield.
6 Deeds HP  8484 West Yorkshire Archives Service, Wakefield.
7 Census 1841 1311 Roundhay Reference Library, Leeds.
8 Census 1851 2316 Chapel Allerton  Reference Library, Leeds.
9 Census 1861 3357 Chapel Allerton Reference Library, Leeds.
10 Census 1871 4574 Chapel Allerton, Reference Library, Leeds.
11 Leeds and Yorkshire Biography V3 p605, Leeds Local History Library.
12 West Yorkshire Archives Service, Leeds.
13 Wilson, R G, *Gentleman Merchants* p205.
14 Soper, J, *Leeds Transport* Vol.1 1830-1902.
15 Deeds 663 477 5402-1872 West Yorkshire Archives Service, Wakefield.
16 Deeds 705 161 1901-1874 West Yorkshire Archives Service, Wakefield.
17 Deeds 737 254 3317-1874 West Yorkshire Archives Service, Wakefield.
18 Leeds Obituaries V2 p85 Leeds Central Library, Local History, Leeds.
19 Yorkshire Evening News BUPA Archives, Leeds.
20 Deeds Vol 45 p784 No 260 West Yorkshire Archive Service, Wakefield.
21 Obituaries Vol 7 p103 , Central Library Leeds, Local History.
22 The Brotherton Library, Private Collection, Parkinson Building, Woodhouse Lane, Leeds.
23 Felsenstain, F, *The University of Leeds* 85/6 Review Vol28 p41.
24 Halliday Wilfrid, J, DUR *Dorothy Una McGrigor Phillips A Memoir.*
25 Deeds 13 287 107, 119 477 164, 174  735 262  West Yorkshire Archive Service, Wakefield.
26 Deeds 111 757 343 West Yorkshire Archive Service, Wakefield.
27 Dept.of the Environment, *List of Buildings of Special Historic Interest*, Leeds 6-28.

## Acknowledgements

I would like to thank especially three people for their help: Mary Darley for her reminiscences of life as a nurse at Roundhay Hall and for the use of her photographs. My mother-in-law, Marjorie Plows for her local knowledge of the changes in Gledhow over many years. And Trevor for his help, especially with the illustrations.

# 3. Rise and Fall of Industrialisation in Burley-in-Wharfedale

*by Pam Shaw*

BURLEY-IN-WHARFEDALE is mentioned in the great national survey of William the Norman in AD 1086. It was written there as Burghelai which means an Anglo Saxon fortified enclosure. It may have been a Roman outpost and later a Saxon settlement, but there is little supporting evidence to substantiate this. But for the development of a cotton mill and later a worsted manufacturing industry, Burley-in-Wharfedale may well have remained a very small hamlet consisting of a few farms, a manorial hall, an inn, a smithy, a water-powered corn mill and a chapel of ease.[1]

**Figure 1.** Greenholme Mills.
*Courtesy of the West Yorkshire Archive Service, Bradford*

The original mill was built in 1792 for cotton spinning by a partnership of Thomas Davidson of Stockton-on-Tees, George Merryweather of Burley-in-Wharfedale and Jonas Whitaker of Leeds. The mill was built about half a mile from the village on the banks of the river Wharfe[2] (Figure 1).

By then, agriculture had begun to lose its leading role in the country's economy with the building of the first village mill in the then West Riding of Yorkshire. The increasing development of the mill industries is substantiated by the Registrar General's Census around that time, which stated that over fifty per cent of the population of Burley-in-Wharfedale was involved in textiles.[3]

There were a number of factors influencing the siting of Greenholme Mills on the banks of the river Wharfe in Burley-in-Wharfedale, the main one appeared to be the availability of adequate water-power, and when in 1811 a further mill was built, it used water which was diverted from the goit of the original old mill to drive the water wheel in the new mill. It was much later that steam power was added to the mill. The second important factor was the supply of workers. Where the labour of children was not available, cottages had to be built to accommodate families, this necessitated easy access

**Figure 2.** Burley-in-Wharfedale 1890. *Used with the kind permission of Image IT, Leeds University*

to local building materials.[4] Stone was readily available and in the case of Greenholme Mills, this could have come from nearby stone quarries on Ilkley Moor. Easy access to transport facilities was crucial, the mill site being only six miles from the Shipley canal network. The building of Greenholme Mills had a social, economic and environmental impact on the development of Burley-in-Wharfedale (Figure 2).

The new six-storey mill was one of the largest in the area, and was run by a labour force of children brought from London. The owners' reasons for employing child labour were explained in the *1802 Act For The Preservation Of The Health And Morals Of The Apprentices And Others Employed In Cotton And Other Mills*. Free labourers could not be obtained except on what was described as being very advantageous terms. For the sake of securing one child spinner, the owners would be obliged to provide housing for a full family without necessarily benefiting from that family labour. Greenholme Mills preferred to use parish apprentices, accommodating them in nearby company lodgings. The children, both boys and girls, were bound as apprentices to serve the firm for several years. In May 1802 Mr Hey, a surgeon from Leeds and Reverend Dikes from Hull, visited Greenholme Mills as representatives of a select committee. Mr Hey submitted a report which stated:

> *The committee resolves unanimously that we will not on any account allow the apprenticing of poor children to the masters or owners of cotton mills or other works of the kind where such poor children shall be obliged to work in the night time, or for any unreasonable hours in the day.*[5]

The children were interviewed singly and of the 260 apprentices, 52 worked nightshift from 7 pm to 6 am without a break, although a meal was served at midnight which they ate whilst working. The Burley mill was given two years by the *1802 Act* to prepare for the cessation of night work for children.[6]

It may be argued however, that the old cotton mill owners performed charitable work. With the exception of the overlookers the mill was staffed by children sent down from the workhouses in London and who had by working in the mills, the advantage of being apprenticed to the trade. When they had served their time many of them settled in Burley, and their families afterwards became their own householders and were otherwise comfortably off. Some of the families living in Burley today may be descendants of the children from the Foundling Hospital and workhouses in London. Besides teaching the children cotton spinning, Merryweather and Whitaker provided food, clothing and lodging.[7] Despite the monetary benefits there was some degree of local opposition to the employment of local children in the mill, which was the driving force behind the mill owners decision to import children from the workhouses. However, many local children were actually moved from normal family life and were totally dependant on their employers, this dependency also applied to domestic workers employed in the numerous large houses in Burley.

In 1810 George Merryweather left Greenholme Mill and moved his cotton spinning interests to Manchester. When this move took place 190 of the young operatives were marched to Manchester to work there. *The Halifax Journal* described the event in some detail, which showed the mill owners in a somewhat different light from previous reports:

> *On Tuesday last the boys and girls, consisting in number 190, belonging to the calico manufactury of Mr Merryweather of Otley, passed through this town on their way to Manchester, to which that gentleman is removing his extensive concern. The cleanliness; healthy appearance; and general cheerfulness of the children, attracted the notice and exited the admiration of every beholder, they were clad in blue uniform, the boys with leather caps, and the girls wearing straw hats, walked hand in hand but were relieved at times on their march by several wagons which accompanied them, wherein were deposited 3,000 penny loaves. By the acknowledgement of everyone who witnessed the procession, it was a sight truly gratifying, and if gratifying to the stranger, to the disinterested spectator - how much more so exquisite must it have been to the feelings of him their Master*

*and Protector, whose head devised and whose heart sanctions the*
*superior comforts of this youthful band-this rising body of industry.*[8]

No children under nine years were employed at the mill. Those under
eighteen years worked eleven and a half hours daily and adults
worked an average of thirteen hours daily. Payment would have been
made on piecework, therefore workers would eat whilst working
rather than take a break. Thomas Brown, who was later the manager
of Greenholme Mills, gave the following information to the Factory
Commissioners in 1883:

> *We colonised our mill originally and have several hundred apprentices*
> *from London; we now have a sufficient supply in the neighbourhood.*[9]

William Fison was related to the famous Norfolk maltsters,
Whitbreads of London. He began his career in textiles at a warehouse
in Cheapside, Bradford. In 1842, his father met a Quaker gentleman,
travelling in the same coach to London. They found that they both
had sons of the same age. Forster, the Quaker gentleman, suggested
that their sons should go into partnership. This resulted in the
running of two firms, Forster and Fison dealing in wool, and William
Fison and Company of Piccadilly, Bradford, manufacturing worsted
cloth. William Fison later married a girl from Burley-in-Wharfedale
whose father, Mr Jonas Whittaker, was the owner of Greenholme
Mills. This match was a major factor in Forster and Fison's interest
in purchasing Greenholme Mills.[10]

On 17 May 1848, Greenholme Mills, were put up for auction at
the *Talbot Inn*, Bradford. The bill of sale included:

> *The estate and mansion house built in fifty acres of parkland, pleasure*
> *grounds, extensive farm buildings, a messuage, 73 cottages and shops*
> *and 140 acres of rich farm land.* [11]

William E Forster and his friend William Fison, both aged 29 years,
purchased the mill and surrounding estate and property. In 1850,
they moved their existing business in Bradford to the Burley Mills.
They changed the purpose of the mill from cotton spinning and
weaving, to the production of worsted.[12] Titus Salt, later Sir Titus
Salt, was also very interested in buying the mill. However, he arrived
one hour too late for the auction, missed the sale and came to build
Saltaire Mill and model village, which was adjacent to the Shipley
canal network, and used extensively for transporting goods at that
time.[13]

One of Forster and Fison's great achievements occurred in the

**Figure 4.** Wharfeside Forster's home.
*Author's collection*

**Figure 5.** Forster's library at *Wharfeside*.
*Author's collection*

1890s, Greenholme Mills being the first mill in the country to install electric lighting, whilst in 1908, Mr W Howard Arnold-Forster invented mechanical doffing, which was introduced into the mill in the same year.[14]

In 1850 Forster married Jane Arnold, the eldest daughter of the famous headmaster Reverend Thomas Arnold of Rugby. Two years later, they moved into their palatial home which they had built near to the mill on the bank of the river Wharfe, naming it Wharfeside, which remains today a private residence (Figures 4 and 5).[15] It has superb views of the river Wharfe and the Wharfe Valley. Fison took up residence in the existing mansion called Greenholme, which was formerly the home of Jonas Whitaker one of the original mill owners (Figure 6). Frederick W Fison who was an MP for Doncaster, owned Greenholme after his father, but by the early twentieth century it was let privately as the old expensive lifestyle had become impossible to maintain.[16] It was demolished in 1922-23, the stone being re-used to build houses adjacent to the mill for managers and over lookers. These houses called Great Pastures, were built to a very high standard, having the luxury of a bathroom, three

**Figure 6.** William Fison and family outside Greenholme, now demolished.
*Courtesy of the West Yorkshire Archive Service, Bradford*

bedrooms, a separate kitchen, a parlour, dining room and a good sized garden (Figure 7). Today these properties are privately owned. According to local people employed at the mill between 1919 and 1940, the managers and overlookers were always male. They recall that if anyone was unlucky enough to get on the wrong side of a manager or overlooker, their lives could be made a misery and they might even lose their jobs and inevitably their homes.[17] The only Trades Union recalled was The Overlookers Union, this gave the

**Figure 7.** Great Pasture. *Author's collection*

managers absolute power over the workers. One of the women interviewed, whose father was an overlooker during the 1930s, was born at Great Pastures.[18] Her husband's father had a shop in Menston, providing the clogs for both mill and agricultural workers.[19] A retired headmaster and local historian, Mr F W N Newbould, vividly recalled the clattering of clogs going down the mill road. His father was an apprentice woolsorter, who started work in the early part of the twentieth century at fourteen years old, eventually earning the princely sum of thirty shillings weekly [£1.50]. Woolsorters were very highly skilled, hence the high wages.[20]

Throughout the nineteenth century, education was a burning question, and in Forster's early days, long before his marriage into the Arnold family, he repeated again and again that he would strive to get the children of the working classes out of the gutter by educating them. In fact, the inscription at the base of Forster's statue in London reads: 'To his wisdom and courage, England owes the establishment throughout the land of a national system of elementary education'. In 1861, Forster entered Parliament and by 1865 he had become the Minister of Education. He saw the *Endowed School's Act* 1869 safely through all its stages and became the architect of the *Elementary Education Bill 1878* (Figure 8).[21] The Act was designed to vastly increase the number of schools leading towards education for all children between five and twelve years. It placed responsibility onto local government by allowing the election of School Boards in areas without sufficient accommodation for all children. Boards had various powers and were allowed to levy a rate to finance and set up the running of new schools and to pass bylaws making school attendance compulsory.[22] In 1837 children in the village were instructed at two pence per week for reading three pence for writing and four pence for a whole course. The board had the powers to waive this fee in cases of hardship.[23]

**Figure 8.** Right Honourable W E Foster. *Author's collection*

In 1856 Forster and Fison built a school adjacent to the mill known as Greenholme Mills School, which was the first of its kind in the country. For forty years until its closure in 1897, the cost of running the school was met by Greenholme Mills. The school was used to educate 'half timers' employed at the mill. 'Half timers' were

children aged between ten and fourteen years and who were now compelled by law to attend school for half of each working day. Three male teachers were employed at the school. There is little evidence to show what, if any, education was given to girls, but in 1882 a public meeting was held in the Burley Lecture Hall to consider the advisability of forming classes for girls and women.[24] The Township School was built in 1862, which was patronised by non-conformist families and maintained close links with Greenholme Mills School. The West Riding Education Authority took over responsibility for the school from 1904 until its closure in 1926.[25] More recently the Township School was used by Bradford Education Authority as a Craft and Design Training Centre for teachers and in 1995 the school buildings were sold to a property developer and tastefully converted to office premises and a private dwelling. The original village school built in 1838 opposite the *Malt Shovel Inn*, (now known as Cutlers), was demolished in the early 1900s.[26]

In the early part of the twentieth century most village children would expect to start their working lives at Greenholme Mills. However, according to the 1881 Census sixty-two per cent of females in the twelve to fifteen year groups were employed as textile workers; boys in the same age group numbered 68 per cent.[27]

A number of people in the village who were employed at Greenholme Mills during the First World War, recollected how they commenced work part-time at the age of twelve, for three shillings and nine pence per week and at thirteen they worked full time earning eight shillings and sixpence for a full week's work.[28] After the First World War the school leaving age was raised to fourteen, and half-time work officially ended. Many women who were previously employed at Greenholme Mills remembered starting their employment in the spinning sheds. After two or three year's experience they could pay ten shillings (50p) training fee for the opportunity to become a weaver. Ten shillings was a large amount of money in those days and some women could not afford to pay. Weaving was very skilled work and pay was by the seventy-yard piece; a good weaver could earn twenty-seven shillings weekly, regarded as an excellent wage.[29] A lady in the village reminded me that late arrival at work meant that the gates were locked and there would be no pay (Figure 9).[30] Village tradition expected women to stay at home after marriage.

One lady interviewed, estimated that 75 per cent of women employed in textiles were married and that half of those may well

**Figure 9.** Group portrait at the entrance gates to Greenholm Mills on Iron Row c1900. *Author's collection*

have been in the twenty to twenty-nine age group.[31] Another interviewee described how women who worked after marriage, when their husbands were already employed, ran the risk of being ostracized by the villagers because of their so-called greed![32] The two world wars relaxed this expectation whilst the men were away, and demand for cloth was high. But after the wars, especially the first war, women were returned automatically to unpaid, under valued household work. Former weavers recalled how the mills were famous for the production of true blue serge. The cloth was used for ladies and gents suits and it was woven in grey and black and sent away to be dyed, probably to the Bradford Dyer's Association. One lady recalled weaving cloth for the Royal Canadian Mounted Police and the Manchester and Liverpool Police.[33] By the late 1920s shower proof tropical suiting became the mill's speciality. Many villagers today recalled Greenholme Mills providing a shop selling both uniform material and wool. The shop was called 'Cockatoo' (Figure 10).[34]

In 1801 the population of Burley was

**Figure 10.** The remains of the entrance to 'Cockatoo'. Greenhome Mills shop. *Author's collection*

**Figure 11.** Iron Row today. *Author's collection*

842, and by 1901 it had grown to 3,310. This growth was due to the availability of employment at the mill, and in 1921 the Burley Urban District Sanitary Commission passed plans to build twenty-six council houses which would be available to rent.[35]

Forster and Fison also provided rented accommodation for their mill workers. These are still sited throughout the village including West Terrace, North View, Spring Gardens, Park Row and Iron Row. Iron Row was originally called New Row, and its present name was adopted when the Luddites, a band of people intent on destroying machinery in the 1812 to 1818, became active. New Row had direct access to the mill and iron guards were fitted over the windows as a means of protection. Iron Row today still has stone floors and stairs and the ceilings are an unusual barrel shape, probably to accommodate machinery for the weaving which often took place in the upstairs rooms (Figure 11). There was no comparison between these terrace properties and those built at Great Pastures. In the main, they had two rooms up and two down with outside toilet facilities; but the rents were low and the provision of a house was usually linked to employment and wages. Today these homes are also privately owned. Iron Row is a much sought after area, and the small cottages today sell in the region of £100,000. Older residents recalled that in 1966, sitting tenants were paying rents between twelve and sixpence and twenty-five shillings weekly. One gentleman recalled that Forster and Fison would provide free land to those employees who were prepared to build their own houses, and his grandfather who worked at the mill, took advantage of this by paying £75 to have his house built privately.[36]

The mill had a great influence on the village especially whilst under the ownership of Forster and Fison, both of whom cared about education and social and political justice (Figure 12). They gave many benefits to Burley which otherwise the village might never have had. This was clearly demonstrated by their interest in and patriarchal attitude towards the community. They were one of the first mill owners in the country to provide a dining hall and holidays for their workers. These holidays were very much appreciated by the workers and in September 1849, following a holiday outing, an address conveying the workers' thanks, was spontaneously presented to the firm. It read:

**Figure 12.** William Edward Foster 1818-1886, painted by Henry Tamworth Wells RA. *Used by permission of the Reform Club, Piccadily, London.*

*Gentlemen, We, the undersigned in your employ, desire to express our sincere and heartfelt thanks for the very great kindness shown by you to us in our Saturday's excursion. We beg to assure you that but one feeling pervades every bosom, and that is satisfaction. The comfort of the arrangements, the diversity of the entertainments, and the liberality and condescension of our hosts, shall ever be remembered by us with lively feelings of gratitude and thankfulness.*

*We hope that this party, combined with other arrangements which you are so nobly and generously making for our comfort, may all tend to stir us up to renewed diligence, and conduce to the general welfare of all..*

*We are, gentlemen, with every feeling of respect and thanks,*
*Your Grateful Workpeople.*
*Bradford, September 3rd 1849.*[37]

Besides providing employment and housing, Foster and Fison were actively concerned with the education, welfare and the leisure of their employees and in 1856 built a lecture hall, (now the Queen's Hall), with the new Greenholme Mills School adjoining. This hall was designed to encourage and promote useful leisure pursuits and it was also one of the first of its kind in the country. The hall was primarily for the benefit of the workers at the mill, with a room was set aside for reading and provided daily with newspapers and books. It was seen as a place where villagers might have a comfortable place in which to assemble for lectures, meetings, concerts and kindred functions. The hall was used for silent film shows, which was the highlight of the week, especially for children. The films were changed twice weekly and were shown Mondays, Wednesdays, Thursdays and Saturdays, at a cost of one pence or two pence, depending on the seating. The hall's maintenance and repairs did not cost the rate-payers a penny. The whole expenditure in that direction was met by Forster and Fison.[38] The Queen's Hall was purchased by Burley Urban District Council in 1935 for £3,600 and is still very much used today. The mill owners also felt that there were too many public houses in Burley, so they provided a coffee shop at the junction of Back Lane and Main Street for the young men of the village, ostensibly to keep them out of mischief! [39]

In 1862, most of the workers at Greenholme Mills were provided with a railway trip to the London Exhibition at the expense of the firm. They had to walk to Apperley Bridge Station, approximately six miles away, and were followed by a wagonette to pick up the weak. They were all met by Forster and stayed in London overnight, a Mr Thomas Cook helping with the arrangements. He was later to become founder of the internationally famous travel agents Thomas Cook and Company. [40]

A dinner was held in 1892 at the *Midland Hotel* Bradford, to celebrate the 50th anniversary of the establishment of Greenholme Mills.[41] In 1899 to mark the Diamond Jubilee of Queen Victoria, William Fison made a gift in perpetuity, of a recreation ground to the village. It was reported in the *Wharfedale and Airedale Observer* on Friday, 30 June 1899:

> *Through the characteristic generosity of Mr W. Fison, the model village, as Burley in Wharfedale has not inappropriately been called, has provided a public recreation ground which will not only supply a present need and meet a future demand for years to come, but will be a permanent memorial of the jubilee. Formal possession of this munificent gift was given on Saturday last, the anniversary of the Queen's Coronation.*[42]

Working at the mill was hard and the hours long, therefore holidays were eagerly anticipated. Christmas Day, Boxing Day, Easter Monday, Whitsuntide Monday, two or three days in August and two or three for Burley Feast, was all the workers could expect before the First World War. Gradually, the holidays were increased so that the few days in August became a full week and the whole mill would shut down. Firms such as Forster and Fison did not pay holiday wages to their employees prior to the Second World War. Workers in the 1920s and the 1930s who wished to do so, paid into a 'Thrifty Fund', which they could draw out prior to the August Bank Holiday. In 1929, Mr Ben Mason, the Honorary Secretary and Treasurer of the Greenholme Mills Work Peoples Savings Club, reported that payments out for the year, including Easter, Whitsuntide and the Burley annual holiday week in August, totalled approximately £700, which was a striking testimony to the thriftyness of the Burley operatives! For those who had saved enough money, a holiday in the favourite resorts of Blackpool, Morecambe or Scarborough was possible, otherwise day trips in a charabanc might be preferred. The annual weekly shut down of the mill was a time when mill workers could enjoy some leisure time together. Many of them rented rooms at the seaside and bought their own food, which the landlady would cook for them. In this way whole families were able to enjoy a full week's holiday which otherwise they would not have been able to afford. In 1931, Forster and Fison also provided the motor transport for Boy Scouts and their equipment to camp under canvas at Redcar, whilst the Girl Guides elected to camp in Filey.[43]

The Rt Hon William Forster died on 5 April 1886, aged 68 years. Following a memorial service in Westminster Abbey he was buried in God's Little Acre Cemetery in Burley-in-Wharfedale, and in 1892 a fifteen foot high Celtic stone cross was erected in his memory by subscription from Burley residents. Following Fison's death in 1900, a similar cross was erected by the village in his memory. Both crosses are facsimiles of the ancient Columba's Cross on the Isle of Iona in Scotland. The crosses stand side by side today in front of the Queens Hall in Burley Main Street (Figure 13).[44]

**Figure 13.** The memorial crosses outside the Queen's Hall. *Author's collection*

Between 1851 and 1871, the Registrar General's Census of Population, recorded that 60 per cent of Burley's workforce was employed as textile operatives. By 1881 the number had fallen to less than fifty per cent. One thousand people were employed at Greenholme Mills in 1871, 800 in 1877, and 700 in the years 1889 to 1908. Subsequent directories do not give itemised figures, however, there are references to the fact that the inhabitants of Burley were chiefly employed in spinning and the manufacture of worsted.[4] Using this information it can be estimated that approximately 700 workers at least were employed at Greenholme Mills during the First World War. Employment would have been easier to find at that time as the government would expect textile manufacturers to increase their productivity in order to meet the extra needs of wartime contracts, for example, khaki cloth for armed forces uniforms. These years were inevitably boom years, and as in many manufacturing industries uncertainty and losses would have been temporarily shelved, large profits would have been made although this would not necessarily have been reflected in the wages of the workers.

By 1921, the percentage of textile workers in Burley-in-Wharfedale had been reduced to twenty-eight per cent and by 1931 it had fallen to twenty-seven per cent but textile work remained the predominant occupation in the area up to 1931.[46] Although textile work was still predominant in the village, the census returns give no indication as to whether the textile operatives listed were actually employed at Greenholme Mills. There may have been a number of people who travelled into Burley-in-Wharfedale from surrounding areas, for example, Ilkley, Otley and Addingham to work at the mill, and people in Burley-in-Wharfedale could have been employed in textiles in other areas. The records also reveal that forty-five per cent of females in the village were employed in textile work and twenty-seven per cent in domestic service. This included those working in the many private mansions, hotels, health hydros in Ilkley or at Scalebor Park Psychiatric Hospital in Burley. The building of the hospital in 1902 also played an important part in providing occupation for people in Burley which in turn influenced the building of more houses especially in the areas of Norwood, Grangefield and Lawn Avenue. By the late 1900s the hospital had virtually closed, the site being earmarked for residential development.

The post First World War boom years were followed by an inevitable decrease in the demand for cloth both at home and abroad. This produced severe losses in the textile trade and by 1927 the Greenholme Mills overdraft stood at £70,000. Five years later Barclays Bank refused to

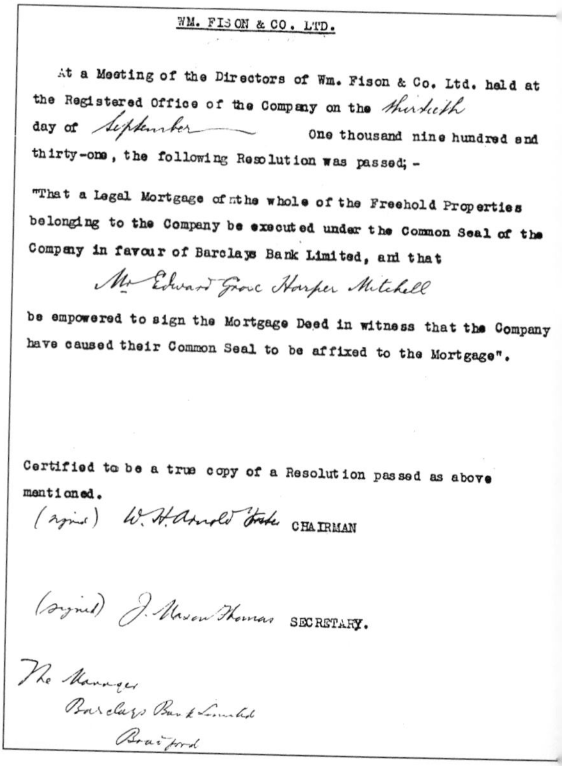

WM. FISON & CO. LTD.

At a Meeting of the Directors of Wm. Fison & Co. Ltd. held at the Registered Office of the Company on the thirtieth day of September One thousand nine hundred and thirty-one, the following Resolution was passed; -

"That a Legal Mortgage of the whole of the Freehold Properties belonging to the Company be executed under the Common Seal of the Company in favour of Barclays Bank Limited, and that

Mr Edward Grove Harper Mitchell

be empowered to sign the Mortgage Deed in witness that the Company have caused their Common Seal to be affixed to the Mortgage".

Certified to be a true copy of a Resolution passed as above mentioned.

(signed) W. H. Arnold Forster CHAIRMAN

(signed) J. Mason Thomas SECRETARY.

The Manager
Barclays Bank Limited
Bradford

**Figure 14.** Mortgage papers 1931.
*Courtesy of the West Yorkshire Archive Services, Bradford*

support a request for further borrowing. Reorganisation became inevitable. The mill was mortgaged by the Midland Bank and strict controls were imposed on spending; and many of the Greenholme Estate houses were put up for sale (Figure 14).[47]

In May 1929, Forster and Fison were forced to reduce wages for all employees. The 600 workers who remained at the mill accepted one shilling and sixpence in the pound wage reduction and further reductions were noted in the firm's 1931 minute books.[48] The only union at that time remained the Overlooker's Union for the foremen. There was no official support for the ordinary workers, but there was never a recorded strike or serious dispute at the mill.[49] By 1931, unemployment was recorded in Burley-in-Wharfedale as consisting of ninety six males and twenty six females, or just over seventy per cent of the total village work force.[50] In 1933 an unemployment committee was formed to help co-ordinate welfare efforts; twenty-four allotments were made available to the unemployed and distress vouchers of two shillings and sixpence (12½p) were offered to needy families (Figure 15). An appeal was made for furniture and physical activities arranged, especially for the young men :

*Who were out of work and apt to let themselves go and are losing mentally and physically, all the time they are out of employment, it is hoped to brace them up with physical exercise, which of course will be entirely optional.* [51]

There was no recorded provision for women who were unfortunate enough to be unemployed. The older generation in the village recalled working short time during the 1930s depression and one lady remembers how men had to work night shift in the spinning sheds. As this was

**Figure 15.** Help for the Unemployed and the issuing of distress vouchers in 1933 as recorded in the *Ilkley Gazette*.
*Author's collection*

### HELP FOR UNEMPLOYED.

A public meeting will be held in the village next week to discuss the question of assisting local unemployed.

A deputation from the Burley branch of the British Legion waited on the Urban District Council on Monday, after the public business of the meeting had been transacted, and asked for the support of the Council in the provision of facilities for physical and mental recreation for the unemployed.

Seen yesterday, the Chairman of the Council (Mr. R. Gossop) said he would call a public meeting one day next week, to appoint a committee who will formulate a scheme.

"At the Council meeting, Major McQueen gave a resume of suggestions put forward by the Legion," said Mr. Gossop. "Broadly speaking, the idea is that the young men who are out of work are apt to let themselves go, and are losing, mentally and physically, all the time they are out of employment. It is hoped to brace them up with physical exercises, which, of course, will be entirely optional, and help them in every way we possibly can.

"While the Council received the idea with sympathy, we cannot, of course, use Council funds in this connection, but an appeal will be made for subscriptions, and the organising committee will be drawn from all denominations in the village.

"All the details will be outlined and discussed at the public meeting held next week."

### DISTRESS VOUCHERS.

The Distress Committee of the Burley Unemployment Welfare Scheme have decided that eight half-crown vouchers should be distributed to deserving cases in the village this week, and a similar number next week. This brings the total number of vouchers distributed to 40, which was the number authorised by the full committee. Another meeting will be held shortly.

traditionally women's work, it was very much resented by the make workers. In contrast, long hours of overtime were worked during the Second World War to meet the new demand for cloth.[52]

During the inter-war years, male workers in Burley-in-Wharfedale were employed in textiles, printing, engineering, agriculture, commerce and local government. The 1921 census showed 19.7 per cent worked in textiles, 13.5 per cent in metalwork, 12.4per cent in agriculture and 9.3 per cent in commerce. A decade later the 1931 census revealed twenty-one per cent worked in textiles and only 6.8 in engineering. More males had moved into commercial distributive trades and local government, a trend that remains today, necessitating people commuting to the nearby cities of Leeds and Bradford to gain employment.[53]

Those who worked at Greenholme Mills in the 1950s recalled the introduction of new machinery and the production of synthetic fibres, but despite these attempts to modernise, the mill was forced to cease production on 26 October 1966.[54] This was partly due to escalating costs, lack of capital investment and a renewal of fierce competition from foreign markets. The slump in textiles affected textile manufacturers throughout the country and was evidence of the British industrial decline. A serious fire at the mill on 8 July 1966 was extensively reported in a local newspaper, but the actual closure in 1966 provoked little interest.[55] The Greenholme Estate, including the mill, was put up for sale by auction in twenty-two lots at the Queen's Hall, Burley in Wharfedale on Friday, 6 September 1968. (Figure 16). It was purchased privately prior to auction, for an agreed figure of £70,000.[56] Most of the dwellings have since been

**Figure 16.** Papers rellating to the sale of Greenholme Mills 1968. *Courtesy of Dacre, Son & Hartley*

WJH/JS

25th March.1968.

Messrs. H.M. Dawson & Co.,
1. Piccadilly,
Bradford. 1.

Dear Sirs.

re Greenholme Estate. Burley-in-Wharfedale.

We are pleased to inform you that on behalf of our mutual clients. Messrs. illiam Fison & Co. Ltd., we have agreed to sell the above Estate to Messrs. oadland Properties Ltd. Of High House. East Ayton. Scarborough. at the sum of 0.000, subject to contract, and we enclose herewith a plan showing the Estate as rounded by the red line excluding the properties coloured in purple. The rights of y are shown in brown.

We also enclose a schedule of the Field areas and, in some cases these will fer slightly from the areas shown on the Ordnance sheet where alterations have en place since the Ordnance sheet was printed. e.g. where intermediate boundary ces have been moved.

We confirm that the following properties are included in the sale:- Block nprising 68 & 70. Main Street and Flats above 68a and 70a; also cottage at rear .2. Iron Row. The terrace of cottages Nos. 1/29 Iron Row, odd numbers. together h the plot of land at the rear as shown on the plan. Cottage at the corner of ltherbank and Main Street – see plan. Farm and cottages at Greenholme, apart from s. 3. 4 & 5, which are being sold to Mr. Green. The farm buildings and garages. od Lodge; also the fishing rights. Mill premises including the lodge. Nos.4, 6 &16. at Pasture. No.7, Great Pasture.

Please note the following are expressly excluded from the sale:-

(a) Garage block at the end of Great Pasture comprising 4 garages.

(b) The balance of the claim for compensation for the loss of development value consequent upon refusal of planning permission. When this compensation has been paid. there will no further claim holding attaching to the land..

**WEST RIDING OF YORKSHIRE**

Leeds 12 miles Bradford 10 miles

Excellent, well maintained Industrial Premises of approximately 133,000 sq. ft. in unique situation close to trunk road affording easy access to Lancashire and West Riding towns. Vacant possession offered but large demand for tenancies also affords scope for **High Yield Investment.** Adequate loading and parking facilities

Reasonable price on application to:

**DACRE, SON & HARTLEY**

Chartered Surveyors, Chartered Auctioneers and Estate Agents
3 and 5, THE GROVE, ILKLEY. Tel.: 3366 (4 lines)
and at **Otley, Keighley** and **Skipton**

**Figure 17.** Greenholm Mills today. *Author's collection*

sold. Today the mill remains standing, a visible reminder of a former thriving industry on which local economy depended. It now serves as a trading estate divided into independent letting units (Figures 17&18).

**Figure 18.** Gate house to Greenholme Mills today. *Author's collection*

Burley-in-Wharfedale had already begun to lose its identity because of two local government reorganisations. The first when it ceased to be Burley Urban District Council in the 1930s (becoming part of Ilkley Urban District Council), and in 1974 when it became incorporated into Bradford Metropolitan District Council, even though its post code is given as LS, which is Leeds.[57]

In the days when Greenholme Mills were active, Burley was a village where everyone knew everyone else. Working at Greenholme Mills developed a sense of shared experience and cohesiveness for people living in Burley-in-Wharfedale. Apart from working in the same place villagers took their holidays at the same time, tended to visit the same resort and share the same leisure facilities. The community was largely united by kinship, friendship, self-containment and a sense of solidarity and belonging. Sadly, worsted manufacturing lives only in the memories of those who once worked at the mill; the industrial core of the village has disappeared. Burley-in-Wharfedale has become a village of commuters.

### Notes and References

1. Speight H *Upper Wharfedale*, Elliot Stock, London 1900 p 140.
2. Ingle G *The West Riding Cotton Industry 1780-1835*, Unpublished Ph D. Thesis,1980, Bradford University p 583. Quoted with full permission of the author and Bradford University J B Priestley Library.
3. Registrar General Census, Reference Library, Bradford.
4. Ingle G *op cit* p 178.
5. Ingle G *op cit* p 583.

6. Ingle G *op cit* p 199.
7. Ingle G *op cit* p 122.
8. Ingle G *op cit* p 118.
9. Ingle G *op cit* p 123.
10. Ingle G *op cit* p 118.
11. *Sale Documents 1848*. Fison Collection West Yorkshire Archive Service Bradford.
12. Fieldhouse J *Bradford 1978*, Watmough Ltd, and City of Bradford Metropolitan Libraries Division p 157.
13. Speight H *op cit*, p 152.
14. Fieldhouse J *op cit*, p 157.
15. Fieldhouse J *op cit*, p 158.
16. SpeightH *op cit*, p 148.
17. Interview with Doris Lomax 2000.
18. Interview with Barbara Hargrave 1989.
19. Interview with Dick Hargrave 1989.
20. Interview with Mr FWN, Newbould 1989.
21. Fieldhouse J *op cit*, p 160.
22. Interview with Mr FWN Newbould 1989.
23. *Ibid.*
24. *Ibid.*
25. *Ibid.*
26. Interview with C Jackson 2000.
27. Registrar General Census 1881 Reference Library Bradford.
28. Interview with C Jackson 1989.
29. Interview with B Wood 1989.
30. Interview with C Jackson 1989.
31. *Ibid.*
32. *Ibid.*
33. Interview with Doris Lomax 2000.
34. Interview with FWN Newbould 1989.
35. Registrar General Census 1801 and 1901 Reference Library Bradford.
36. Interview with D Stirk 1989.
37. Speight H *op cit,* p 153.
38. Interview with FWN Newbould 1989.
39. Burley Urban District Council minutes 1935. Reference Library Bradford.
40. Interview with F.W.N. Newbould 1989.
41. *Ilkley Gazette*, 9.1.92.
42. *Wharfedale & Airedale Observer*, 30.6.1899.
43. *Ilkley Gazette*, 9.8.1929, 16.8.1929, 7.8.1931 and 14.8.1931.
44. Speight H. *op cit*, p 151.
45. Registrar General Census Papers 1851, 1871, 1877, 1889 and 1908. Reference Library Bradford.
46. *Ibid* 1921 and 1931.
47. Minutes Book 1931 Fison Collection. Reference Library Bradford.
48. *Ibid.*
49. Speight H. *op cit*, p 154.
50. Registrar General Census Papers 1931. Bradford Reference Library.
51. *Ilkley Gazette* 3.2.1933.
52. Interview with C Jackson 1989.
53. Registrar General Census Papers 1921 and 1931. Reference Library Bradford.
54. *Ilkley Gazette* 26.10.1966.
55. *Ibid* 8.7.1966.
56. Sale Records, Dacre Son and Hartley, 6.9.1968.
57. Interview with FWN Newbould 1989.

## Acknowledgements

I wish to express sincere thanks to everyone in Burley-in-Wharfedale who agreed to be interviewed. I also acknowledge the invaluable support and encouragement of both Dr G Ingle and Mary Laurenson. In addition I would like to pay tribute to Mrs P Henshaw of the J B Priestley Library University of Bradford, Bradford Reference Library and the staff of West Yorkshire Archives, Bradford whose combined help was also invaluable. I am also indebted to my husband for his help and support in researching the history of Greenholme Mills. Thank you also to Phil Skerratt and Jane Shaw for their computer skills. Finally, a special word of thanks goes to Lynne Stevenson Tate, for her professional guidance and optimism.

# 4. THE END OF THE HILL

## *by Maisie Morton*

IN UPPER ARMLEY, right on the border with Bramley was a small cluster of houses. This was Hill End. A secret sort of place. Its secrets are safe now. Too late to ask people about the interiors and occupants of the different dwellings. Official records merely confuse. Census returns give no house numbers and start in a different place each time. Poll books only give the names of those entitled to vote. Directories miss people out and give wrong names to places. Attempting to reconstruct the place on paper is like doing a giant jigsaw with at least a third of the pieces missing. Once it must have been a busy, bustling place with lots of workers, many children and with close relatives living in neighbouring cottages or in the nearby hamlets of Upper Heights, Lower Heights and Hill Top (Figure 1). Farming and clothmaking kept people busy in each place. The fields and paths ran between the four small groups with little interruption. By the 1900s however, it was mainly residential, quiet, and known by visitors for its spectacular views of Farnley, Morley, Drighlington and Tong, which made it possible to see weather coming before it arrived. At Hill End one said hopefully 'It's clearing over by Tong'. The sunsets were lovely - the winds less so.

When the Leeds, Bradford and Halifax Junction Railway was opened in 1853 it served to isolate the hamlet from its neighbours at Lower Heights and Upper Heights, even though the management provided a corrugated iron footbridge and a farm access bridge. However, there were still several ways to get to the place. One was from Hill Top along Hill End Road, always known as 'The Lane'. The lane, about 400 yards long, was merely a mud track in winter and a dust track in

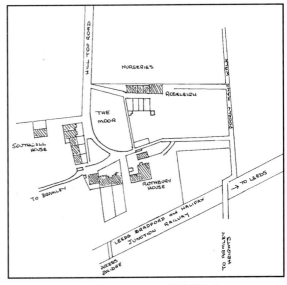

**Figure 1.** Plan of the hamlet of Hill End.

summer, until the 1920s when it became a metalled road which stopped abruptly when it reached the hamlet. Another way was along an ancient pathway running parallel with the lane, known locally as 'Poorly Man's Walk', so named, the story goes, because convalescing or ageing men would bring stools and sit in the sunshine, their backs against the high boundary wall of Westfield House (Figure 2). At the end of the wall was a sharp bend and then the path continued for a further 300 yards or so, crossed the iron railway bridge and hurtled down to Armley Heights and finally to Farnley Beck. Just before the reaching the bridge, another path branched off to the right, sloping upward to the hamlet of Hill End. It passed in front of a row of houses and ambled off through a stile to 'Jim Watt's Bottoms' and so to Bramley. I believe Jim Watt was a farmer called James Watmough. The rest of the name - probably geographical.

The group of houses was, literally, at the end of the hill which peaked at Hill Top, and lay around a quite steeply sloping patch of grass known as The Moor'. Towards the end of the 1800s it was, together with the surrounding fields and houses, rather grandly referred to in documents as The Hill End Estate. Hill End Road, as a compacted dirt road continued around around three sides of the moor, which later incomers were inclined to call 'The Green' as though it were a village green in a rural sense, just awaiting the Morris Dancers who would have certainly fallen over on the rough ground. It was common land which is probably why the metalled road only went to its rim and it had been a public tenter ground. This was where newly woven and treated cloth was, in past days, fastened by tenter hooks to large wooden frames and stretched out to dry and shape in the fresh air.

**Figure 2.** The path from 'Poorly Man's Walk' up to Hill End in winter. This shows Roseleigh and the cottages on the SE side of the moor, the bungalow, the ash tree, the tennis court and what had been John Elley's field. Far left are 'The Homes' and far right the Nurseries.

**Figure 3.** Hill Top Moor in the year 2000.

Armley, described in early directories as being 'chiefly inhabited by clothiers', had several of these public tenter grounds, as had Wortley and Bramley. In Armley these pieces of land were often known as 'Moors'. Hill Top Moor lay at the border of Armley and Bramley adjacent to a quarry. The moor itself and the outlines of the quarry are now rough scrub land (Figure 3). Little Moor has faired well and is now a park at the junction of Wortley Road and Town Street (Figure 4). Nearby Armley Moor, lying between Town Street and Theaker Lane is where the once renowned Armley Feast is held at the beginning of each September (Figure 5). There

**Figure 4.** Armley Moor, now a park in 2000.

**Figure 5.** Armley Moor, where the Feast is held in 2000.

**Figure 6.** The remodelled tenter ground in Theaker Lane with seat in 2000.

was another smaller tenter ground in Theaker Lane, which has become part of a long strip of grassland dividing new housing from the road. A seat is there, which bears an uncanny resemblance to one which used to be at Hill End (Figure 6). Kirby in *Armley Through the Camera* mentions the many weaver's houses on Redcote Hill, now vanished, where there was another public tenter ground, again next to a stone quarry. The Gott family enclosed these within their boundary wall in exchange for other land which they owned as part proprietors of the Canal Company. This became Whingate Park, more familiarly known as 'Charley Cake Park'. Kirby also mentions houses in Ridge Road which used to be weaving shops. They were close to a long narrow tenter ground which partially disappeared with the building of the turnpike from Bradford, now Stanningley Road. There was another at the junction of Wortley Road and Whingate, now built upon and one down Canal Road or the former Airegate Road. There were at least four private Tenter Closes with houses - two on Armley Ridge Road, another on Hall Lane and one at the top of Swallow Hill bordering on Wortley. There were probably several more which have now vanished. When their use as tenter grounds was over, the larger spaces like Hill Top Moor and Armley Moor were used for public meetings, political and religious and also travelling entertainers.

Hill End changed remarkably little through the years. The moor lay on a north west by south east axis but just north and south is used here for ease of reference. According to the Armley Enclosure Award of 1799, the closes around and abutting the moor were held by James Graham, John Elley, Jno Musgrave, Jonas Gamble and Wm Whitelock.

James Graham of Kirkstall was born in November 1853, second son of Thomas Graham of Edmond Castle. He was MP for Carlisle and a man of some public standing. He was married to Anne Moore, an heiress and daughter of the Reverend Moore of Kirkstall and became a baronet in 1803. He died in 1825 and was succeeded by his son Sandford. He held much property in Armley and other districts of Leeds but his allocation immediately adjoining the hamlet on the west, were Foot Gate Closes, Farr Close and Near Close. The tenants were Samuel Mirfield, Thomas Stead and Abe Halliday.

John Elley is a missing jigsaw piece. Little seems to be known about him. He could have been the John Elley born to John and Hannah Elley of Hunslet Lane, Leeds in 1769, but there is no proof. However, he does not appear to have been an Armley man and is referred to in the Award as Mr Elley. He too, had some land on the west side of the moor: Far Close, Near Close, Upper Close, Low Close, and housing. All were tenanted by Samuel Mirfield and Josua North. Elley also held a square of land bordered by Near Close on the west, Jonas Gamble's patch to the north, Jno Musgrave's on the east and Wm Whitelock's to the south.

John Musgrave was a butcher and held Old Geldard Close, Low Geldard Close, Upper Close, and some housing, all on the north of the moor, and two closes on the east. He himself lived at Upper Close and other housing mentioned was occupied by Roberts and 'others'. The Musgraves were an old, well respected Armley and Wortley family. They were farmers, yeomen and connected with the wool industry. John had four other allotments of land in different parts of Armley.

Jonas Gamble, son of George Gamble of Farnley was born in 1730 and held a small patch of land adjoining the moor and between it and John Elley's little unnamed square of land. He also had housing on the west tenanted by Foster and 'others'. His family, mostly farmers, held property at nearby Armley Heights but also had a good deal of land in Farnley. Gamble Lane runs from the valley up to Farnley. There is also a Gamble Hill Estate in Bramley.

William Whitelock was the person appointed Commissioner to carry out and make awards for the enclosure. He allocated quite a bit of property to himself in this area including the land directly south of Hill End. One of his allotted closes, called Far Ing, covered what later became part of the playing fields of West Leeds High School bounded on one side by 'Poorly Man's Walk' and Heights Lane on the other. It was later cut through by the railway. His *Hieghts Estate* [sic] ran together with Graham's and Elley's land down to Heights Lane and Armley Heights. Before he died around 1810 Whitelock had acted as Commissioner for thirty eight enclosures all over Yorkshire but particularly in the old West Riding. It would be interesting to know what land he had allocated to himself in all these places.

The enclosure plan shows buildings only on the north and west sides of the moor but by 1846 a township map shows six more cottages off the south east corner of the ground. Exactly when these cottages were built is one of the missing jigsaw pieces. They were certainly built before 1841 as the census for that year gives eighteen houses in the hamlet, six of them unoccupied. The next four decades all have the same number of houses - eighteen, a number which varies little through the following years. Sometimes one house was made into two - sometimes two were changed into one but otherwise little altered. The number of occupants did vary.

Around 1800 the hamlet was home to Josua North, Abe Holliday, Samuel Mirfield, Thomas Stead, Jno Musgrave, Roberts, Foster and two lots of 'others'. It is impossible to say how many 'others' there were, or how large a family any of them had. An educated guess would suggest that the 'others' consisted of five more families making a total of twelve. In 1819 some of the Graham land passed to George Kindersley, and the tenants were John Briggs, Thomas Page, William Squire, George Wray, William Sykes, John Wade and Robert Thompson but the size of their families is not known.

### Table 1 Levels of occupancy between 1841-1891

|  | occupied houses | unoccupied | occupants |
|---|---|---|---|
| 1841 | 12 | 6 | 61 |
| 1851 | 14 | 4 | 67 |
| 1861 | 17 | 1 | 81 |
| 1871 | 18 | 3 | 88 |
| 1881 | 17 | 1 | 92 |
| 1891 | 17 | 2 | 89 |

The figures above are as accurate as can be made owing to the vagaries of the census ennumerators as mentioned earlier. It is also sometimes difficult to make out which houses are actually at Hill End and which are on Hill End Road. The writing doesn't help. There are at present no available figures for the total number of inhabitants for the following years but the area did become almost entirely residential and by the 1960s when it became certain that the hamlet really was to be demolished, the number of occupants in each house was in most cases only one or two.

The occupations of the people who lived at Hill End also changed throughout the years. Around 1800 there was a butcher, farm workers and certainly cloth workers. As less important people are not mentioned in early directories or poll books, the census of 1841 is the first real chance to find out what work ordinary people were doing.

### Table 2 Occupations as shown in the Censuses from 1841 to 1891

|  | Cloth | Agriculture | Bricks | Coal | Iron | Shoes&boots | Currier | Other/retired | Total inhabitants | Children twelve or under |
|---|---|---|---|---|---|---|---|---|---|---|
| 1841 | 23 | 1 |  |  |  |  |  | 3 | 61 | 21 |
| 1851 | 23 | 1 |  |  | 1 |  |  | 11 | 67 | 20 |
| 1861 | 22 | 1 | 5 | 3 | 1 | 1 | 3 | 3 | 81 | 29 |
| 1871 | 17 | 2 | 2 | 7 | 2 |  | 3 | 7 | 88 | 34 |
| 1881 | 8 | 1 | 3 | 1 | 1 | 3 | 2 | 28 | 92 | 30 |
| 1891 | 6 | 1 | 1 | 1 | 3 | 3 | 5 | 15 | 89 | 31 |

*Other occupations included chemists, tailoresses, machinists, teachers, clerks, joiners, a postman, an architect, a glazier, a sawyer etc. Non-working wives are not included in these figures.*

Most of the cloth workers were weavers but there were also slubbers, burlers, fillers, carders, warpers, pieceners, steamers, and of course the manufacturers themselves. No child under twelve was actually working but the large number of children is quite astonishing. Much later, between 1918 and 1945, the local children living in the hamlet apart from those living in 'The Homes' could almost have been counted on the fingers of one hand, but back in 1871, of the eighty eight inhabitants, an astonishing thirty four were children of twelve or under. One couple, a James Brookesbank and his wife had nine offspring aged between twenty-one years and one year, together with the nineteen year old wife of one of the older sons. They were all in one cottage.

The west side of the moor underwent most changes. There was at least one farm with barns, outhouses, a private well and an access bridge over the railway. This was worked by Joshua Briggs, the son of John Briggs. He had bought the farm from Sir Sandford Graham. In 1871 his own son Joshua inherited five cottages with stables, mistals and outbuildings and it seems that, at that point, three of the cottages became Rothbury House. This younger Joshua, was a bookseller and his wife and daughters started a Day and Boarding School in what must have become a reasonably roomy house with, according to the 1891 census, ten rooms. He, his wife and three sons, seven daughters and two other teachers were living there at the time of the 1881 census, but in the mid eighties the school moved into another large house with garden in Armley Town Street, which was probably a more convenient site. It was known as 'Miss Briggs's' for many years and was where children of parents who could afford to pay for all the extras - paper, pencils, painting, sewing and so on, were educated. Rothbury House, two cottages, barn, stable and outbuildings known as the Hill End Estate was sold to Hannah Crowther of Pudsey who then, in 1893, sold to the banker Richard Wilson of Westfield House. By 1891 there were two households tenanting Rothbury House.

On the same side of the moor, from very early times, there was also a weaving shed. William Austin, a clothier, appears in a poll book of 1807 and his son Thomas Austin is first named as a cloth manufacturer in a directory of 1822. William disappears from Hill End sometime after the 1851 census. Two other residents describe themselves as cloth manufacturers employing men in 1851 but it is not possible to say whether they actually used part of this particular building. It was here that most of the people living round the moor were employed in various capacities connected with cloth making. To begin with there were three dwellings on ground level. These were eventually made into one, with two working floors above, similar to another weaving shed at Hill Top. The weaving must have been done in this building as the windows of the surrounding cottages were too small to afford sufficient light for home weaving. When the factory was bought in 1895 by Richard Wilson, it was described as a warehouse and house. That the cloth industry must have moved away, is indicated by the lack of suitable workers living around the moor. The building was pulled down and Wilson had two semi-detached brick houses built in its place, one slightly larger than the other. These, the last houses to be built in the hamlet, had their backs facing the moor. The front of the houses had a view over Farnley and were nicely faced with stone, which was rather a waste as the houses were not visible except from a considerable distance. Wilson made several other changes on this edge of the moor. Two other cottages were made into one which also looked towards Farnley; three cottages were made into two and a barn was demolished. Privies, coal places, and pigsties were added. At his death his executors sold the property to each tenant.

By the end of the 1800s the north side of the rectangle consisted of three small cottages with single mullioned windows, two larger houses and another house slightly to the rear. At one point this row was called Ivy Terrace but the name seemed to fall into disuse. For a time the two larger houses were made into one and in the 1920s were used as a Children's Home. They were unusual in that to reach the front door you crossed a little bridge from the flagstone pavement over a sunken playground. During the Spanish Civil War, the home was used to house refugee children from the Basque area and afterwards reverted to two dwellings. The house to the rear is another lost piece of the jigsaw. A guess is that this was the much altered house, owned by William Musgrave back at the time of enclosure, called at one time Beverley Cottage and eventually becoming Southwell House. It did at one time belong to the Board of Guardians who administered the Bramley Union Workhouse, as did the cottages and houses on that side of the moor.

The terrace of homes on the south-east corner of the moor, backed on to a high stone wall behind which were nursery gardens and greenhouses, on land which had belonged originally to John Musgrave but was eventually bought by Richard Wilson. This row of cottages underwent the fewest changes. I can only speak with certainty about the interiors of these particular houses as I never entered any others around the moor. As grandchildren of the

**Figure 7.** 'The Moor' looking SE towards the four cottages and Roseleigh, 1958.

Rhodes's at Roseleigh, we were not encouraged to mingle, but I have been told that the three older cottages on the north side were very similar.

The six cottages, built before 1841 were then inhabited mostly by weavers (Figure 7). In 1874 William Rhodes, a joiner living temporarily at Shadwell, and out for a walk with his wife and son, 'happened' across Hill End (Figure 8). Given the distance from Shadwell and the hidden nature of the place, the gentle Sunday afternoon walk seems unlikely, but one must respect family traditions. They liked the place and bought the cottages and the land in front of them - land which had been allocated to Jonas Gamble by the enclosure and had since been owned by Isaac Akeroyd and his nephew, John Bailey Akeroyd. The two cottages furthest away from the moor were to be pulled down and a larger brick house constructed, designed by William Rhodes' son, Frederick William who was an up and coming architect and it was to replicate the one they were presently living in at Shadwell (Figure 9). I believed every word! However, Frederick William, who certainly did become a well respected architect, being responsible for the plans for well over 8000 houses in West Leeds alone, was only thirteen at the time of the 'walk'. It is therefore possible that the alterations to property at Hill End which were proposed by William Rhodes in 1877 and 1878, was when work first started.

**Figure 8.** William Rhodes with his eldest grandaughter Mabel, my mother, c1890.

**Figure 9.** Frederick William Rhodes, son of William in his office c.1900.

The plans for this work are presently unavailable as they are fragile. Frederick William was articled in 1880 and the family were certainly living at Hill End in 1881 (Figure 10).

The new house became Roseleigh and the garden was quite a show place with lawns, an orchard, a vegetable plot, a carpet garden, a rose garden, rockeries, a greenhouse, a henrun and a much loved summerhouse. Familiarly known as 'the bungalow', this summerhouse had two rooms, casement windows, a balcony and was sturdy and warm enough to sleep extra visitors as, although built of wood, it was double thickness (Figure 11). A huge ash tree in the garden could be seen for miles around. Purchase of further land in 1910 from Richard Wilson's executors gave the garden a tennis court, a field (the land which had been allocated to John Elley by Enclosure) and access to 'Poorly Man's Walk' (Figure 12). It also enabled a scullery to be added to the house on the ground floor which to a child's eye always looked as though it was about to fall off on to the tennis

**Figure 10.** Roseleigh c.1949

**Figure 11.** The bungalow and Roseleigh, c.1900

court. Until about 1960, Roseleigh was the venue for many tennis and garden parties, both private and in aid of Whingate Methodist Chapel, which the family attended regularly ever since its inception by Joseph Pearson, William's father-in-law. There are still ladies, now possessors of bus passes, who remember attending Brownie meetings on warm summer evenings in the garden of Roseleigh, playing in new mown hay and going home delightedly clutching bunches of marguerites from the garden. In those days the back-to-back houses of Whingate had no gardens.

The house itself had two large bedrooms and a boxroom large enough to take a single bed. At some date a bathroom had been made out of part of one of the bedrooms and was tiled with Burmantofts faience and was my grandmother's pride and joy. Years later I found a few spare tiles in an outhouse. They were spider ridden, cracked and mouldering but I was told they were much too valuable to use for hopscotch. Spring water must have been used, as mains drainage did not arrive until the mid 1920s. I cannot ever remember the house without the bathroom.

**Figure 12.** Maisie (the author, left) and cousin Margaret Rhodes c1937-8.

When William Rhodes died in 1891, his son Frederick William inherited, and before moving to the newly built 'Aberdeens' in Whingate, his widow Mary lived for a short time in the house next door, No 21. A doorway, said to have been cut through a built-in wardrobe in the main bedroom, gave ready access. I looked in the wardrobe when I was sure Grandma was out, but never found any sign of the door, just a smell of mothballs. The relative heights of No 21 and No 23 would have meant access steps being built in No 21. On the ground floor was a sitting room and a living room and a small hallway floored with Minton tiles. There was a cellar kitchen, quite light and dry with a range and sink. This was the domain of the servant. There was also a larder, a keeping cellar and coal cellar.

Each of the four cottages had a small patch of garden at the other side of the brick road which gave access to the large wooden gates of Roseleigh. This was a continuation of the dirt road, and a narrow flagstone footpath connected the houses. At the bottom of these gardens and reached only by going right around the near edge of the moor, was a privy. It was a very long distance to walk especially in inclement weather, even when flushing toilets arrived. The dwellings were what were known as an 'up and a down'. They had a living room, a bedroom and a cellar (not counted as a room in census records) so the number of rooms - two - as given in 1891 for three of these cottages is correct. As all them were exactly the same size, so it is rather a surprise that in 1891, Benjamin Dean who lived at No 15 and whose family had lived at Hill End for many years, claimed to have four rooms. He must have partitioned his bedroom - but accommodating himself, his wife and six children in 1881 in a house that size must have been a huge problem. His was the first house in the row but there was no evidence of an out-shot or lean-to ever having been built. It is very difficult to imagine how poor Hannah Dean coped and not surprising really that Benjamin was a widower by 1891. Even in that year, there were five adults aged between thirteen and forty-eight living in the two rooms.

On photographs the bedroom windows of the first two cottages, No 15 and No 17 show some sign of having originally been about twelve inches wider than those in the other cottages, No 19 and No 21. The bedroom had a plain sash window at the front, an open staircase rising in one corner and no underdrawing or false roof. In time, some tenants made a second miniscule bedroom by a partition and in even more recent times, a back bedroom window was inserted in each house. These offered little extra light, facing as they did, the high stone wall which surrounded the nursery. The staircase rose almost immediately from just inside the outer door. Again, later occupants had sometimes added a partition to make a minute hallway. The living room had a fireplace and a sink. There was also a cellar with stone steps probably also open. All very basic so far, but the cellar was vaulted in such a way that it seemed as though there was a tunnel extending through all the cottages in the row. At the bottom of the stairs, let into the rough, uneven brick floor, was a place for coal and a trough with cold fresh water running through it. The water would have run initially through all six cottages. When the two were pulled down to build Roseleigh the water must have been used in the cellar kitchen and then culverted in some way. Obviously spring water, it never seemed to dry up. It is unlikely to have been used in any home manufacturing process given that the trough was on floor level and quite small - little larger than a kitchen sink and there was no natural light. It could only have been for household use. The nearest public well was at Hill Top but, in those days anyone who could afford it had small wells in their cellars, just as Joshua Briggs had one in his own garden. Very many years later, after the whole of Hill End had been demolished, the authorities said that the land was useless for building because of the many springs - a problem which one hopes has now been solved. As water would have been needed for the manufacturing processes in the weaving shed/factory, that too must have been drawn from springs. The Farnley Beck was far down in the valley.

This last row of houses changed the least, but still poses a problem. Back in 1874 there were six cottages. According to the deed  'Now in the several occupations of Thomas Hall, George Wainman, John Ramsey, George Austin, Benjamin Dean, Joseph Ramsey, and A B Coldwell'. Surely that makes seven occupants for six cottages? In 1881 George Wainman (his father had lived there before him), John Ramsey, Benjamin Dean, George Austin and William Rhodes are living in the terrace. What happened to Thomas Hall who was sixty-six in 1874 and his wife; Joseph Ramsey twenty-nine and his wife and two children and the mysterious A B Coldwell who appears nowhere else? William Rhodes was a gentle, loving, godfearing man.  Surely they were not just evicted.

Little happened here between the two World Wars. There was certainly no industry, but seldom were there any houses empty. Some families were second and third generation. People now lived there but went elsewhere to work. The houses and gardens were cared for and little disturbed the calm. After the last war however, everything began to run down. Young people, who in the century before would have stayed and moved into another house in the hamlet on marriage, went away to get work. The older people began to feel that the lane seemed to be getting longer. So many things became more difficult. There were rumours of a road going through but nobody knew its destination. Roseleigh and the cottages became infested each summer with a plague of minute flies which completely covered grandma's beautiful tiles. In wet weather the cellars of Roseleigh became inches deep in spring water. The showpiece garden, always hard work to maintain, now became a burden and gradually, all around the moor, even the older people moved away to stay with relatives or to find more labour-saving accommodation. Then in the mid 1960s came the compulsory purchase orders.

Hill End  vanished completely and new housing now covers the whole area - the hamlet and the fields. It has been named 'St Mary's Park' after the nearby Hospital which used to be the Workhouse. 'The Hill End Estate' would have been more historically accurate but perhaps 'Estate' doesn't have the right connotations. A small oblong of grass around an access footpath at the end of Hill End Road is all that remains of the moor. I was probably alone in feeling glad to see it go. As the only relative still living in Leeds but not at Hill End, I found caring for the two elderly Rhodes ladies who still lived there, and fighting an endless battle with the garden was very tiring. But for many people it was the end of an era and it did not take long for nostalgia to turn it into a sort of paradise. Several years ago there was quite a lively correspondence in the *Yorkshire Evening Post* in response to a letter from a past resident, all telling of idyllically happy hours spent there.

One Rhodes lady moved in 1966 and the other in 1967 - one from a cottage and the other the other from Roseleigh. The family had been there a hundred years and there was a strong feeling of loss. Forgotten were the flies, the weeds, the ever growing lawns, the rundown feeling, the bitter winters, the general inaccessibility. A nostalgic trip back after the houses were gone filled even me with misery. The big ash tree in the garden, once such a brave landmark had disappeared. Because of tipped rubbish, nettles and dock plants, it was impossible to distinguish the site of the houses, or make out where the tennis court or the greenhouse had been. It was as though Roseleigh and Hill End itself had never existed. This spanking new estate is surely better than that dreadful devastation and who knows maybe one day someone digging in their garden may come across the two stone cannon balls from the rockery which I believe were relics of the battle of Adwalton Moor, found and brought to Hill End by my great grandfather William Rhodes who was born near there; my sister's engagement ring lost before the war; a scrap of Burmantofts faience; a Minton tile, or some other memento of the past. And just sometimes, if I am visiting one of our city's parks and smell geraniums, I am reminded of grandad's greenhouse, or if working in my own garden. Once the local children are in school and all is quiet, I can feel again what it was like as a child, gently swaying on our swing, day-dreaming and hearing nothing but silence; and for a moment nostalgia reigns. Fortunately, it doesn't last.

My thanks are due to family and friends for shared memories, to Rene Dussome and John Goodchild for their ready help and to Frank Haiste who lived as a child at Hill End, for his informative letters and the gift of photographs. My special thanks are due to Mr Teifi James, MRCP., FRCS., FRCOphth., for his skill and unfailing kindness.

## SOURCES

Armley Enclosure Award and plan (1793). Registerd 1800 WRRD B20 p256.
Township Map of Armley 1846. Photocopy found in effects of Mrs Alys Strother. Provenance untraced.
Correspondence from *Yorkshire Evening Post*. Cuttings in effects of Mrs Alys Strother. n.d.
*Armley Through the Camera*, compiled by T Kirby, 1901.

# 5. THE LOST VILLAGE OF LOTHERTON

## by Dave Weldrake

LOTHERTON HALL ESTATE is situated on the Magnesian Limestone belt which runs up the eastern side of the modern county of West Yorkshire. It has been a popular visitor site ever since it was given to Leeds City Council for a museum in the 1930s. However, prior to the estate being emparked in the early 1800s Lotherton was a village complete with manor house, church and a village street. This is how the settlement is shown on a map produced by Thomas Jeffreys in 1775. It is intended in this article to examine some of the evidence for the development of this community and to make a partial reconstruction of the layout of the field system around that village.

### Early beginnings
It would be impossible to say with any certitude when the first people came to settle on the Magnesian Limestone belt. Archaeologists tend to believe that the first major land clearances for farming occurred in the Neolithic period, some 4000 years ago. Occasional flint tools are sometimes found in the area, and a flint working site has recently been identified at Boston Spa.[1] Indeed, agricultural surpluses built up in Lotherton and its surrounding area may have helped to feed the work force engaged on the construction of the vast Neolithic religious complex at Ferrybridge, some fifteen miles to the south. This included a henge (a banked and ditched enclosure, similar to that surrounding the monuments at Avebury in Wiltshire), a number of circles with wooden, rather than stone uprights, and several barrows or burial mounds. Fuller exploitation of the landscape would have taken place during the Bronze Age. Little trace of their settlement now remains, but a Bronze Age cremation urn was recovered from a site at Barwick Road, Garforth.

### Iron Age/Romano-British Lotherton
The first real glimpse that can be gained of the developing landscape around Lotherton comes from what may at first sight seem an unexpected source - the air. It is often possible to see things from an aeroplane which cannot be seen from the ground because one is too close to them. Particularly noticeable in this respect are what are

known to archaeologists as cropmarks. These can often be seen as
green lines against a field of ripening corn. The green lines indicate
the presence of buried ditches: the roots of the crop growing over
them can get down into the looser soil of the buried ditch and the
plant will stay green longer than plants in adjacent areas. These lines
can then be traced and mapped out to give a view of a now vanished
agrarian landscape.

When this technique is applied to the area surrounding Lotherton
Hall, it becomes evident that the landscape was farmed in antiquity
almost as heavily as it is today. From the air a patchwork of small
field enclosures and trackways becomes evident. On the occasions
when it has been possible to investigate such enclosures
archaeologically, they have generally turned out to be Iron
Age/Romano-British farmsteads. A number were investigated during
the construction of the A1/M1 link road to the south of Leeds.[2] A site
at Aberford Road, Garforth, revealed a sequence of enclosures which
have produced  one of the largest numbers of fragments of Roman
pottery from a rural site in West Yorkshire. A small cemetry was also
found on the site.

### The Anglo Saxon settlement of Luttringtun

One of these small Romano-British farmsteads may have grown into
a villa which in turn may have formed the nucleus for the Anglo
Saxon village of Lotherton which had come into existence by at least
963 when it is mentioned in a land grant of King Edgar's.[4]
Alternatively, the Saxons may have come along and seen some ruined
structure and used it as a quarry for their own buildings. This seems
to have been a very common practice in this part of West Yorkshire.
For instance the medieval predecessor to Castleford parish church
stood adjacent to a Roman fort. Ledsham church has the remains of
a Roman altar showing in its stone work, and some of the stones at
Bardsey have Lewis holes, a device for lifting large blocks, which was
apparently unknown to the Saxons.[3] That this may have been the
process at Lotherton is indicated by the presence of what appears to
be Roman tile among the stones of the present Lotherton Hall
chapel.

At the time of the charter the village was known as Luttringtun.
The first element is the personal name 'Hluttor'. The 'ing' part
means 'followers of' and 'tun' is a settlement or farmstead. Therefore
the original name of the village was 'the farmstead of the people of
Hluttor'.[5]

In 963 King Edgar granted the estate to one Aeslac and as part of the legal transaction a circuit of the boundaries of the township are included. This is particularly fortunate as Lotherton is absent from the usual source for the shape of Saxon England, the Domesday Book, compiled in 1086. This is probably because Lotherton was one of the six berewicks (dependants settlements) of Sheburn-in - Elmet mentioned, though not named in Domesday. The boundary details given in the charter are therefore the only glimpse we are likely to get of this Saxon settlement.

Even then the picture is not as clear as might have been hoped. The southern boundary along the natural line of the Bragdale valley seems fairly clear, as is the eastern and northerly boundaries, along the line of Woodhouse Moor Rein, one of the great system of presumably prehistoric dykes which cross the line of the present A1 at Aberford. The western boundary, however, remains the subject of some debate. The charter states that it follows the course of the herepath or military road. Farrar assumed this to be the Roman road, the predecessor to the modern A1. More recently Long has suggested that the herepath may in fact have been along the line of what is now Ranger's Walk, but this would appear to conflict with boundaries of the modern settlement.

## An enigmatic find

With one possible exception, no Saxon material has ever been recovered from Lotherton itself. The exception is a finger ring found last century and now in the Ashmolean Museum. It was described as being found somewhere between Aberford and Sherburn, a description which would fit well with the present Lotherton estate. The ring is clearly of Saxon origin and bears the motif of the Agnus Dei or Lamb of God. Round the inside is the inscription AEDELSWID REGINA (Aethelswith Queen). Aethelswith was the elder sister of Alfred the Great and was Queen of Mercia from 842/4 to 874/5. How a ring bearing her name came to be found in Yorkshire is something of a mystery.

## Lotherton Hall Chapel

The oldest building now standing on the site is the modest chapel of ease located next to the entrance to the Hall itself (Figure 1). The first mention of the chapel here occurs in a report written by Parliamentary Commissioners at the time of Cromwell who state that:

*There are two chapels in the parish* [Sherburn] *viz. Lotherton and Micklefield. To the first belongs the town of Lotherton and part of*

**Figure 1.** Lotherton Chapel from the south. *West Yorkshire Archaeology Service*

*Aberford. It is distant two[sic] miles from the said parish Church, and hath neither minister nor maintenance belonging to it. We think fit that that part of Aberford in the Chapelry of Lotherton be annexed to the parish of Aberford. We think it not fit to have the said Chapels made parish Churches, there being no considerable number of parishioners to resort thither.*[8]

On architectural grounds the chapel can be said to be much older, probably dating back to the 1150s. It bears an overall resemblance to Adel church on the north side of Leeds. It is however, lacking in Adel's elaborate decoration, reflecting the difference in status between the two structures. Adel has always been a parish church, whereas Lotherton was never one. It was established for the convenience of residents wishing to hear mass without having to walk the six miles to Sherburn, but all other services - baptism, marriage and burial - would take place there and the fees for the performance of these services would go to Sherburn church.

The walls of the chapel are built of roughly coursed stone. Presumably the outside of the building would have been rendered to hide this rough work. Other attempts would have been made to enhance the appearance of the building. For instance, the capstone over one of the small 1150s slit-like window has had its outer face scored with radiating lines to make it look like a more elaborate segmented arch The effect is somewhat spoiled by the fact the stone has been set askew (Figure 2). It make one wonder whether the stone might once have topped a

**Figure 2.** Window in south wall of Lotherton Chapel, The capstone has incised lines imitating the appearance of a segmented arch. *West Yorkshire Archaeology Service*

window on an earlier Saxon church on the site and has been reused here for effect. The possibility that there may have been a Saxon church is not totally out of the question. To be a thegn or lord in the Saxon period a landholder had to fulfil certain property qualifications, one of which was to build a church on one's estate. If Aeslac had pretentions to grandeur when he acquired Lotherton in 963, he may have done exactly that.

The south door of the chapel is relatively plain and could belong equally well to a Norman or Georgian phase of building. However the north door of the chapel, usually unnoticed by visitors, is more elaborate (Figure 3). It clearly belongs to the 1150s and would seem to represent the former principal entrance to the structure. This in itself is rather unusual. In most churches the principal entrance is the south door and it would normally be this door which would be selected for architectural development. The north door was often regarded with superstition and the north

**Figure 3.** The north door of Lotherton Chapel. This is more elaborate than the door on the south side. (See Figure 2).
*West Yorkshire Archaeology Service*

side of the churchyard was often considered an unsuitable place to be buried as it lay in the shadow of the church. One wonders therefore why the north door at Lotherton has been so treated. Could it have been that the street of the village lay immediately to the north of the chapel, roughly along the line of what is now the exit from the Estate? This is certainly the impression one gets from the Jefferys map, and if this is so the main entrance may have placed where it is as a convenience to the villagers.

## Lotherton Hall Cottages

On the opposite side of the estate road to the chapel on the corner of the stable courtyard are Lotherton Hall Cottages. This title is something of a misnomer for the structure is anything but a cottage, being two full stories high with accommodation under the roof. According to the schedule of listed buildings the main structure dates to the early 1600s with additions later in the century. At first this seems a little difficult to believe, but a closer inspection of the exterior of the building will show the scar of a blocked up doorway (Figure 4) and windows which have been made smaller. Previously, the blocked-up door would have lead from the village street into a lobby fronting onto a central chimney stack. Visitors would then have to go either left or right to enter the principal ground floor rooms. Behind the chimney stack is a large oak staircase, the lower part of which has been restored but the upper part still has its Jacobean timbers intact.

This structure is clearly too large for a simple workers cottage and so another reason for its existence must be sought. In a medieval or early post-medieval village there are only a few possibilities for a house of this size. It could be a vicarage, but as has already noted the chapel at Lotherton never achieved the status of a church in its own right and so there would not have been a vicar resident in the village. It could be a dower house, where a widowed lady of the manor lived while the new lord of the manor took over the manor house, but this would assume the existence of a larger house elsewhere on the site. For this there is no evidence. All in all it therefore seems more reasonable to assume that Lotherton Hall Cottages were the earlier manor house on the site and that they became down graded to the status of labourers' accommodation when the predecessor to the present Hall was built.

**Figure 4.** The blocked up main entrance to Lotherton Hall Cottage.
*West Yorkshire Archaeology Service*

### The tenants' houses
No trace of the other houses indicated on the Jeffreys map now exists. Presumably they were demolished when the Estate was emparked and the tenants moved away, perhaps to that part of the township which borders onto the Great North Road in the northern part of the village of Aberford. However, the outline of two of the tenements can still be seen delineated by low earthen banks in the area of field now used as a car park.

## The field system

Part of the medieval field system also survives in the car park and in the present deer park on the opposite side of the road (Figure 5). It make its presence known to motorists as a series of undulations which cause vehicles to bounce uncomfortably across the grass. These undulations are the remains of ridge and furrow, the medieval form of cultivation and can be seen continuing across the access road into the deer park. They are often visible where arable land has been emparked, since in the absence of modern earth moving machinery, it would have been too much of a chore to level the land. It was therefore merely left to go to grass.

> *These ridges were the basic divisions of the great open fields which surrounded the medieval village. From documentary sources it can be established that Lotherton had three of these: East Field, in part of which the present house now stands West Field and North Field. However, these large field in turn acquired their own subdivisions. Perhaps even by the fifteenth century these large open fields may have been encroached upon, certainly areas within them had acquired their own name if not their own fences. In a land grant of 1453, we find mention of land which 'lay in the North Field .... abutting le Stocking at the east side and le Greystones at the West.'* [9]

In this instance 'Le Stocking' is not the garment but is derived from the Old English word 'stoccing' meaning a clearing. The present Stocking Lane which branches off the Aberford - Towton Road (or High Road as it is referred to in medieval documents) was the lane

**Figure 5.** An aerial photograph of Lotherton Hall Estate. The lines of the ridge and furrow can clearly be seen as corrugations crossing the park. *West Yorkshire Archaeology Service.*

which led to this enclosure.

The Tithe Award map of Lotherton also mentions a number of other place names which may have survived from the medieval period . There is, for instance, a Cherry Trees Flatt in the North Field, a Tithe Barn Flatt adjacent to Colliery Lane and a Coney Garth and a Coney Garth Plantation on opposite side of the road leading into Aberford. Conies are rabbits and were often kept in special warrens by Norman landlords so the two Coney Garth names may indicate the site of a medieval rabbit warren, rather than the home of feral rabbits.

## Conclusion

From such indications as these it becomes possible to build a skeleton outline of the layout of the village as it might have been laid out before it was emparked: a small cluster of houses lying alongside the principal street of the village, the manor house and chapel at the southern extreme of the street. Around this nucleus are the three open fields, some parts of which are already being encroached upon. The full picture may never be fully known, but out of these few scraps of evidence a ghost of a lost village emerges to tantalise us with hints of its former presence.

### Acknowledgement

This article grew out of work undertaken at Lotherton in the summer of 1995. The author would like to thank Julia Wynne-Throe (Leeds Countryside) for granting access to those parts of the estate not normally open to the public. I would also like to thank the West Yorkshire Archaeology Service for permission to use photographs taken at the time to illustrate the article.

### Notes and references

1. Barnes M  pers.com.
2. Roberts I 1996, 'New link to the Past', *Archaeology in West Yorkshire* Issue 6, 1996.
3. Ryder P *Medieval Churches of West Yorkshire*, 1996.
4. Farrer W  *Early Yorkshire Charters Volume I*, 1996.
5. Smith A H  *Place Names of the West  Riding of Yorkshire,* 1961.
6. Farrar W  *Early Yorkshire Charters*, 1916.
7. Long M H 'Sherburn' in Le Patourel H E H, Long, M H and Pickles, M F *Yorkshire Boundaries*, 1993.
8. Cited in Kirk G E  'Lotherton Chapel', *Publications of the Thoresby Society*, Volume 26, 1922.
9. Brown F D W (ed.), 10909, *Yorkshire Deeds.*

# 6. A Brief History of the National Institute of Houseworkers, Leeds 1951-1972

*by Christine Nolan*

LET'S FACE IT, NOBODY LIKES to clean the loo, and women who clean in private households clean more than most. The majority of these women often work in a hidden economy. Invisible from statistics and society in general, they frequently work for low pay which is cash in hand, and without employment contracts, sickness benefits, or any other benefits that the majority of workers take for granted.

Because they are working in the hidden economy, they have no power and nobody to protect their rights. They do a very important job, servicing the nation's households, enabling other men and women freedom to pursue their own careers, and as such they do a job that has low status and little reward.

My interest and curiosity in the history of domestic service stems from my own personal experiences. My mam was in domestic service from the age of fourteen, when she had to leave the North East to go into service in London. Later she worked as a cleaner in private houses into her seventies, in order to supplement her income as most cleaners do. When my own children were young I also went out cleaning other peoples' houses for eight years. Cleaning fits round children's school hours and is mostly part time work, thus enabling women to pick the children up from school. Which is another reason why some women choose this type of work, as well as supplementing their income.

When I returned to education years later as a mature student, while researching for my degree I chose to study the history of charwomen in the last century, but soon discovered that very little information existed on these women's lives. Part of my research entailed interviewing women who cleaned in private households and to record their history, in order to preserve it. Cleaners who clean in private houses are women without a voice and I wanted them to be heard.

Domestic labour has been neglected partly because of its invisibility. Housework seldom appears in official accounts as Allin states:

*Census of employment which provides the accurate benchmark figures on which the Department of Employment realigns the industrial and employment estimates does not include women in private domestic service...*[1]

After the Second World War, the then Minister of Labour, Ernest Bevin, requested a report to be done on the organisation of domestic labour, in order to provide training for domestic employment of women leaving the services and war industry. The report was undertaken by two women, Miss Florence Hancock (later to become a Dame) a leading Trade Unionist, and Miss Violet Markham who devoted all her life to the women' issues and said:

*Domestic work has for years lived under the shadow of lack of status, long hours and poor pay ...*[2] (Figures 1&2)

As a result of this report, the National Institute of Houseworkers was set up in July 1946 at 53 Mount Street, London. In 1951 a centre of the National Institute of Houseworkers was opened in Leeds at 9 Newton Road, Chapeltown (Figure 3). The institutes main aims were to raise the status, and regulate the working conditions of domestic workers, and to turn domestic work, which had been the Cinderella of women's occupations, into one of the most respected and sought-after jobs of them all.

**Figure 1.** Miss Florence Hancock.

**Figure 2.** Miss Violet Markham, who with Miss Hancock drew up the report which led to the founding of the National Institute of Houseworkers.

In order to achieve this, they proposed that suitable training in any kind of housework be undertaken at training centres in England, Scotland and Wales. Those who went through the training successfully were awarded a Diploma which would make the students Associate Members of the NIH. They would find the right

**Figure 3.** Frontage of 9 Newton Road, Chapeltown.

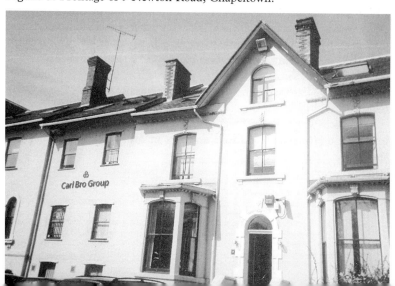

job for each holder of the Diploma, and keep in touch with the students to give help and advice when necessary. These were the ideals, in reality it is questionable whether these aims were achievable. Ernest Bevin said

*The institute...has got to show our women and girls that, with proper organisation, domestic work is a skilled trade, which has a great contribution to make to the wellbeing of the nation...*[3]

Training at the institute lasted six months, for the over seventeens and eight months for the fifteen and sixteen year olds. In the late 1940s and early 1950s, there were resident and non-resident students. pre-Diploma Worker Candidates would have completed an eight months course which was followed by a year of continued training in employment. Experienced Worker Candidates were women who, by virtue of their experience of domestic work, either in their own homes or in private employment, reached Diploma level without further training. The training was carried out at fully equipped centres like the one at Newton Road. Advertisements for students would appear in the *Yorkshire Evening Post* (Figure 4). From these it appears that apart from training in all aspects of housework, a more general education was included (Figure 5). The institute carried out its own time study for household tasks (Figure 6). From my own personal experience of cleaning in the 1960s, and for the majority of women in my research, cleaning a living room took a great deal longer than in the time study, one woman who I interviewed writes acidly about her experiences of being a house cleaner for others...

Figure 4. Advertisement for students, The National Instutute of Houseworkers, 1954.

# Take a Training in Homecraft

## and gain the N.I.H. Diploma

New courses begin at Dan-y-Coed, the SWAN-SEA Training Centre, on :

**4th May and 2nd September**

6 months' training for the over-17s
8 months for the 15 and 16-year-olds

*Application forms and further information can be obtained from : Miss M. L. Cooke, Area Officer, 56 Charles Street, Cardiff.*

Figure 5. Training Plan, The National Institute of Houseworkers.

## TRAINING PLAN

The course will last 26 weeks (during the six months' training, holiday leave with allowances will be granted for 8 days including public holidays). Students will receive training for 30 hours in each week, and in addition will do 14 hours' practical work weekly.
The course will be divided into three parts :—
A.  Practical Training.
B.  General Education.
C.  Practical Work in selected households.

| | | |
|---|---|---|
| A.  PRACTICAL TRAINING. | approximately 460 | hours |
| 1.  The place of the houseworker in the household and in the community .. | 20 | hours |
| 2.  Health Education, First Aid and Home Nursing | 60 | hours |
| 3.  Household Organisation | 185 | hours |
| 4.  Cooking | 90 | hours |
| 5.  Laundrywork | 60 | hours |
| 6.  Needlework and other craft | 45 | hours |
| B.  GENERAL EDUCATION. | approximately 139 | hours |
| 1.  Books, dramatics, music and art | 94 | hours |
| 2.  Citizenship and social studies | 45 | hours |
| C.  PRACTICAL WORK IN SELECTED HOUSEHOLDS. | | |
| To be done in suitably selected households during the last 4 months of training | 125 | hours |
| D.  TESTS FOR DIPLOMA | 10 | hours |

| TIME | | | NOTES |
|---|---|---|---|

**B. FIREPLACES AND DOMESTIC BOILERS**

**1. Laying and Lighting Fire.**

| | *Daily* | 5 mins. | These times are for a modern grate, but up |
| | *Weekly* | Up to | to ten minutes extra may be needed for an |
| | | 10 mins. | old-fashioned grate with blackleading. Extra |
| | | | time must be allowed for filling the coal |
| | | | scuttle and carrying it from the fuel store. |

**2. Domestic Hot Water Boiler.**

| | *Daily* | 10-15 mins. | This time includes the work entailed in daily |
| | *Weekly* | 10-20 mins. | maintenance. |

**C. BEDMAKING**

| One single bed made single-handed. | 5 mins. | The kind of mattress influences the time taken. |
| One single bed made single-handed with linen change. | 10 mins. | Time is saved if a double bed is made by two workers, but very little time is saved if two workers make a single bed, though some energy is saved. |

**D. CLEANING**

**1. Living Room** (taken to mean the room that the household uses most).

| | *Daily* | 10-15 mins. | |
| | *Weekly* | | These times do not include doing the fire- |
| | (with vacuum cleaner) | ½ hour | place. The time will vary in summer and |
| | (without vacuum cleaner) | 1 hour | winter in most households. |

**2. Bedroom.**

| | *Daily* | 5-10 mins. | These times do not include bedmaking (see |
| | *Weekly* | | " C," Bedmaking.) |
| | (with vacuum cleaner) | ¼ hour | |
| | (without vacuum cleaner) | ½ hour | |

**3. Bathroom and Lavatory combined**

| | *Daily* | 10-15 mins. | |
| | | (+5 mins. if separate) | |
| | *Weekly* | 20-30 mins. | |
| | | (+10 mins. if separate) | |

**4. Kitchen, Scullery and Larder**

| | *Daily* | Up to ½ hour | The time given is for a busy kitchen, omit- |
| | *Weekly* | 1-1½ hours | ting work on domestic hot water boiler. |

For health reasons, it is particularly important to give adequate time to 3 and 4.

**5. Hall and Stairs**

Furnishings, floorings and amount of space to be cleaned vary so greatly that it is impossible to give times.

**E. CARE AND CLEANING OF HOUSEHOLD EQUIPMENT**  1 hour

Usually spread over the week.

**F. LAUNDRY WORK**

**1.** One week's personal laundry for one houseworker excluding overalls and aprons.  1-1½ hours

This time includes washing and ironing and will vary according to the season.

**2.** Complete family wash for six people, done by one person.

The time varies with the age and occupation of the members of the household, the district in which the household is situated, the time of the year, and the drying facilities.

(a) *Washing*
   (i) With a washing machine (sheets included).  1-3 hours

This time includes care and cleaning of washing machine and wringer after use. The kind of washing machine has consider-able influence on the length of time taken.

   (ii) Without washing machine (no sheets).  3-4 hours
(b) *Ironing*
   Without sheets.  3-4 hours

**3.** Ironing a man's shirt.  10 mins.

Time varies with different materials.

[ 5 ]

**Figure 6.** Timed Household Tasks, The National Institute of Houseworkers.

*The woman of the house wrote for a well-known magazine, even wrote a book about how to cope with running a home, and hers was a tip. It took five hours to do the bathroom and living room. It used to turn my stomach unblocking the loo, pots piled into high heaven, clothes dumped in every room. Many's the time I would find half an onion dumped in the overfilled ashtrays. And I dreaded the times when anyone in the house had a cold, I had to go round picking up tissues in all the rooms. The only reason I stuck it out was it fit round the kids hours and she left me along to get on with it.*[4]

In May 1953 *The Houseworker*, the monthly journal of the National Institute of Houseworkers (price 2d in old money) reported two services operating in Leeds NIH. The Home Help Services of the local authorities - designed to meet domestic emergencies, and the Daily Houseworkers Service that is the subject of this article.

The Daily Houseworkers Services supplied a pool of part-time domestic workers to work in private households. The Annual General Report of June 1949 notes:

*The setting up of Daily Houseworkers services has shown that in a most varied group of towns experiences workers are willing to come forward to take the examination for the Diploma in order that they may be employed under conditions of a guaranteed week with the Daily Houseworkers service and the institute 'behind them'.*[5]

Clearly, some students felt the move to regulate the wages and conditions and raise the status of domestic work with the Diploma and Houseworkers Service, was a step in the right direction. Two experienced houseworkers expressed their views:

*Lots of people seem to think that people who work at any form of housework are beneath the office-workers and so look down on them. However, with this scheme of the NIH and their Diploma, together with a standard of work and conditions this may change.*[6] *Housework is a neglected trade, to win a Diploma will help people to realise that this kind of work is worth considering.*[7]

However having a Diploma and regulated wages and conditions and a smart uniform did not address the main problem that domestic labour is still predominantly then, as now, women's work (Figure 7). Most domestics do a double or treble day cleaning to or three households including their own as well as

**Figure 7.** Uniform worn by Associate Member of the National Institute of Houseworkers.

having the major responsibility for raising the children. Ironically, the jobs which have been transferred from the home to the workplace, such as childcare, are overwhelmingly done by women, but that is another matter.

The main idea behind the Daily Houseworkers Service was to link

**Figure 8.** Standards of Wages & Conditions of Work (for Associate Members of the National Institute of Houseworkers and pre-Diploma Workers).

## Standards of Wages and Conditions of Work.
(For Associate Members of The National Institute of Houseworkers and Pre-Diploma Workers).

### MINIMUM WEEKLY WAGE.
For Women Workers of 18 years and over with Diploma.

| | NON-RESIDENT £ s. d. | RESIDENT £ s. d. |
|---|---|---|
| Age 18, with less than 6 months experience | 3 4 0 | 1 14 0 |
| After 6 months experience | 3 7 6 | 1 17 6 |
| After 12 months experience | 3 11 6 | 2 1 6 |

For Women Workers under 18 years.

(a) With Diploma

| | NON-RESIDENT £ s. d. | RESIDENT £ s. d. |
|---|---|---|
| Under 17 years 6 months | 2 13 6 | 1 11 0 |
| 17 years 6 months and over | 3 0 0 | 1 13 6 |

(b) Pre-Diploma Workers (After training, during period of practical experience).

| | NON-RESIDENT £ s. d. | RESIDENT £ s. d. |
|---|---|---|
| First 6 months (or till age of 18) | 1 18 0 | 1 0 6 |
| Second 6 months ( ,, ,, ,, ) | 2 2 0 | 1 2 6 |

For non-resident workers the charge for meals supplied will be agreed with the householder in individual cases.

**Working Hours—Adults.**
The normal working week for resident workers will be 48 hours, and for non-resident workers, 44 hours. A spreadover of 96 and 88 hours per fortnight, respectively, may be mutually agreed. Overtime will be paid at time plus $\frac{1}{4}$ for the first three hours and time plus $\frac{1}{2}$ thereafter.

**Working Hours—Workers Under 18 years.**
Resident workers will work 44 hours and non-resident workers 40 hours. No overtime will be worked.

**Free Time.**
Workers will have one day and a half per week free, but work will be spread over a seven day week to meet the need for essential Sunday work.

**Holidays.**
Workers will have a fortnight's holiday with pay per annum for the first five years, and three weeks after five years. Resident workers will receive pay at the non-resident rate during holiday periods. In addition, workers will be free on public holidays or will be given time off in lieu if mutually agreed.

**Accommodation for Resident Workers.**
The worker should have, as a minimum, a separate bed-sitting room, which is adequately heated, and have access to the bathroom.

all the housecleaners together. An inspector from the Institute visited prospective employers in order it was felt to place the work where she fitted in with the householder. It was explained to each employer that they had to accept the wage rates and conditions of employment of the Institute's Associate Members, that were laid down by the Board of Directors in October 1946 after consultations with the National Union of Domestic Workers, the Household Service League of the National Council of Women and some individual branches of the National Federation of Women's Institutes. The householder paid the Institute [2/7d] for each hour the housecleaner worked and the wage rate for the houseworker was then agreed (Figure 8). As the Daily Houseworkers scheme was self-supporting with no grants and subsidies the charge to the employer was important in funding the scheme.

In the Annual General Report for 1953-4, the funding for the NIH was decreased in 1952, which led to a reduction in the number of Diploma examinations. To prevent these changes having a knock-on effect on the Daily Houseworkers services and the Home Helps, arrangements were made that pre-Diploma students would be taken on a temporary basis until their examination was taken. These arrangements came into force in June 1953. The reduction in the number of exams taken did however cause a set back in the earlier part of that year. The number of hours worked in private households was reduced to 491,455. This was 600 hours below the figure for 1952-3. Members of the Daily Houseworkers Service attended on average 1,656 households each week, during this time period. A wage increase was not possible during this financial year.

The National Institute of Houseworkers held its third National Conference in Leeds on 7 July 1953 at the Devonshire Hall of Residence of the University of Leeds. It was attended by the Lord Mayor of Leeds, and a report on the action taken after the 1952 National Conference was read out.

On the question of a student's contract, the chairman reiterated the difficulties of having a written contract, which in the 1950s could not be enforced legally, but assured the Conference that the Board of Directors would continue to give the matter consideration. The Conference approved the action taken on a number of other resolutions, which included references for Daily Houseworkers, a bicycle allowance to Daily Houseworkers, and visits to prospective householders by District NIH Officers.

A major concern among the 1953 delegates was that the NIH needed a policy of encouraging the Local Education Authorities to introduce training schemes for the NIH Diploma. Mrs Pesky (Leeds Associate Member) said, 'That training was as necessary for young girls as for boys'. And she was supported by Mrs Williams of the Welsh Joint Committee, who agreed that as authorities were prepared to pay for training for University courses and technical courses for industry, they should support domestic training in the same way.

In 1956 the National Institute of Houseworkers moved to 17 Cookridge Street (Figure 9). All that remains of the Institute is the front door. By this time things were beginning to change. Netta Wray had first hand experience of working for the NIH Daily Houseworker Service in Leeds in the 1950s (Figure 10). She was a young married woman with six children to look after, and lived in Middleton in Leeds. She is now eighty-two with a wicked sense of humour and we spent the morning together while she told me all her tales about working as a housecleaner for the NIH. Netta's view is different from the written sources.

Netta remembers going to 17 Cookridge Street, to pick up her job sheet for the week with a list of householders on it. She told me that the NIH office was a small room on the first floor, which was

**Figure 9.** Frontage of 17 Cookridge Street.

originally the Girl Guide Headquarters. She remembers that a Miss Hall and Mrs Copper worked for the Institute. Netta saw the advertisement in the *Yorkshire Evening Post* and applied for training as an Experienced Worker Candidate. When I showed Netta a picture of the 1940s uniform with the cap (Figure 7) and told her about the training that had taken place in the fully-fitted kitchen in the past at Newton Road, her exact works were 'I was robbed, my uniform was a wrap-round number in heavy material. It was mucky green with fawn on it and a badge on the pocket with NIH written on it.' Netta's training consisted of one week with a Mrs Childs at St Helens Lane, Lawnswood. She remembers she baked a cake, did some hand washing and she received a diploma and a dark

**Figure 10.** Netta Wray, Associate Member of the National Institute of Houseworkers in the 1950s.

green badge with NIH engraved in gold lettering on it.

Netta worked four mornings a week in different households and was paid 2/6d [12.5p] an hour plus fares. She travelled on two buses from Middleton all over Leeds. One of her employers, where she cleaned once a week, used to pile the pots up in the sink and in the cooker in the kitchen from Sunday. The house was filthy she says 'But I needed the money or I would have walked out'. Employer number two, she says, 'Were not short of a bob or two, but you couldn't get any money out of them'. They never had any money. They had to empty the children's money boxes to pay her. Netta says she used to lay in wait for the employer to come home to pay her. 'She was hoping I had gone home, so she wouldn't have to pay me'. Also this employer referred to Netta as her maid if anyone called at the house, which deeply insulted Netta as she says, 'She was no-one's lackey'. So after only a few months she left that particular employer.

Netta recalled other employers from her NIH days, one telling her to use the tradesman's entrance. In another household, the three old ladies she worked for refused to put the heating on until Christmas. It was freezing in the house and she had to carry big bowls of cold water from the bathroom to wash a big linoleum kitchen floor. Finally, in 1958, Netta decided to go freelance. While still working for the NIH, she came across a gem of an employer who appreciated how hard she worked. They asked Netta if she wanted them to pay her 2/6d [12.5p] plus the money her employer paid the NIH for her services. Netta agreed with the mutual agreement and she ended up better off financially. She gave up her other NIH jobs and stayed with that employer for twenty years.[8]

During 1960-61, the Daily Houseworkers Service was operating in six centres around the country and employed, at the end of the financial year, 326 workers who supplied during the year 311,3999 hours of service to 1,033 households. The total income covered expenditure with a small surplus. The householder charge was increased to 3/4d per hour from 2/7d. The charges became effective in the summer of 1960. Although the financial position remained satisfactory, the number of hours of work was falling, which was causing concern. It appears that women were not willing to go out cleaning to earn a living by this time period, as more jobs were opening up in other areas, such as retail and the service sector.

In my research ninety-nine per cent of women in my study said they only went out cleaning because it fitted around school hours, thus saving the problems of finding childcare and paying child minders, if they had dependent children. Lack of affordable childcare today is still a big problem for working mums on low pay. This, coupled with lack of qualifications and the inability to afford time and loss of income, is a major problem for a lot of women who would like to return to education. The findings from my research from the nineteenth century to the present day, highlight the fallacy that women worked for 'pin money'. They work to supplement the family income in the majority of cases.[9]

From the Annual General Report of 1961-62, it is clear that this was a period of reassessment for the Institute. New fields of development were being explored, as well as advice, services and training in whatever field of domestic work was needed. At the same time, the general aims to raise the standard and status of the domestic worker, whether employed in private households, hospitals, educational settings or commercial establishments were still being expounded. The headquarters of the Institute moved from London to Boston Manor Road, Brentford, Middlesex (Figure 11).

The daily houseworker service was still having problems recruiting workers, at the same time as a general increase in the number of householders requiring more housecleaners. So, as a result of these developments, a survey was undertaken with consultations with domestic workers and householders. It was decided to increase the weekly full-time wage for Associate Members (women with the Diploma) to £6 per week in order to attract more housecleaners. The service charge to householders increased from 3/4d to 4/3d. At the end of the financial year (prior to the new rates coming into operation) 308 workers in the Daily Houseworker Service had given 292,977 hours of service to 958 households.

By the 1964-65 annual report, the Daily Houseworker Service was continuing to lose workers. The number of cleaners was now down to 266 and the number of householders had fallen to 870, in parallel with the number of service hours worked 267,000, a 3,977 decrease on the 1961-62 report.

It was noted in the report that the Institute had not been able to keep abreast of the wastage of workers. The directors of the Institute were concerned by the numbers of householders that were making private arrangements to employ the Institute's Daily Houseworkers, without due regard to the obligations on both parties under the law to pay National Insurance Contributions. My research endorses the

**Figure 11.** New Headquarters, Boston Manor House, Brentford.

fact that then, as now, the majority of cleaners working in private households work in the hidden economy. Ninety-nine per cent of those who took part in my study worked on a cash-in-hand basis, to supplement family budgets.[10]

In March 1964, Dame Florence DBE, retired after being Chairman of the National Advisory Council since 1959 and in June of that year, at the Civic Hall in Leeds, Alderman Mrs L Taylor, Lord Mayor of Leeds, presented Diplomas to students. The presentation was attended by 200 guests followed by tea at the Civic Hall.

The name of the National Institute of Houseworkers changed in 1969 to the National Institute for Housecraft (Employment and Training Ltd.) Many changes had taken place from the Institute's early days in the 1940s. Not least among these had been the trend leading away from the private household to institutional placings such as hospitals and the like. Dame Florence with her breadth of vision and forward thinking understood and accepted the changes arising from the results of post-war Britain in 1945. The fundamental aim of the Marham/Hancock Report to raise the status of domestic work through training and a recognised national standard was the foundation on which the National Institute was formed and remained until the Institute's closure. The Leeds branch of the National Institute for Housecraft (Employment and Training) closed its doors in Leeds in 1972.

### Notes and References

1. Allin P, Hunt A, *Women in Offical Statistics, The Changing Experience of Women*, Oxford 1987.
2. Markham V, The Houseworker Journal, No 2, March 1948.
3. Bevin E, Leaflet, *The National Institute of Houseworkers Archive* HD 6072, TUC Library, North London University.
4. Interview with Netta Wray, 9.3.2000.
5. The Annual General Report, June 1949, The National Institute of Houseworkers.
6. *Ibid.*
7. *Ibid.*
8. Interview with Netta Wray, 9.3.200.
9. Nolan C, 'Being Taken to the Cleaners, Small scale study of women who clean in private houses 1898-1990', unpublished dissertation, author's own collection.
10. *Ibid.*

### Acknowledgements

My special thanks to Netta Wray, who allowed herself to be interviewed for this article, who helped me to record a piece of oral history that would otherwise have been forgotten. I would like to thank Christine Coat and Bridgit librarians of the TUC Library, North London University, for their assistance and patience. My deepest thanks are reserved for my husband Trevor for his complete belief in me as a writer and his constant supply of cups of tea in the early hours when a deadline beckons.

# 7. The History of the Leeds Dental Institute School of Dentistry

*by Dr Harold Saffer BChD. LDS*

THE LEEDS DENTAL SCHOOL and Hospital was first established on 27 July 1905. It consisted of a single Dental Department on the second floor of the newly completed Leeds Public Dispensary (Figure 1). The first patients were admitted on the 13 March 1905, and such was the demand for dental treatment, that by 1913 over 2000 patients were being seen annually.

In 1906, the Hospital was recognised by both the University of Leeds and the Royal College of Surgeons as a School and Hospital, where students could receive the necessary training in dental mechanics and the clinical practice required for the Diploma in Dental Surgery (LDS). The first students were admitted in 1907 (two in April, and five in October). The total number of staff at the Dental Hospital consisted of thirteen local dental practitioners and a dental technician. The Dental Department of the Public Dispensary became part of the University of Leeds in 1914, and the formal appointment of the members of the Dental Hospital staff as University Lecturers took place between 1906 and 1914.

In 1920, the Dental School moved from the Dispensary to part of the Infirmary (Figure 2), taking care of over 18,000 patients in that

Figure 1. Leeds Public Dispensary 1904-1920

year. During the next few years, as a result of the expansion of the Dental School, and pressure from the Infirmary for the return of their accommodation, a new Dental Hospital was built in Blundell Street (Figure 3). It opened in 1928, at a cost of £42,000. There was an initial intake of thirty students a year, and in the first year over 24,000 patients were seen. Professor T Talmage Read was appointed as the first chair of Clinical Dental Surgery in 1931, and later became Warden of the Dental School and Hospital.

With the introduction of the National Health Service in 1948, the Dental Hospital became part of the United Leeds Hospitals. In 1953 lack of space and an enormous increase in the number of patients necessitated an extension of the rear of the Blundell Street premises. Four years later an apprenticeship scheme for dental technicians and a training plan for chairside assistants were introduced. In

**Figure 2.** Leeds General Infirmary 1920-1928

addition, the first Dental Administrator, James (Jimmy) Ross, a former student and lecturer, was appointed. In 1959 Professor Hopper replaced Professor Read as chair. In 1968, as a result of increased demand for Orthodontic treatment (correction of irregularities and abnormalities of the teeth), a separate department was established in Woodhouse Lane. Further demand necessitated

**Figure 3.** Leeds Dental School & Hospital (Blundell Street) 1928-1978

extension into neighbouring Fenton Street in 1970.

Twelve months later plans for a new Dental School and Hospital were approved. Building commenced in 1974 and was completed in 1978 (Figure 4), at a cost of more than £8 million pounds. In 1979 a school for the training of dental hygienists was established. In 1985 following Professor Hopper's retirement, Professor Basker became the new Dean of the Dental School. Professor Hume succeeded Professor Basker in 1990 and is Dean at the present time. Since 1985 a complete refurbishment has taken place and there has been constant updating of equipment.

I was a student at the Leeds Dental School from 1944-49, and upon qualification in March 1949 (Figure 5) worked as a House Surgeon for four months before being called up to the Army for National Service as a Dental Officer. I recall vividly being interviewed by Professor Read, the Dean of the Dental School. He was a tall, dignified, charming man, who commanded instant respect from all who knew him. He was extremely well qualified, having both Medical and Dental Degrees, and having obtained Prizes in virtually every examination in his Medical and Dental undergraduate years. He had a phenomenal memory and was a brilliant lecturer and surgeon.

The intake of Dental Students at that time was only twelve, because of conscription to the Armed Forces. There were two courses; a four-year Diploma Course (Licentiate in Dental Surgery LDS), and a four and a half year Degree Course (Bachelor of Dental Surgery BChD). Those students, who were awarded the BChD, were also awarded

**Figure 5.** Graduation day, March 1949.

**Figure 4.** Worsley Medical & Dental Building (officially opened 1979)

the LDS. The curriculum for the Degree comprised two pre-clinical, and two and a half-clinical years. During the first pre-clinical year, Biology and Dental Metallurgy were taught at the University, and at the Dental School we had lectures and practical work in Dental Mechanics and Prosthetics. The lecturer was Mr Turrell, and my Dental Mechanics Instructor was Mr Schofield, (nicknamed 'Stiffy'). He was slight of build, very serious, and extremely kind and helpful. He was a first class technician and had an abundance of patience with those students (myself included), who found moulding wax, casting plaster of paris, and soldering and swaging metal, rather more taxing than studying the facts and figures of Physics, Chemistry and Mathematics. Those who were successful in the Examinations at the end of the first year (1st BChD) went on to the second year. One or two dropped out at this stage, usually because they felt that the course was not for them.

In the second year, Anatomy, Physiology, and Biochemistry were taught at the Medical School, in addition to continuing our training in Dental Mechanics and Prosthetics at the Dental School. At the end of the second year, the highly important Anatomy, Physiology, and Biochemistry (2nd BChD) and Dental Mechanics and Dental Prosthetics Examinations were held, and successful students went on to the clinical years. By this stage one could see 'the light at the end of the tunnel', and indeed, the vast majority of students going into the third year became Dental Surgeons.

In the third, fourth and fifth clinical years we treated patients, and in addition, were taught Medicine, Surgery, Pharmacology, Pathology and Bacteriology in the Medical School. We were taken around the Wards in the General Infirmary to give us an insight into General Medicine and Surgery, and attended Clinics such as Ear, Nose and Throat. I recall also, attending post-mortem clinic. In addition to all these activities we had lectures and practical work in Anaesthetics, Dental Anatomy, Periodotology, Orthodontics and of course, Operative Dental Surgery. We were also assigned to Extraction Clinics, where we were taught extraction of teeth under both general and local anaesthesia.

During lunchtime and other breaks from lectures etc., some students could be found at the nearby *George* pub, enjoying liquid refreshments! Others could be spotted at the Student Union, and a few at the Medical School Library. The Annual New Year's Eve Dental Ball was in great demand by dental students, nurses from the General Infirmary, medical students and indeed students from all other University faculties. It was always a sell-out and over subscribed.

Clinical work was carried out in departments associated with the following dental specialities. In the Prosthetics Department, we were given instruction on the replacement of natural teeth by artificial substitutes, including the use of plastics, precious and non-precious metals, and porcelain. Also, we were taught how to construct obturators for the treatment of cleft palates, radium application for the treatment of cancer, splints for fractures of the jaws, and artificial eyes, ears, and noses. The mechanical work was, in the main, carried out by dental technicians, and the practical clinical work on the patients by students under supervision.

The main work carried out in the Oral Surgery Department was extraction of teeth under local and general anaesthesia by students under supervision. Our principal tutor for Local Anaesthesia was Mr Cocker, and for General Anaesthesia Mr Frank Southam. Minor oral surgery, for example: - removal of buried roots, cysts, impacted teeth and so on, also took place in this department, generally by House Surgeons or senior students under supervision. More complicated surgery was generally undertaken by Professor Read at his weekly operative clinic, at which senior students had to attend. These mandatory sessions afforded invaluable instruction, and I, personally, looked forward to them immensely.

I vividly recall the Professor occasionally pause, and ask us all a question pertinent to the case in hand. He would stand erect, upper front teeth lightly biting his lower lip, listen intently to an answer and either nod affirmatively, or, if the wrong answer had been given, look around for another student who would dare to give an opinion. His favourite expression was 'temporise'. By this, he meant to impress upon us all to interrupt a procedure if either the patient or operator had 'had enough', and then later complete the work when both patient and operator would be rested, or, to keep something under 'observation'. A question he would often ask was 'What are the causes of post-operative pain?'

Those students who remembered to answer 'The three Is sir', would get an instant affirmative nod, and a smile, for good measure. The three I's were - Infection, Injection, and Injury. This profound teaching was to stay with me throughout my career.

The Conservation Department was concerned with the preservation and restoration of the natural teeth by fillings, inlays, and crowns, and the replacement of teeth by bridges. Preliminary instruction was given to students in such conservation by the use of extracted teeth mounted in a manikin or 'phantom head'. Textbook cavities were prepared using a foot engine, operated by a system of pulleys, which caused the rotation of a stainless steel (later substituted by the much harder wearing diamond) bur in a handpiece. The speed of the latter was determined by the power of the student's foot. This was an ideal way to introduce the student to the intricate and delicate techniques required, for the amount of tooth substance removed was directly proportional to the rotation speed of the bur. If too great a speed was produced, damage could occur to the tooth pulp (which contains the nerve and blood vessels) and/or the soft tissues of the mouth, if the student's hand were to slip.

As the students became more proficient, they graduated to the use of an electric engine for this purpose. We all, of course, looked forward eagerly to being allowed to use an electric engine, as it not only completed the work more quickly, but was also a welcome relief for our tired feet. I recall the envy of my fellow students when I was permitted to use an electric engine after only one month of 'pedalling', because I had damaged a ligament in one of my knees. A demonstrator examined the prepared cavities at each stage of the filling process, and, if satisfactory, the record card was signed as evidence of being allowed to proceed to the next stage. In cases where the decay involved the living pulp tissue, endodontic treatment was carried out. This involved complete removal of the pulp, (or sometimes incomplete removal, known as pulpotomy), control of infection, and replacement by inert materials, such as Gutta Percha.

A specified number of all types of fillings, crowns, and bridges, had to be completed before the student was permitted to take the final examination in conservation. Periodontal treatment was also undertaken in this department, as were Orthodontics, and Children's Dentistry. With the advancement of Dental Science, and the demand for the latter aspects of Dentistry, Periodontal, Children's Dentistry, and Orthodontics, were later to become individual specialities.

Periodontal treatment involved the treatment of diseases of the supporting tissues of the teeth, and soft tissues of the mouth. Acute infections required urgent treatment, and chronic infections resulting in advanced periodontal disease, (or pyorrhoea, as it was called then, and, literally, meant the presence of generalised pus), were treated where possible, and referred for extraction when treatment was not possible. Children's Dentistry, and Orthodontics, were also treated in this department.

House Surgeons and students under supervision initially saw all patients in the Examination Department. All those who required X-rays were transferred to the X-ray Department. The patients returned to the Examination Department and were then transferred to the appropriate department for treatment.

I recall a number of lecturers and demonstrators. Professor Read taught Oral Pathology, Oral Bacteriology, and Oral Surgery. Mr Marcus Hollings, who had been appointed assistant to the Professor in 1931, was in charge of the Conservation Department, and Mr Shaw and Mr (Jimmy) Ross were his assistants. Mr Cocker taught Dental Anatomy, and Local Anaesthesia. Prosthetics was in the capable hands of Mr Woodhead. Mr Frank Southam was in charge of Extractions and General Anaesthetics, and, finally, Dr Wilkinson and Mr Jason Wood looked after the Orthodontic Department. 'Block' Woodhead, as he was affectionately called, was renowned by generations of dental students for being the man to get hold of in times of 'emergency'. This was when students and demonstrators alike were unable to remove an impacted wisdom tooth, or buried root. The call went out for 'Block', and sure enough, the 'emergency' was soon over.

Students were divided into two groups in the Orthodontic Department. Dr Wilkinson was in charge of one group, and Mr Wood the other. The two men had different methods of teaching. Dr Wilkinson's philosophy was relatively old fashioned, whilst Mr Wood used more modern techniques. I regret not having had the benefit of instruction in the more modern techniques, (though, fortunately, post-graduate studies in the United States rectified that), but I would not want to have missed the privilege of having been one of Dr Wilkinson's pupils. He was a very small, extremely genial man, and was always smiling. He had a private practice in Park Square, and listed many titled families amongst his patients. He used to tell generations of dental students how he had qualified in Medicine, Dentistry and Law, and had practised all three. If any medical and legal colleagues, therefore, should tell us how difficult their work was, we should quote him, and tell them that Dentistry was the most difficult and exacting. He was a truly amazing man, and was able to treat his own teeth, injecting the Local Anaesthetic himself.

During years three and four, examinations (3rd BCHD) were held in Dental Anatomy, Pharmacology, Medicine, Surgery, Pathology and Bacteriology, and Anaesthetics. In the fifth year,

**Figure 6.** 'Ginger' Saffer during National Service, Cairo 1951.

final examinations were held. These included Oral Surgery, Conservation, Oral Pathology and Oral Bacteriology. Those of us who were successful then went our separate ways. Some were appointed House Surgeons, and the remainder were quickly claimed by the Armed Forces (Figure 6), having been exempt whilst studying.

In almost half a century since graduation I have seen the changes that have taken place, as the result of the combined effects of fluorine and greater public awareness of the importance of oral hygiene, and the regular attendance at the dentist's surgery. I well recall seeing numerous extractions being carried out in both the Local Extraction and General Anaesthetic Departments, whilst I was a student and house surgeon. This was also the case whilst I was an Army Dental Officer, and subsequently when I was an anaesthetist in the school clinics of Leeds and the West Riding of Yorkshire and a general practitioner in the Harehills, Hyde Park and Park Row and Park Square areas of Leeds (Figure 7). After leaving the army I spent a year doing post-graduate children's Dentistry in New York, and there, too, witnessed the ravages of dental decay in children.

However, since the advent of the use of fluorine, as described above, the incidence of decay fell dramatically, so that the daily

**Figure 7.** A typical dental surgery, March 1963.

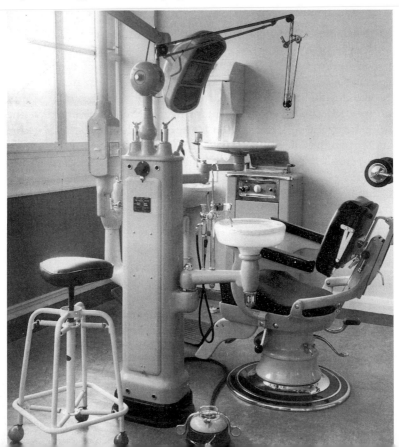

General Anaesthetic sessions, involving numerous full and partial clearances, single and multiple extractions for the relief of toothache, became a thing of the past. In fact, in my final years of practice, extractions were very rarely carried out and the General Anaesthetic machine, together with the old foot engines of fifty to sixty years ago, became museum pieces.

General Anaesthetics are not now permitted to be carried out in general practice, because it is considered safer to have extractions under General Anaesthetic carried out in hospitals and centres where modern means of resuscitation are present.

As a result of the decrease in the number of extractions being carried out, and the improvements in filling materials and conservation techniques, crowns, bridges, veneers and implants have replaced partial and full dentures. Cosmetic dentistry is therefore in great demand. Also, as a result of the speciality of periodontics, fewer teeth are being lost because of gum and other oral tissue problems. Implantology is also a speciality, which is much in demand.

Other improvements during my career include the use of rubber gloves and facemasks to prevent cross-infection, central suction to remove excess saliva, ultrasonic scalers to provide rapid removal of calculus [tartar] deposits, cosmetic dentistry, and more efficient sterilisation of instruments by the use of autoclaves instead of boiling water.

In addition, advances in technology have resulted in the use of lasers, digital radiography, magnification lenses, and even microscope attachments. Eye strain is now a thing of the past, as with the magnification produced, the tiniest pulp canals, root orifices, and margins for fillings and crown and bridge work can now be seen easily, making the finished article unbelievably perfect. Mouth mirrors can also have an extremely tiny camera attached to show the work being carried out on the teeth on a television screen in the surgery, so that the patient can view the whole procedure.

Looking back, I enjoyed my many years in practice, and always attended post-graduate courses to keep up to date with advanced techniques and improved materials. Even after retirement, I have maintained my registration, and such has been my interest, I still attend post-graduate lectures.

### Notes and References

An article by J H Ross B.ChD. entitled The first pupils (date unknown), supplied by Leeds Dental School Library.
A History of the Dental Hospital/School/Institute at Leeds, The Newsletter of Leeds Dental Alumni Association, 1999.
University of Leeds School of Dentistry Prospectus, 1999.

### Acknowledgements

My sincere thanks to the *Yorkshire Evening Post* Newspapers and the Dental Hospital Reference Library for allowing me to use their photographs and reference documents.

# 8. Dream Builders: The Thompsons of Golden Acre

*by Tony Shelton*

*There are dream builders as well as brick builders and the dream builders
really lay the foundations for the brick builders.*

THE STORY OF BLACKPOOL, *A Clarke, 1923*

AT THE EDGE OF ST JOHN'S CHURCHYARD, Roundhay,
under a tall yew, stands a family memorial (Figure 1). It is made of
black and grey polished granite and takes the form of a classical temple
with a domed roof graced by a stone dove of peace. The black base has
space for a whole dynasty of inscriptions but carries only three:

IN LOVING MEMORY OF A DEAR HUSBAND AND
FATHER
HERBERT WRIGHT THOMPSON
FELL ASLEEP SEPTEMBER 8TH 1928 IN HIS 61ST
YEAR
"LIFE'S WORK WELL DONE"

ALSO ANNIE ELIZABETH,
WIFE TO THE AFORESAID
BORN JAN 6TH 1871, PASSED TO A HIGHER LIFE,
FEB 7TH 1943

ALSO FRANK TEMPLE THOMPSON, SON OF THE
ABOVE
PASSED ON 20TH AUG. 1950 AGED 53 YEARS

**Figure 1.** The Thompson family
memorial, proud to be different
and marking a rise and fall in
two generations.

The Thompsons are not famous but in their hey-
day they became well known in Leeds as
entrepreneurs who helped make the modern city,
reflecting and helping to fashion their changing
times. They built several hundred houses, the
*Parkway Hotel* and, after creating the first Golden
Acre Park, provided, out of necessity, the land for
the second. In two short-lived generations they
gained and lost wealth and experienced both
success and failure. For all this and for the
memories they created, the Thompsons deserve to
be better remembered.

**Figure 2.** Concord Street, off North Street: the location of Herbert's 1992 joiner's yard (*Slater's Directory*, 1892); the only street in the old Leylands district to survive to the present day with most of its buildings intact.

### East Side, West Side, All Around the Town[1]

Herbert Wright Thompson was born on 27 June, 1868 in Recovery Street, Burmantofts to Ann (formerly Wright) and Reuben, an illiterate stonemason.[2] Herbert became a joiner but was evidently ambitious and by the age of twenty-four he was running his own firm which soon expanded into general building (Figure 2).[3] His first projects included lock-up shops on Skinner Lane, built in about 1892, and four houses on Sholebroke Avenue, Chapeltown, started in 1893.[4]

On 13 April 1895, Herbert married Annie Eliza Temple at St George's Church, Leeds. Annie was born in 1871 to Annie Jane (formerly Welburn) and Wilson Temple, a boot maker who lived in a back-to-back in Jermyn Street, one of the 'alphabet' streets off Kirkstall Road. The new couple first lived in Sunny Bank Street, a mixed city centre community of shops, tradesman and modest residencies (Figure 3).[5]

Before long, though, Herbert had established a family tradition of occupying, prior to selling, new houses in his own developments: this was clearly an economical way of putting a roof over Thompson heads. By 1896, his firm was erecting large numbers

**Figure 3.** Sunnybank Street, Herbert and Annie Eliza's first address. It was demolished in the early years of the last century to make way for the construction of Calverley Street, Leeds Civic Hall and gardens and the Brotherton Wing of the Leeds General Infirmary. The site of its southern end now lies within the city's new Millennium Square. Buildings from Herbert's time, which still stand, are shown solid. *Based on OS 1908 edition.*

**Figure 4.** Herbert's houses: a) The Sutherlands and Comptons, Harehills, built in the 1890s; the architect was Charles Dodgson of Roundhay Road; b) The Crossflatts, Beeston Road, built in the 1900s.

of back-to-back and through terraced houses in the expanding Harehills Lane area: the Sutherlands, Stanleys and Brownhills are all Thompson-built(Figure 4).[6] It was at 170, Harehills Lane, that Frank Temple, the Thompson's only child and the main character in this story, was born on 6 February 1897.[7]

By the end of the century, Herbert was busy developing on the edge of the city at Beeston: between 1903 and about 1912, he built several hundred houses in the Crossflatts area, off Beeston Road. At the same time, he ventured into the select suburb of Roundhay. There, from 1904 to about 1925, he built a mixed row of shops and houses (including one for the family) now known as Street Lane Parade (Figure 5).[8]

**Figure 5.** Herbert Thompson's Street Lane Parade; at the end, slightly smaller than their neighbours, are what were originally the four houses of Queen's Terrace, the Thompsons' home for twelve years.

**Figure 6.** a) Three of the Thompson villas on Old Park Road (with a later infilling); b) Kornah, Old Park Road, the family home until 1930; built in 1916 by Herbert and designed by Luwee Harris, somewhat in the Arts and Crafts vernacular style pioneered in the 1890s by architects such as Voysey and Lutyens. Its generous exterior proportions were matched by its interiors, which boasted wood panelling and imposing fireplaces. Many features have been retained including, in the kitchen, the bells with which the Thompsons would summon their servant(s).

Some twelve years later Herbert provided his family with a permanent home, also in Roundhay, to match their established wealth and status. Shortly before the First World War, Herbert had taken advantage of the sale of the late Charles Ryder's Gledhow Hill estate. As part of a complex deal the Leeds Corporation gained land for Roundhay School (opened in 1926) and a strip for the widening of Gledhow Lane (1915) and Herbert was able, so it was later reported, to offer the mansion and gardens for the use of convalescing wounded soldiers.[9] For himself he acquired a piece of prime building land fronting on to Old Park Road and Ryder Gardens. There, from 1916 until the early 1920s, he built seven detached villas. The Thompsons soon moved into the corner house, Number One, Old Park Road, and named it Kornah (Figure 6).10

The 'new look' of Kornah and the other Old Park Road houses is the work of Luwee Harris, an architect closely associated with the Thompsons and their projects (Figure 7). Harris was born in 1866 and trained in private practice in York and Leeds before moving to London in 1887. He returned to Leeds around the turn of the century and built up his own successful architectural and surveying practice. His commission, for the Street Lane development, led to others for the Old Park Road houses, the Hawksnest estate in Alwoodley and, from the late 1920s, the Golden Acre Estate and Golden Acre Park, of which more later.[14] He lived in Bramhope and became a member of Wharfedale Rural District Council and Joint Hospital Board.[11] He is best remembered, though, for a family tragedy. In 1932, Luwee junior, his son and partner, drowned in the Golden Acre lake in the park designed by his father.[12]

**Figure 7.** The Thompsons' favourite architect, Luwee Harris, senior with his wife Elizabeth. *Courtesy of Betty Maiden*

### You Ought to be in Pictures [13]

After the war, Herbert's house building continued, but at a slower pace. Much of his energy was now diverted to his new business, the renting and distribution of silent movies, in association with his brother Charles. He later moved into cinema ownership, too, buying the Harehills Picture House. In those early days the movie business was decidedly risky but there were fortunes to be made and Herbert could now afford to take chances.[14]

The films themselves were of dubious quality. An easy-to-follow recipe was laid down, not without tongue in cheek one hopes, in the *Bioscope* magazine in 1922:

> *...certain things can always be relied on to please such as romance presented with sincerity. Baby scenes always get over. Even the lowest mental types enjoy peeps into furrin parts...women especially like a good cry. But the end must strike a happy note.*[15]

Into this chaotic business entered the young Herbert Wilcox, a one-time journalist and professional billiards player. In 1920 Wilcox founded a distribution company, Astra Films, and, in the same year, came to Leeds. He announced a 'gigantic producing scheme' in partnership with Herbert Thompson, who set up his own production company to produce films for Astra at the London studios of the British and Colonial Kinematograph Company. Their first film, *The Breed of the Treshams* (1920), starred stage actor Sir John Morton Harvey.[16] However, in 1922, Wilcox moved on to greater things and, in a long career, founded Elstree Studios and the British National Film Company, produced many prominent British films and made a star of Anna Neagle who he eventually married.[17]

With director Kenelm Foss, Thompson continued to produce films at the same speed with which he had once built houses. Most were based on sentimental novels and stage melodramas, all, according to film historian Rachael Low, 'tasteless and made with complete contempt for the audience'.[18] They included *The Virgin Queen* with Lady Diana Manners which was partly shot at Temple Newsam, *All Roads Lead to Calvary*, Dicky Monteith and, in 1921, numerous *Wonderful Adventures of Pip, Squeak and Wilfred*. One of Herbert's last films, *The Romance of Old Baghdad* (1927), was not well received though: by then public taste was outgrowing the silent movie formula. The actors were little, if ever, known unless you count illustrious-sounding names like Manora Thew, H V Tollemache and J Nelson Ramsaye. But Thompson films provided early chances for some who would achieve prominence in theatre and film: Miles Malleson (*The Headmaster*), Zena Dare (*No 5 John Street*) and Fay Compton (*House of Peril*).[19]

### Down the River of Golden Dreams[20]

Herbert Thompson's last and most ambitious building project was very much a father and son venture. Frank had spent much of the First World War in Egypt as Private M2 177360 in the Royal Army Service Corps and, on his return to Leeds, had joined his father's businesses, enjoying at the same time the lifestyle of a rich man's only son with the prospect of a substantial inheritance.[21] He became the

**Figure 8.** Young man about town Frank Thompson (centre) and friends in the 1920s with his Crossley 25/30 tourer, a large (15 feet long) and expensive (£1375 in 1920) status symbol; the model was also used by royalty. Donated in 1985 by Mrs Smith-Goode, now courtesy of Eric Cope; information from Mike Worthington-Williams, *Classic Car Mart* magazine.

centre of a 'fast' set of most similarly well-to-do friends, some of whom were later to be persuaded to invest in his ventures (Figure 8).[22] He acquired a fine car, a wife, Lillian Christine Harling (formerly Vogel) and the first of many fine houses, Dyneley Hall in Bramhope.[23]

In 1925 Herbert acquired 300 acres of poor-to-middling farmland between Adel and Bramhope: Blackhill Well Farm and Breary Grange Farm were remnants of the old Cookridge estate, which had been broken up in 1919.[24] There were houses to be built and another fortune to be made. The land became, on paper at least, the Golden Acre Estate after, it was said, the colour of the local stone (Figure 9).[25] The prospects looked favourable since the market for

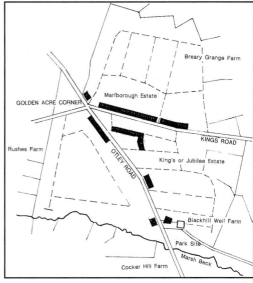

**Figure 9.** The development of the Golden Acre Estate as planned by the Thompsons. The houses built are shown as solid shapes. Based on building plans held by West Yorkshire Archives Service, Leeds.

owner-occupied houses was beginning to grow: the post war economy was improving, building societies were becoming more generous and city dwellers were developing aspirations to a life in the country.[26]

Luwee Harris was commissioned to draw up plans for three large estates of detached and semi-detached houses with such prestigious road names as King's and Marlborough.[27] The inhospitable-sounding Marsh Lane which ran through the middle of two planned estates was given its present name of King's Road.

**Something to Remember You By**[28]

All was set for the Golden Acre Estate to become a Yorkshire 'Metroland' but in 1928, before many houses could be built, the 'well known builder... who had made Leeds the great film city it is..' suddenly died.[29] The business passed to his widow and son. In 1930, Annie Eliza sold Kornah and moved to Scarborough.[30] As for Frank, it was later said by his employee Henry Haigh that he became richer by some £128,000, the equivalent of £4-5 million at today's values.[31] Opportunity beckoned.

IMPORTANT DAY FOR VETERANS.

Lord Mayor to Open New "Headquarters" on Woodhouse Moor.

**Figure 10.** Herbert's memorial: a) Donor Frank Thompson and recipient, probably Mr GH Clapshaw, secretary of the Woodhouse Moor Veterans' Association, inspecting the new Woodhouse Moor shelter in 1935. Courtesy Yorkshire Post Newspapers; b) the building in 2000, converted to a Tandoori take-away after a period as The Pavilion, a women's photography centre.

The son would often pay public tribute to his father, recounting that he had 'built most of Beeston, Cross Flatts, the Compton Road district and a lot of Holbeck' and in 1935 he presented the city with a permanent memorial. In 1933, the Woodhouse Moor Veterans' Association had approached Frank Thompson for an estimate for constructing a veterans' shelter on Woodhouse Moor. 'I quoted them nothing,' said Thompson; 'I thought it was a very worthy cause'. The resulting building was spacious with large windows, a veranda and clock tower, all in 'Old English' style. It was opened on 22 July by the Lord Mayor, Alderman Hemingway, who said that there was no better way for a man to keep the memory of his parents green. The shelter would, said the Lord Mayor, 'be cared about and used forever' but, as with many a politician's oratory, this was hope dressed as prediction.[32] The shelter still exists but only after a fashion (Figure 10).

**It's the Talk of the Town** [33]

Meanwhile, in 1928, there was also another, more exciting venture, a dream of his late father's, the creation of the Golden Acre amusement park (Figure 11). Frank travelled across the Atlantic to collect ideas from Coney Island, the acme of amusement parks and, after two or more years of planning and construction, the Golden Acre Park was opened just in time for Easter 1932 by the Lord Mayor, assisted by stage star Jack Buchanan, and a grand firework display. Attendances reached up to 30,000 on the first Whitsun holiday weekend and 175,000 in the first season.[34] In 1933 Thompson sold the park land and fixtures to the new Golden Acre Park Co Ltd in return for cash, shares and a managing director's salary of £500 a year.[35] Success looked assured, though not that of

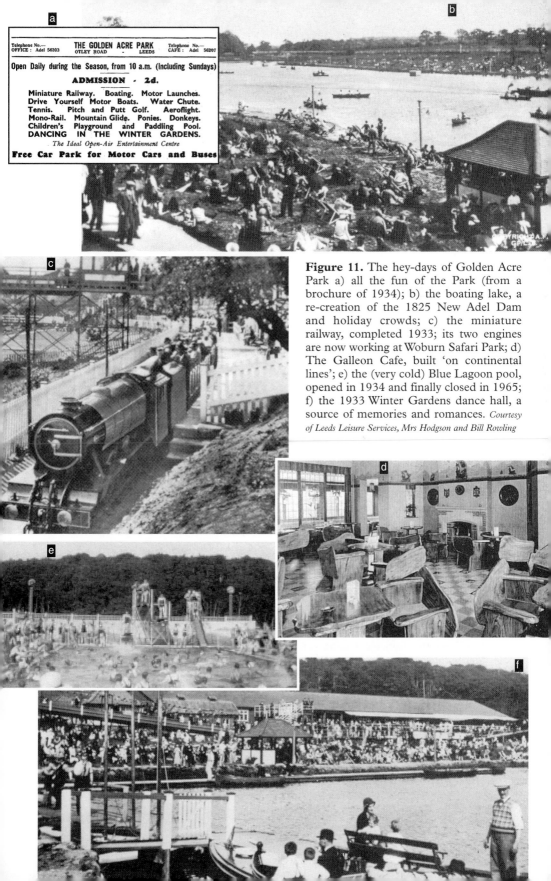

**Figure 11.** The hey-days of Golden Acre Park a) all the fun of the Park (from a brochure of 1934); b) the boating lake, a re-creation of the 1825 New Adel Dam and holiday crowds; c) the miniature railway, completed 1933; its two engines are now working at Woburn Safari Park; d) The Galleon Cafe, built 'on continental lines'; e) the (very cold) Blue Lagoon pool, opened in 1934 and finally closed in 1965; f) the 1933 Winter Gardens dance hall, a source of memories and romances. *Courtesy of Leeds Leisure Services, Mrs Hodgson and Bill Rowling*

Thompson's 'Happy Hour' amusement arcade in
Kirkgate Leeds. This opened and closed within the
year, having attracted local criminals and police
concern.[36]

### Life is Just a Bowl of Cherries [37]

During the first years of the 1930s, Frank Temple
Thompson lived the life of a successful
entrepreneur. He had a new wife too, whose tastes
matched his own. His first, short-lived, marriage
had ended when Lilian divorced him and in 1929
he had married Alice May Campbell. May's first
marriage, to Captain John Erwin Campbell, had
produced a son, Kenneth, born in 1919, but had
also ended in divorce. Frank became a 'good
stepfather' to Kenneth whose name was changed to
Thompson.[38] In about 1931, the new couple moved
from Dyneley Hall (always May's favourite house)
into Red Roof, a large Thompson-built detached
villa on Kings Road which boasted a specially-built
small ballroom[39] (Figure 12). There, for three or
four years, Frank and May lived the life of a wealthy
couple of the new age with, thanks to May, a touch
of show business.

May had been a keen swimmer but in about
1921 an accident in Leeds baths had seriously
damaged her back leaving her with a lifelong and
increasingly severe disability. From then on she
walked with the aid of a stick but that did not
prevent her from treading the boards, appearing in
productions by the Leeds Sylvans and Leeds Amateur Operatic
Society.[40] However, it was as a songwriter that she claimed her

COMPOSER AT WORK

## Leeds Woman's
## New Dance
## Tune

HOW JACK PAYNE
HELPED HER

MISS MAY THOMPSON, of
King's-road, Otley-road,
Leeds, is having one of her dance
tunes featured by Jack Payne's
band.

Miss Thompson is better known as
the wife of Mr. Frank Thompson, the
proprietor of Golden Acre Park and of
the Harehills Cinema.

About a year ago she wrote the words

**Figure 13.** May Thompson
hits the (local) headlines.
From the *Yorkshire Evening
Post* 29.12.1932.
*Courtesy of Yorkshire Post newspapers*

**Figure 12** a) Red Roof, King's Road, Frank and
May's Thompson-built home from 1931 to about
1935 and the frontage flagship of the planned
Marlborough estate. *Courtesy of Margaret Watson*
b) The house in 2000. The ballroom is now a
ground floor flat.

**Figure 14.** Anna Neagle, the popular British film star, with Frank Thompson aboard the Golden Acre train, probably in May 1933 when she launched *May Thompson*, the miniature railway's second engine. Anna Neagle was, of course, the protegee (and later wife) of film producer Herbert Wilcox, once the partner-in-films of Frank's father Herbert. This photograph was taken by the late Roy Neill, a prominent Leeds amateur film-maker of the day, some of whose movie footage of Golden Acre still survives. *Courtesy of Alastair Corson.*

moment in the limelight. She was a accomplished pianist and had written songs since childhood. She played her compositions for friends at Red Roof (Figure 13). In 1932, she scored her first success, a ballad fox-trot called *A Four Leaf Clover*:

> *Only two days later (after writing the song), when dining in London, she was presented with a glass four leaf clover and later was given a four-leaf clover plant. She looked upon these incidents as favourable omens.* [41]

Her greatest success came in 1934 when she and her latest opus were introduced to none other than Gracie Fields. *I'm a Failure* (a prophetic title, perhaps, in view of later events) was injected into the latest of Our Gracie's films, *Love, Life and Laughter,* a light-hearted treatment of the Nell Gwyn story. [42] On the strength of this, it was recorded by the bands of Roy Fox, Ray Noble (vocal by no less than Al Bowlly), Jack Payne and Jay Wilbur. [43]

May and Frank clearly loved show business and show people and May's friendship with stars of stage and screen brought many to Red Roof, including Anna Neagle, Gracie Fields, the film comedian Sidney Howard, Charles Laughton and May's special friend Ivor Novello (Figure 14). Some would be enticed to the park, too, to perform openings, pose for press photographers and mingle with visitors. (Figure 15). [44]

**Figure 15.** Teddy Brown a renowned xylophonist, vocalist and Café de Paris bandleader, was a popular visitor to Leeds theatres and to Golden Acre and introduced May to Gracie Fields.
*Courtesy of Bill Rowling.*

## If I had a Talking Picture of You [45]

May had seen the world, too. Much of her first marriage had been spent farming in Kenya and she had travelled to India. It was her idea to combine her wanderlust with Frank's interest in the movies by making a travel film of a trip to Palestine and Egypt.[46] Its motives were scientific, patriotic and, no doubt, commercial. Thompson's motto was 'Keep the British film flag flying' and his aim to outdo the best that Hollywood could produce. Moreover, the whole enterprise was underpinned by a moral purpose. 'People are getting tired of so much slapstick, dope drama and sex plays,' he pronounced in 1931. The thousands of feet of film were edited into a three-part talkie, said to be the first to be made by a Leeds man. There were shots of Marseilles, Cairo, Luxor, the Garden of Gethsemane, Jericho and a Jerusalem sunset scene of shepherds and their flocks which might, according to a breathless reviewer, 'have been composed by an artist who wished to convey to the spectator that time had stood still for centuries...' There were also 'human, amusing or charming incidents' and May's commentary contained, according to Frank, 'what the Americans call wisecracks', possibly helping to compensate for the lack of sex. *There and Back* received a trade showing in 1932 at the Leeds Rialto but, to date, no trace can be found of what would now be a fascinating glimpse of the Near East of seventy years ago. There was talk of another filmic journey, to the Rocky Mountains, but it is doubtful if this ever came about.[47]

## You Can't Have Everything [48]

From his father Frank had inherited the Harehills Picture House, which served for a while as his business address, and an interest in buying more cinemas including, it is said, the Capitol, Meanwood.[49] In 1937 he acquired the Cottage Road cinema in Far Headingley, intending to replace it with a new cinema on the nearby St Anne's Road allotments. Plans were submitted for a prestigious building in half-timbered style, supposedly in keeping with the neighbourhood,

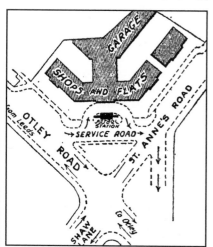

and with parking for 140 cars. The owners of the Lounge cinema, just around the corner, felt threatened. Louis Mannix, who worked there, suspected Thompson, a 'spectre on the horizon', of being well in with the city fathers, of oiling the wheels by providing the Woodhouse Moor Shelter.[50] Opposition to the cinema development was mounted

**Figure 16.** Thompson's fall back plan for the St Anne's allotments, Headingley, 1938. From *Yorkshire Evening Post* 10.6.1938. *Courtesy Yorkshire Post Newspapers*

and the planning application refused by the city council, largely on traffic grounds. In 1938, needing to make a return on the cost of the land, Thompson put in a new plan for shops and flats with a garage (Figure 16). Ingenious to the last and no doubt taking heed of the news from Munich, he offered to add an underground bomb and gas proof shelter. The council's Air Raid Precautions Committee welcomed this and the plan was approved in principle but never built. The Cottage Road cinema was soon sold to today's owners, Associated Tower Cinemas.[51] During the war, Thompson was to make one final attempt to gain permission for a new cinema but this proposal, for a site at Golden Acre Corner, had no chance of success.[52]

### You're a Builder Upper[53]

Much of what we know about Frank Temple Thompson comes from the local press. He used the local papers in a very modern way to promote his preferred image, that of a successful businessman, patriot and benefactor (Figure 17). He dressed the part, too, never being photographed in anything but an immaculate suit with well-trimmed and brilliantined hair. He is said to have been a flambouyant figure with a 'John Wayne' swagger, a big man, especially to those, like Gracie Dring who remember him from their childhood. When she was six years old, Thompson chose her as his dancing partner to inaugurate the Cocoanut Grove dance floor at his *Parkway Hotel*.[54]

Those close to Frank Thompson witnessed his kindness but as an employer he was a shrewd, hard taskmaster, capable of sharp mood swings and, according to some of his workers, not over-generous. General staff at Golden Acre Park received no more than £3 a week for six days (including Sunday) with plenty of unpaid overtime.[55] Henry Haigh, son of William, the last tenant of Blackhill Well Farm,

*Introduction*

In publishing this new Brochure giving some particulars of the attractions to be found at Golden Acre Park, I wish to thank all previous visitors for their patronage, and to express the hope that they have always enjoyed themselves to the full.

To others who have not yet spent any time in the Park, my colleagues and myself extend a hearty welcome and assure them that they will have " The Time of Their Lives."

In past seasons we have been successful in giving thousands upon thousands of people many a happy hour ; we have laid ourselves out to provide amusements and entertainment cheaply and healthily and intend to continue this policy.

During the coming season old friends will find new pleasures awaiting them. Newcomers will marvel at the variety and completeness of our plans for their entertainment, and this Brochure has been prepared to give them just a few details of the wonderful times they may expect.

We look forward to seeing you all this season. Don't fail to pay a visit to Yorkshire's Premier Pleasure Park . . . your first visit will not be your last !

*Managing Director.*

**Figure 17.** The Frank Thompson presence: the characteristic powerful glare for the camera (his smile was never captured in his middle years) together with a sample of his publicity. From a 1935 Park Brochure. *Courtesy Bill Rowling.*

worked at the park for some years collecting takings, helping with maintenance, manning the entry kiosks and driving the miniature train. At the age of ninety-one, he recalled an example of Thompson's attitude to workers and to expenditure. The versatile Henry had been instructed to service one of the railway engines, manufactured by Hudswell Clarke's of Hunslet, a job which took the whole of one Sunday:

> *Then Thompson rolls up about five o'clock...he opens his wallet and n'owt but five pound notes. He says 'I can't give you 'owt now, I haven't any change'.* [Later] *he gave us ten bob apiece - and it would have cost him a guinea an hour at Hudswell Clarke's.*[56]

Thompson was, however, capable of generous and friendly gestures. When the Winter Gardens ballroom had been completed in only 6 weeks he treated all the 180 workers involved to a slap-up dinner.[57] The Mawson family of neighbouring Cocker Hill Farm instance his presenting the Parkway's first pint to Joe Mawson as he ploughed in the fields across the road and a congratulatory telegram sent to Tom and Sybil on their wedding day in 1943.[58]

Henry Haigh observed the convivial side of Thompson, as he liked to be called by intimates, and his fondness for drinking with his business associates:

> *Well it used to be laughable on a night - about six o'clock you'd see them all come out of the office, Thompson, Beevers* [his head clerk], *Scott* [Arthur Scott the company secretary] *and one or two more and then off to the Three Horseshoes at Headingley.*[59]

There were evenings, too, spent in the company of architect Luwee Harris, sampling his home-made beer. Others invited to these sessions would run the risk of arriving home in the small hours very much the worse for wear.[60]

Business, family and friendship all tended to become mixed. Thompson-built houses provided homes for May's mother and for the Lennard family. Bob Lennard, a skilled joiner and foreman, had begun his career working for Herbert and went on to help build houses on the Golden Acre Estate and create the park and to manage maintenance at the *Parkway Hotel*. He and his wife, Florence were also friends of Frank and May and they built up a fine collection of souvenir gifts from the Thompsons travels: Margaret Watson, the Lennards' daughter remembers 'a miniature Empire State Building, a ten-gallon hat, a picture of Nice and a mini-camel from Egypt'. In 1930, when Bob and Florence married Thompson not only sent them a telegram but also sold them Hillcrest, his newly-built house by the park entrance, and lent them the necessary £900.[61]

## Darn That Dream [62]

In about 1935 the Thompsons moved house again to Ladywell House in Oakwood, but, by now, signs were appearing that all was not well with Frank's business affairs.[63] The Golden Acre estate had proved a failure with slow sales and only a handful houses to show for all the planning (Figure 18). Evidently the market was not there for relatively expensive houses in such an isolated location. By the mid-thirties, development had virtually come to a stop.[64]

As for the Golden Acre Park, it had probably never made a useful profit and it might well have been a drain on the company's resources. It may have attracted large crowds but only at holidays and sunny weekends. The park was difficult and expensive to get to and many of those who managed to visit had little, if any, money left to spend there.[65] Golden Acre may have given pleasure to thousands but no company can survive on happy memories alone.[66]

More ominously, there were questions about Thompson's health. These became public in 1936 with an advertisement inviting tenders for the management of facilities at the Park while he rested and went abroad on medical advice.[67] He was, it announced, seriously ill and his condition would not have been helped by the stress and strain of progressing yet another project. At least as far back as 1933, he had hatched a scheme for a hotel at Golden Acre but had repeatedly been refused a licence, thanks to sustained opposition from religious and temperance groups. However, in 1936 the justices at last granted a provisional approval, allowing building to commence. By 1937

**Figure 18.** A development too far: some of the Kings Road houses, still set in empty fields. These together with a few houses on Otley Road (now Leeds Road) are all that materialised from the ambitious plans for the Golden Acre estate.

Thompson was back in harness and the new hotel, named in succession the *Lakeside*, the *Fairway* and, finally, the *Parkway* opened on 25 November 1938.[68]

As one Thompson venture opened, though, another closed. The 1938 season was Golden Acre's last (Figure 19). The official announcement made in January 1939 cited, as the reason, the preservation of the rural amenities of the new hotel, amenities which, it turned out, were to include a 'garden city' in the abandoned park, a select estate of villas round the lake.[69] To promote this new development, the company's name changed to The Golden Acre Estate Co Ltd but the war intervened before any plans could move off the drawing board. The site was requisitioned by the War Office and the 'garden city' was never heard of again.[70] The war years set the seal on Frank Thompson's decline. By 1941, his position was bleak enough for bankruptcy to be mooted and for him to have to call in the loan to Bob Lennard and re-possess the house.[71]

Since 1937 Thompson had been turning to his only other source of income, the sale of undeveloped Golden Acre estate land which was still in his, as opposed to the company's' ownership. Parcels were offered to other builders but with only partial success. The prospect of war was doing little for market confidence and its outbreak put a stop to all private building.[72] It would, therefore, have been as a last resort that, in 1943, Thompson offered to Leeds city council his own unsold

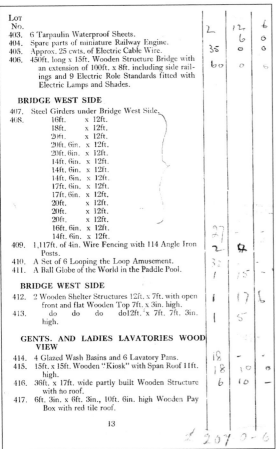

| Lot No. | | | | |
|---|---|---|---|---|
| 403. | 6 Tarpaulin Waterproof Sheets. | 2 | 12 | 6 |
| 404. | Spare parts of miniature Railway Engine. | | 6 | 0 |
| 405. | Approx. 25 cwts. of Electric Cable Wire. | 35 | 0 | 0 |
| 406. | 450ft. long x 15ft. Wooden Structure Bridge with an extension of 100ft. x 8ft. including side railings and 9 Electric Role Standards fitted with Electric Lamps and Shades. | 60 | 0 | 6 |
| **BRIDGE WEST SIDE** | | | | |
| 407. | Steel Girders under Bridge West Side. | | | |
| 408. | 16ft.     x 12ft. | | | |
| | 18ft.     x 12ft. | | | |
| | 20ft.     x 12ft. | | | |
| | 20ft. 6in.  x 12ft. | | | |
| | 20ft. 6in.  x 12ft. | | | |
| | 14ft. 6in.  x 12ft. | | | |
| | 14ft. 6in.  x 12ft. | | | |
| | 14ft. 6in.  x 12ft. | | | |
| | 17ft. 6in.  x 12ft. | | | |
| | 17ft. 6in.  x 12ft. | | | |
| | 20ft.     x 12ft. | | | |
| | 20ft.     x 12ft. | | | |
| | 20ft.     x 12ft. | | | |
| | 16ft. 6in.  x 12ft. | | | |
| | 14ft. 6in.  x 12ft. | 27 | | |
| 409. | 1,117ft. of 4in. Wire Fencing with 114 Angle Iron Posts. | 2 | 2 | |
| 410. | A Set of 6 Looping the Loop Amusement. | 3 | | |
| 411. | A Ball Globe of the World in the Paddle Pool. | 1 | 15 | |
| **BRIDGE WEST SIDE** | | | | |
| 412. | 2 Wooden Shelter Structures 12ft. x 7ft. with open front and flat Wooden Top 7ft. x 3in. high. | 1 | 17 | 6 |
| 413. | do   do   do   do12ft. x 7ft. 7ft. 3in. high. | 1 | 5 | |
| **GENTS. AND LADIES LAVATORIES WOOD VIEW** | | | | |
| 414. | 4 Glazed Wash Basins and 6 Lavatory Pans. | 18 | | |
| 415. | 15ft. x 15ft. Wooden "Kiosk" with Span Roof 11ft. high. | 18 | 10 | 6 |
| 416. | 36ft. x 17ft. wide partly built Wooden Structure with no roof. | 6 | 10 | |
| 417. | 6ft. 3in. x 6ft. 3in., 10ft. 6in. high Wooden Pay Box with red tile roof. | | | |

13

207 0 - 6

**Figure 19.** A catalogue of failure: soon after Golden Acre Park closed, its fixtures and fittings were auctioned, realising just over £3,000.

*Courtesy Margaret Watson*

**Figure 20.** Out of adversity: part of today's Golden Acre Park, sold in straitened circumstances by Frank Thompson to Leeds city council. The site, virtually derelict in 1946 after six years of wartime neglect and military use, has since been developed and expanded to become one of the city's finest parks.

land and, on behalf of the company, the site of the park, all for £18,000. The council took possession in 1946 (Figure 20)[73].

## Somebody Else is Taking My Place [74]

By 1943, when his mother, Annie Eliza died, still optimistically hoping for an early peace, the company was largely in the control of a syndicate of local businessmen. In December of that year, in a letter to his fellow directors, Thompson formerly surrendered his sword:

> *In consideration of having been permitted to remain as the acting managing director of the Parkway Hotel and for the requirements of the debenture holders...I hereby undertake to observe the following conditions...*[75]

Under those conditions, he was now but an employee of the company with a salary of £10 a week and, to add to his humiliation, all cheques, catering instructions and expenditure over £2 had to be approved by the accountants, Messrs Whitfield and Co. He was, though, allowed the free use of two rooms for himself and May and another for his son Kenneth when he returned from Navy leave and there was free food too but not drink which had to be paid for weekly out of his salary. In 1945, the company changed its name to The Parkway Hotel (Leeds) Ltd and, not long after, Frank Thompson severed all connection with his creation, never to benefit from its profitable post-war years.[76]

### The Show is Over [77]

Frank Thompson's health was now poor and he and May faded from view. They were still living in some style, though, buoyed up by rental income from many of the houses built by Herbert. Frank employed Lockwood, a chauffeur for May, whose disability was taking its toll, and a secretary, Arthur Scott, once the secretary of the Thompson company.[78] There were fine addresses, too: in 1941 The Grange, Old Park Road, in 1943, the Parkway then The Croft, Bramhope and, in 1945, The Gables, Boston Spa and the *Savoy Hotel*, where the Thompsons stayed during visits to London.[79]

His last address was also a hotel, the *Granby* in Harrogate. There on 20 August 1950, he died of the long term heart condition which had probably led to his departure abroad in 1936; a 'long distressing illness, borne with the utmost fortitude,' said the death notice. In the papers his demise rated but a column inch or two, a brief account, culled from the files, of the life of a man with 'the Hollywood touch...whose business activities have always held a passing interest for the man in the street' but now a forgotten man, a relic of a vanished pre-war world.'[80] The funeral of the 'adored husband of May' took place at St John's church, Roundhay on 24 August. Attendance was 'by gentlemen only, at the request of his widow, whose pride prevented her from being seen in a wheelchair and whose attendance would have been doubly painful. Within a year Ivor Novello died too, a second devastating blow for May.[81] A year later the will of the 'late proprietor of the Parkway Hotel' was published. The inheritor of a builder's fortune left but £10,078 net.[82]

May survived Frank by some ten years, living alone in a flat in Horsforth.

**Figure 21.** With an independent air...Frank Thompson promenading at Cannes in the late 1930s. *Courtesy of Dorothy Thompson*

## Thanks for the Memory [84]

In style, Frank Thompson was very much a creature of his time, the restless, uncertain thirties. In his *English Journey* of 1934, J B Priestley identified three Englands existing side by side.[85] The old rural England was to be found, perhaps, in the old Cookridge estate whose decline was exploited by the Thompsons. The nineteenth century industrial England, of little houses, mills and grim cities, was epitomised by Leeds, whose masses provided the customers for Golden Acre Park. Thompson inhabited Priestley's third England, born in America, that of arterial roads, bungalows, cinemas, dance halls and swimming pools. Had it not been for economic depression, war, ill health and the vagaries of the market, he might have been one of the great, as opposed to merely interesting, figures in the history of Leeds.

There will, though, always be Thompsons, people with the energy and ideas to change the world and make our lives richer. The successful, perhaps the lucky, ones become rich and famous; the others are quickly forgotten, their works soon anonymous but then, as Max Beerbohm wrote: 'There is much to be said for failure. It is much more interesting than success'.[86]

### Notes and References

Abbreviations used: CEBP - building plans submitted to the City Engineer in West Yorkshire Archives, Leeds; DLC Dibb Lupton Collection (Miscellaneous) in WYASL; DPOPR - deed papers relating to 1, Old Park Road, courtesy Glen and Elizabeth Eltringham; LCCDGAP - deed papers for Golden Acre Park held by Leeds City Council; LLIS - Leeds Libraries and Information Service (Local Studies, Central Library); RIBAL - Royal Institute of British Architects Library Information Service; WYASL - West Yorkshire Archives Service: Leeds (Sheepscar); YEN - Yorkshire Evening News; YEP - Yorkshire Evening Post; YP - Yorkshire Post.

1. Song by Charles Lawler and JW Blake, 1894.
2. Birth certificate; the site of the back-to-backs of Recovery Street is now part of the 1950s Lincoln Green housing estate, near St.James' Hospital. Later the press would report that Herbert (his son too) was a native of the village of Shadwell: whether the family moved there or merely attempted to disguise humble origins is not known.
3. *Slater's Directory*, 1892.
4. CEBP, WYASL
5. Marriage certificate; We Remember the Alphabets, Doreen M Wood, 2000 and *Robinson's Directory*, 1897. Other neighbours in Sunny Bank Street included Jane Robinson, a draper, wardrobe director, cycle maker, whitesmith, cashier, newsagent, chapel and Thomas Thompson (perhaps a relative).
6.. CEBP, WYASL
7. Birth certificate.
8. CEBP, WYASL and DPOPR.
9. DPOPR and YEP, 29.8.1933.
10. DPOPR; electoral rolls, LLIS; LCCDGAP. That part of Gledhow Hill estate, which included the site of the Old Park Road houses, was originally part of the Nicholsons' Roundhay Park estate, which was sold in 1863 to ironmaster James Whitham and acquired by Ryder in 1887. Thompson also sold plots on the north side of the newly widened Gledhow Lane.
11. CEBP, WYASL, RIBAL. Harris had offices in Boar Lane.
12. There are many newspaper reports on the accident, inquest and funeral, eg: YEP 20.5.32, 27.5.32, *Leeds Mercury* 19.5.32; also recollections in *YEP, Old Yorkshire Diary*, 1980s.

13. Song by Dana Suesse and Edward Heyman, 1934.

14. Rachael Low, *The History of the British Film Industry, 1918-29*, Allen and Unwin, 1971; YEP 10.2.32.

15. Rachael Low *op cit.*

16. *Ibid.*

17. Brewer's Cinema, Cassell, 1995. Wilcox retired in bankruptcy in 1964 and died in 1977.

18. Rachael Low *op cit.*

19. *Ibid* and National Film Archive who hold several Astra films in their collection. Kelly's Directory, 1920 shows Astra Films with offices in Queen Victoria Street, Leeds (now part of the Victoria Quarter) and, in 1925, Astra Films (Yorkshire) at King Charles Croft; Charles Thompson had offices in Albion Street. Pip, Squeak and Wilfred also featured, if the author's post-war childhood memories serve him correctly, in a Daily Mirror strip cartoon.

20. Song by Nat Shilkret and John Klener, 1930.

21. *YEP* 13.2 32; electoral rolls (absentee voters list), LLIS; YEP 31.8.31.

22. Conversation with Minnie Bradley whose brother was a fringe member of the Thompson set despite being warned by his father that he wouldn't be able to 'keep up', a prophecy proved correct when Clifford had to decline an invitation to invest in Golden Acre Park.

23. LCCDGAP; Thompson's second marriage certificate,1929; conversation with Tom Mawson; telephone directories, LLIS; WF Seals, *A History of the Township of Bramhope*, 1976. Dyneley Hall was built in 1865 and previously owned by a pram manufacturer. Thompson appears to have owned the Hall up to at least 1937 but not to have lived there after about 1931.

24. Don Cole, Cookridge, *The History of a Yorkshire Township*, 1980 and other books on the local history; Cookridge Estate papers in WYASL and courtesy of Richard Perkin. Tony Shelton Golden Acre Estate Breary Grange farm - notes on property history in WYASL & LLIS (information from Philip Redfearn)

25. Letter from Margaret Watson to author, 1999.

26. E Robinson and L Keeble, *The Development of Building Estates*, Estates Gazette, 1952 contains a useful near-contemporary description of inter-war private housing market conditions and development methods.

27. CEBP, WYASL.

28. Song by Arthur Schwartz and Howard Dietz, 1930.

29. YEP 5.9.1931.

30. LCCDGAP

31. Conversation with Henry Haigh recorded in c 1985 by Eric Cope and Ron Redman, as part of their research into Golden Acre and its miniature railway.

32. YEP 29.8.33, 16.3.35, 22.7.35, 25.7.35.

33. Song by Jerry Lewison, Al Neiburg and Mary Symes, 1934.

34. YP 26.3.32; Yorkshire Observer 26.3.32; *YEN* 17.5.32, *YEP* 9.2.33.and conversations with Joan Duffield and Richard Perkin; letter from Margaret Watson. The Park occupied part of Golden Acre estate land (a small area of Blackhill Well Farm) and part of nearby Cocker Hill Farm, which Thompson bought from the Leeds Industrial Co-operative Society.

35. LCCDGAP and company documents held by WYASL. Thompson's fellow company directors were his mother, Annie Eliza, and Arthur Scott, the company secretary. The Golden Acre Thompsons are not, as has been suggested, related to the family of the same name who own the Blackpool Pleasure Beach (letter to author from Geoffrey Thompson, BPB managing director).

36. Conversation, 2001 with Cecil Foster who worked at the 'Happy Hour' and at the Park.

37. Song by Ray Henderson and Lew Brown, 1931.

38. Marriage certificate, Frank and May Thompson, 9.2.29. and conversation with Dorothy Thompson. John Erwin Campbell was a captain in the Royal Warwick regiment and during his marriage to May, a farmer in Kenya. Public attitudes were softening but it was not until the Matrimonial Causes Act of 1937 that slightly easier procedures were brought in. David Thompson, *England in the Twentieth Century*, Penguin, 1965.

39. LCCDGAP and Thompson letterhead (see Fig 12) Red Roof was sold to the managing director of Schofield's department store and changed hands again in 1972 when it was converted into three large flats. Information from Philip Redfearn.

40. Conversation with Dorothy Thompson and *YEP* 15.2.34.

41. *YEP* 29.12.32.

42. *YEP* 10.2.32, 29.12.32 and 15.2.34.

43. Brian Rust, *British Dance Bands on Record*, 1911-45, 1989.

44. From a variety of press items and pictures (eg YEN 10.5.33) and conversations with Dorothy Thompson, Joan Duffield, Sybil Mawson and others (1999). Ivor Novello's own house, bought in 1927 was called Red Roofs.

45. Song by Ray Henderson, BG De Sylva and Lew Brown, 1929.

46. Conversation with Dorothy Thompson and *How Would You Like a Zebra Steak? A Leeds Woman, YEP* 9.8.35.

47. *YEP* 22.8.31, 31.8.31, 5.9.31, 10.2.32 and 13.2.32, which contains a description of the technology of the novel 'synchronised talkie accompaniment': *By means of a fluctuating beam of light…tiny marks are transformed into small electric currents. These…are increased by means of electrode valves until they have the power to operate the loudspeaker.*

48. Song by Harry Revel and Mack Gordon, 1937.

49. YEP 10.2.32; conversations (1999) with Tom Mawson and Gracie Dring who heard that the Thompson had a regular box at the City Varieties. The Harehills *Picture House,* opened in 1912, closed in 1963 and was redeveloped as shops and a rooftop car park. Thompson sold the cinema in or before 1938.

50. YEP 12.5.37; Louis Mannix, *Memories of a Cinema Man,* Associated Tower Cinemas, 1988; Robert Preedy, *Leeds Cinemas Remembered,* 1980; conversation with Gracie Dring, 1999.

51. CEBP WYASL and *YEP* 3.5.37, 12.5.37, 24.1.38, 10.6.38; letter from Chris Ure, Associated Tower Cinemas. When his cinema application was refused, Thompson appealed to the Minister of Health (then the arbiter of planning appeals) but the refusal was upheld.

52. CEBP, WYASL

53. Song by Harold Arlen, Ira Gershwin and EY Harburg, 1934.

54. Conversation with Cecil Foster, 2001, and Gracie Dring, 1999.

55. Conversation with Cecil Foster and letters from Albert Paylor, Brian Holmes to Leeds Leisure Services and the author.

56. Henry Haigh's conversation, c 1985, with Eric Cope and Ron Redman.

57. *YEP Old Yorkshire Diary*, 1980s.

58. Conversation with Tom, Sybil and Ted Mawson, 1999.

59. Henry Haigh's conversation c1985, with Eric Cope and Ron Redman.

60. Conversation with Joan Duffield, whose father once attended one of Harris's 'tastings', 1999.

61. Letter from Margaret Watson, 1999.

62. Song by Jimmy Van Heusen and Eddie de Lange,1939.

63. YEP 9.8.35 and electoral rolls, LLIS conversation with Cecil Foster.

64. Information from Ken Horn and from CEBP, WYASL. The last building plans for Kings Road were submitted in 1937; some houses remained unsold when war broke out and one was offered for as little as £400, less than half the original price.

65. Many witnesses stress the problems caused for visitors by travel and expense of admission charges.

66. Golden Acre was not alone in its fate: during the 1930s, many American amusement parks failed, maimed by the Depression, and, nearer to home, two prominent West Riding examples at Honley and Hipperholme closed just before the war. Peter Bennet, *Blackpool Pleasure Beach, A Hundred Years of Fun,* Blackpool Pleasure Beach, 1996; Douglas Taylor, West Yorkshire Amusement Parks, *Yorkshire Archaeological Journal* Vol 58,1986.

67. *YEN* 16.10.36.

68. *YEP* 9.2.33, 8.2.34, 7.2.35, 2.36 and 26.11.38; CEBP, WYASL. The hotel's architect was not the usual Luwee Harris but Hayward and Maynard of London.

69. *YEP* 24.1.39, YP 27.1.39.

70. Correspondence in LCCDGAP; company papers, WYASL.

71. Letter from Margaret Watson, 1999.

72. YEP 26.11.41 and 6.9.46; correspondence in LCCDGAP; conversation with Michael and Susan Pierce; CEBP, WYASL. One parcel of land was sold to Smith's, builders of Otley: just before the outbreak of war, they laid footings and, soon after the war, completed the houses of King's Drive. These were the only builders to buy land from the Golden Acre estate and succeed in developing it. During the war, Thompson submitted revised plans for his unsold land on each side of Otley Road, possibly to help boost its value, but these came to nothing.

73. LCCDGAP; Several witnesses have described the park as it was in 1946: ruined buildings, overgrown gardens and the lake reduced to a marsh.

74. Song by Russ Morgan, Dick Howard and Bob Ellsworth, 1937.

75. Letter from Annie Eliza Thompson to Bob Lennard, 1943, courtesy of Margaret Watson; company papers, OLC WYASL; conversations with Paul Steele (*Jarvis Parkway Hotel*) and Richard Perkin.

76. Company papers, OLC WYASL.

77. Song by Al Dubin, Sam Cosland and Con Conrad, 1934.

78. Conversation with Dorothy Thompson.

79. Directories and LCCDGAP; *The Grange*, a Victorian house, was demolished after the war to make way for flats.

80. *YEP* 21.8.50, death certificate and conversation with Alison Evans.
81. Funeral notice in *YEP* 21.8.50. and Conversation with Dorothy Thompson.
82. Unidentified cutting from 1951, courtesy Margaret Watson.
83. Conversation with Dorothy Thompson.
84. *Ibid*. After the war, Ken and Dorothy Thompson lived in Sutton Coldfield; Ken worked in Birmingham, buying advertising space, initially for the Rank Organisation (a link albeit a tenuous one, with Frank and Herbert's movie activities) and later for WH Smith. In retirement Ken became a volunteeer with the Embsay Bolton Abbey railway. In 1986 he was guest of honour at the topping out of the Parkway extension and in 1987 a commemorative tree was planted. In 1992 his ashes were scattered under that tree, witnessed by Dorothy, her niece, the manager of the Parkway and Joe Maiden, who developed the Golden Acre Park demonstration garden and became a noted radio and TV gardening expert.
85. Song by Leo Robin and Ralph Rainger, 1937.
86. J B Priestley, *English Journey*, 1934; Penguin edition 1977.
87. Max Beerbohm, *Mainly on the Air*, 1946.

## Background Bibliography

Steven Burt and Kevin Grady, *An Illustrated History of Leeds*, Breedon, 1996: indispensable local background.
Tony Shelton, *Leeds' Golden Acres, The History of a Park and its People*, published by Age Concern, 2000, with support from Leeds Leisure Services: an illustrated account of the creation of Frank Thompson's amusement park and of today's botanical park.
Tony Shelton, Episodes in the History of Golden Acre, Thoresby Society 2nd Series Vol. 11, 2001.
Grace Horseman, *Growing Up in the Thirties*, Cottage, 1994.
Peter Dewey, *War and Progress, Britain 1914-45*, Longman, 1997: general economic, political and social background.

## Acknowledgments

I am grateful for the generous assistance of many people and organisations. They include Steve Burt; Don Cole; Eric Cope and Ron Redman, whose earlier research has been invaluable; Leeds City Council: Leisure Services (Parks and Countryside and Libraries and Information Service - Local Studies) and Legal Services; Richard Perkin; Philip Redfern, Dorothy Thompson, John Thorpe (*Yorkshire Evening Post*); Brett Harrison et al, West Yorkshire Archives Service, Leeds and Mike Levine.

# 9. Arthur Ransome: Born in a Romantic Town Like Leeds

### *by Margaret Ratcliffe*

THE COMMEMORATIVE BLUE PLAQUE on the house in Ash Grove where Arthur Ransome, the author of the *Swallows & Amazons* series of children's books was born in 1884, gives little indication of the origin and background of the author whose books are still in print but whose life and work embraced so much more than the series of twelve novels for which he is justly famous (Figure 1).

Ransome lived in Leeds as a child, studied at the Yorkshire College as a young man; visited his mother's home in Leeds in her later years and received an Honorary Doctorate from the University of Leeds where his papers are now housed in Special Collections at the Brotherton Library.

But he was not the first Ransome to be distinguished in Leeds life. On 27 June 1878 his father, Cyril Ransome was interviewed by the Literature Committee of the Yorkshire College (which became Leeds University in 1904) and on 17 July was appointed Professor of Modern Literature and History. Student numbers were small at this time and the Arts subjects were in their infancy at the College then renowned for its more scientific and practical specialties. Professor Ransome was appointed at a stipend of £300 per annum plus two thirds of fees.[1] When interviewed, he had been required to present a 'test' lecture, his subject being 'The Campaign of Waterloo.' In fact, lecturing was one his

**Figure 1.** Arthur Ransome (aged 21) caricatured by his teenage brother, Geoffrey, 1905. *Courtesy: the Lupton family*

A.M. Ransome

Discussing the relation of art to Literature

By an anonymous artist.

**Figure 2.** Mount Preston in the early 1960s, looking south towards the city with the Town Hall very faintly visible in the distance. *Courtesy Leeds University Archives*

specialties and, following his untimely death at the early age of 46 his Obituary in the *Yorkshire Post* on the 26 June 1897 mentioned his talent in this direction commenting:

> As a lecturer Mr. Ransome was singularly clear and instructive and particularly careful to adapt himself to the needs of the backward and the slow…Generosity of temper, sincerity and courage were perhaps the dominant features of Mr. Ransome's character, and made him dear to his intimates.

Indeed, his series of lectures *Our Colonies and India: How we got them and why we keep them,* were published and enjoyed excellent sales, going into several editions.

Aged thirty-one when he came to Leeds, Professor Ransome lived initially at an address in Mount Preston, the site of which is now in the heart of University buildings (Figure 2).

A Master of Oxford University, Professor Cyril had been a private tutor in Rugby, one of his pupils being Prince Alamayu of Abyssina, the son of King Theodore (Figure 3). As a young boy, Alamayu had been brought to England when the capital of Abyssinia, Magdala, was stormed and captured by General Napier in 1868. Queen Victoria took a great interest in the dead King Theodore's son, Alamayu. Moved around within Court circles, he had a spell at Rugby School and at Sandhurst though he never really settled anywhere being lonely and far from home. He had been tutored by Cyril Ransome and declared him to be the only person with whom he was comfortable. On leaving Sandhurst he begged to be allowed to join Professor Ransome in Leeds. Letters passed between Sir Stafford Northcote, then Chancellor of the Exchequer and Professor Ransome who eventually agreed and Alamayu came to Leeds in autumn 1879. Almost immediately he was taken ill. At this time Cyril lived with the Reverend Annesley Powys at what was then 1 Glebe Villas, Hollin Lane (Figure 4). The Ransome Collection at the Brotherton Library contains a sheaf of telegrams from Queen Victoria enquiring as to the health and progress of 'dear Alamayu', a typical example reading:

**Figure 3.** Prince Alamayu of Abyssinia.
*Courtesy: the Lupton family*

> *The Queen would be glad of another report this evening. Her Majesty commands me to send her affectionate remembrances to Alamayu and to assure him of the great concern with which she has heard of his illness and of her Majesty's earnest hope that she may soon hear of his beginning to make real progress to recovery. Please give him my love also.*[2]

This was sent from Balmoral by Strafford Northcote. Quite what the Headingley Post

**Figure 4.** No. 1 Glebe Villas – now No. 2 Hollin Lane where Prince Alamayu died in 1879.
*Author's collection.*

Office must have made of these royal daily missives is not recorded.

Professor Ransome's unpublished autobiography tells us that Alamayu did not recover 'Unfortunately by a foolish act (he went to sleep in the WC in the middle of a cold night) and he caught pneumonia'.[3]

Ransome accompanied the body to the funeral at St George's Chapel, Windsor and arranged for the simple plaque on the coffin which reads:

*Prince Alamayu of Abyssinia. Born April 23, 1861. Died at Leeds, Nov. 14, 1879.*

Cyril met Edith Rachel Boulton, Arthur's mother in Scarborough where he was visiting with his friend, Edwards Banks, a Leeds Solicitor (Figure 5). Edith, ten years his junior, was governess to a clerical family just outside York and after a whirlwind romance, they were married in Shropshire (from where Edith hailed) on 28 December, 1882, the bans being read a Wrangthorne Parish Church, Hyde Park Corner.

While Cyril was an academic, Edith had a more artistic background. Her father, who had emigrated, was an exhibited artist in Australia. Edith's own talent was such that when art lessons were proposed for her, the tutor said there was nothing he could teach her.

**Figure 5.** Edith Ransome, the author's mother.
*Courtesy: the Lupton family*

Their first child Arthur, was born on 11 January 1884 at 6 Ash Grove, off Victoria Road (Figure 6). A modest house (now divided into flats) it is deeper than it appears from the front. In 1884 the house was relatively new. Nine houses only were built on the even side of Ash Grove at that time with open fields at the rear.

Following the birth of another child, Cecily in 1885, the family moved to 4 de Grey Road, the only Ransome house in Leeds not still standing (Figure 7). The first ladies' hall of residence in Leeds in 1913, the terrace was demolished in late 1920s, forming part of the

**Figure 6.** 6 Ash Grove, Arthur Ransome's birthplace.
*Author's collection*

**Figure 7.** De Grey Road, following conversion to a ladies' hall of residence. The Ransomes lived at No. 4, the second house from the right. Now demolished and part of the Brotherton Library site. *Courtesy: Leeds University Archives.*

site of what was to become the Parkinson Building and Brotherton Library.

A second son, Geoffrey, was born here in 1887. Geoffrey went to Rugby School and earlier was at Hillbrow preparation school with the poet Rupert Brooke (Figure 8). He later worked in Edinburgh but, nevertheless, as an adult was familiar with Leeds and fished

**Figure 8.** School play (Merchant of Venice) at Hillbrow, Rugby. Rupert Brooke is standing third from the right and Geoffrey Ransome second from the left. *Courtesy: the Lupton family*

Roundhay Park with Arthur. In 1914 Geoffrey, always interested in
mechanical objects and speed, practised driving a motor car in Leeds
declaring the streets a great test.[4]

Arthur Ransome himself considered Geoffrey a great writer but a
promising life and career were sadly cut down when Geoffrey died in
The Great War in 1918. He was commissioned in the 10th Battalion,
the Yorkshire Regiment of the Green Howards and according to his
memorial at Rugby School:

> *He went to the Front with them in September 1915, and was
> wounded in that month at Loos, where the Battalion suffered heavy
> losses. He was wounded again severely near Armentières, in February
> 1916, doing volunteer duty, which nearly cost him his life. He was
> then attached to the Second Training Reserve and received the rank of
> Temporary Captain. In December 1917, he returned to the Front
> attached to the 13th Battalion and in January 1918, was wounded
> again, but remained on duty.*
>
> *On January 11th, while on patrol in the Cambrai sector, he received
> another wound, of which he died in a Casualty Clearing Station at
> Achiet-le-Grand, on January 15th, 1918. Age 30.*

The Officer Commanding the 13th Battalion wrote:

> *He was wounded in bravely carrying out a difficult and dangerous
> duty, and, although he had a party of men with him, he went forward
> himself with his Sergeant rather than send his men.*

Geoffrey's letters to his mother from the front give beautifully
descriptive, graphic and poignant accounts of life in the trenches.

His sketchbooks have survived and recently surfaced. An artist of
wit, vigour and movement, all his subjects have speed either
illustrated or implied; he was an expert at conveying frantic activity
be it in animals, humans or his real passion – motorcycles and

**Figure 9.** A pen, ink and colour washed sketch from Geoffrey Ransome
signed and dated 1907. *Courtesy: the Lupton family*

automobiles (Figure 9). His portraits of classical and Shakespearean characters or his own contemporaries are almost all caricatures and he usually makes the faces of animals expressive of what they are doing or feeling. An early sketch from his schooldays was published in a motor magazine of the day and of this he was tremendously proud.

Many academic families in the late 1800s gravitated to live in the Otley Road corridor moving ever closer to the nearest clean water supply and we know from Arthur Ransome's Autobiography what childhood was like in North Leeds. He tells of escapades involving 'hapless tutors' around Adel Crags with his young friend Eric Rücker Eddison.[5]

The Eddisons were a prominent, college connected family and the two boys were close friends. Ransome writes:

> ... *We were making for the famous rock on Adel Moor. There was only one way of climbing the perpendicular side of this rock.* [Figure 10]. *We reached the top just in time, rapped the tutor's knuckles when he tried to follow us, and spent the day there in comfort.*[6]

E R Eddison later wrote books himself, now to be found on the fantasy shelves in second hand bookstores. His *The Worm Ouroboros* is described by Ransome as 'a book of strange power, a story of fantastic heroes in a fantastic world, written in a consistent, fastidious prose that seemed devised for that purpose.'[7] In later years Ransome named a pet snake Ouroboros and wrote to both Manchester Zoo and the London Reptile Curator for advice on feeding.[8]

An even more exotic playmate was the Russian Prince Peter

**Figure 10.** Adel Crags, 1904. *Author's collection*

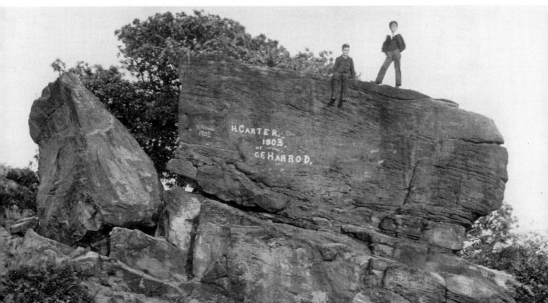

Kropotkin. An acknowledged nihilist, (being one who rejects all religious and moral principles coupled with the philosophic doctrine that nothing has real existence), the term was particularly applied to Russian revolutionaries opposed to all constituted authority. Ransome met Kropotkin at Adel Grange, the home of the liberally minded Misses Ford, who were neighbours of the Eddisons. Concerned for the welfare of girls working in the Leeds tailoring trade, the Ford ladies were activists themselves. Before the suburban spread of housing to Adel, the Grange had its own lake and it was here Kropotkin taught the young Ransome to skate.

Many years later Ransome no doubt remembered Kropotkin when he included an ice skating lesson in his book *Winter Holiday*:

> *You just put your weight on one foot and swing yourself round with the other,' said Dick. 'At least that's what it feels like.' 'Like this,' said Nancy, and swung herself round in the bravest manner while going at full speed, coming down with such a bump that if the ice had been a little less thick she must have gone through. But she picked herself up with a laugh. 'Not quite like that,' she said. 'Lets have a shot at doing it slowly.'* [9]

Ransome was to meet the Prince again in Russia in 1917 and followed his funeral procession in Moscow in 1920.

While the children played, the adults were always occupied. Professor Ransome maintained a busy schedule lecturing, writing and close involvement with many of the leading committees and organisations of the day.

The Yorkshire College Calendar indicates he gave evening and weekend lectures (for which students had to pay 1/6d [7½p]).

He proposed the motion to found The Thoresby Society in 1889, a Society still going strong today whose stated aim is

> *to encourage the study of the history of Leeds and its neighbourhood through an annual programme of lectures and through publications, a library, and excursions organised by the Society to places of interest.*

Professor Ransome was also on the Committee of the Leeds Charity Organisation Society, a well-meaning body, though hardly the forerunner of our present social security system, spending much of its time defending its record of refusing aid!

A notice on the reverse of each annual report warns:

> *You are earnestly requested not to give to beggars either in the streets or at your own doors. If the tale they tell is a true one, their case will*

ELEVENTH ANNUAL

REPORT

OF THE

Leeds Charity Organization

SOCIETY,

1882.

OFFICE—3, OXFORD PLACE.

Leeds:

PRINTED BY A. MEGSON & SONS, BAINES' BUILDINGS, BANK STREET,
1883.

Officers and General Committee for 1883.

President:
THE MAYOR.

Vice-Presidents:
REV. JOHN GOTT, D.D. | REV. PROVOST BROWNE. | FREDK. BAINES, ESQ.

Honorary Treasurer:
JOHN LUPTON, ESQ.

Honorary Secretary:
REV. C. HARGROVE, M.A.

Committee:

A. G. BARRS, ESQ., M.D.
W. H. BROWN, ESQ., M.R.C.S.
EDWARD BUTLER, ESQ.
THOMAS CHURTON, ESQ., M.D.
REV. W. DUNN, M.A.
J. E. EDDISON, ESQ., M.D.
FREDK. HALL, ESQ., M.D.
REV. CECIL HOOK, M.A.
REV. CANON, JACKSON, M.A.
DARNTON LUPTON, ESQ.
JOHN RALPH, ESQ., M.A.
PROFESSOR RANSOME, M.A.
EDWARD WALKER, ESQ.
JOHN WHITING, ESQ.
REV. F. J. WOOD, M.A.

Ladies' Committee:

MRS. BLAIR.
MRS. C. BOUSFIELD.
MISS BROWN.
MRS. J. E. EDDISON.
MRS. W. EMSLEY.
MISS GUNDRY.
MRS. HENDERSON.
MRS. LUCCOCK, (Hon. Spt. Ndlwk.)
MRS. MILLARD.
MRS. G. H. NUSSEY.
MISS PASSAVANT.
MISS STABLES, (Hon. Sec).
MISS TALBOT,
MRS. J. W. WILLANS.

Clerk:
MRS. BROWN, AT THE SOCIETY'S OFFICES.

Inquiry Officer:
WILLIAM BARRETT, 4, ROSEBANK TERRACE.

Bankers:
MESSRS. BECKETT & CO., LEEDS.

Collector:
JAMES SWALE, 22, LOUIS STREET, NEW LEEDS.

Meetings of the General Committee on the first Thursdays in the month at 4 p.m.
Meetings of the Relief Committees every Tuesday and Friday at 4 p.m.

**Figure 11.** Leeds Charity Organisation, Eleventh Annual Report, 1882.
*Courtesy: Leeds City Libraries*

*require more help and care than you can give off hand. If, as is unhappily far more probable, it be false, you not only throw away your money, but by the gift encourage idleness, lying, and vice.*[10]

At the Tenth Annual Meeting in February 1882 held in the Town Hall, Leeds, with the Mayor in the Chair, Professor Ransome seconded the resolution to adopt the report and balance sheet (Figure 11):

*He said an objection brought against the Society was that it spent too much in office work. The Society seemed to fulfil two distinct functions. In the first place it directed charity onto the right road, and in the second it prevented charity from going wrong. It was in preventing it going wrong that a considerable amount must be spent, but he thought the report conclusively answered that objection. Another objection was that they did not relieve the cases of deserving people sent to them. People constantly came to him, as a member of the Committee, and complained that very deserving cases which they had recommended had not been relieved. But on examining these cases it was found, in nine instances out of ten, that they were simply cases of people out of work. The Committee were sorry that they could not help such cases, but the fact that they were £67 to the bad showed that it was out of their power to assist them. The Report distinctly showed that a very large sum of money had been spent in actually helping people, and the cases quoted in the Report showed in what methods it had been applied, and in what directions these good results had been obtained.*[11]

This was an era of soup tickets, begging letters, poor law guardians, children's chemises and asylums. The report details numerous cases which had been investigated. In 1881, 450 cases were relieved and 187 turned out undeserving.

Case No.11380 was one of those relieved:

*In this case the applicant was a young women who was dying of consumption. As one of her brothers was imbecile, and another deformed, it was hard for her father to give her any of the comforts necessary for one in her case. The character of the applicant was exceedingly good and the Society assisted her during her illness, and she was also visited and helped be a Member of the Committee up to the time of her death.*[12]

Cases 7846, 10352, 10354, 10682 and 10759 were less successful.

*This case was sent five times for investigation. It was that of a little girl who was sent out by her parents, under the pretence of selling chips, but really for the purpose of begging. She then told, in the most innocent manner, a pitiful tale of a father killed by falling off a building, and of she and her mother being left to do the best they could. For a long time she evaded detection, by giving false names and addresses, but was at length traced. It was found that her father was in full work as a labourer, that he had been twice convicted for drunkenness, and once for deserting his wife and family, and that he had been summoned five times by the School Board for not sending this girl to school. The mother was in the habit of taking off the girl's shoes and stockings before she sent her out begging. The girl was brought before the Stipendary Magistrate, and sent by him to an Industrial School, until she is 16 years of age.*[13]

The Philosphical and Literary Society continues to flourish. Founded in 1819, its lectures numbered many distinguished persons at its premises in Park Row (now the site of the HSBC Bank) including William Morris (1883-84) and W G Collingwood (1900-01.) John Ruskin's secretary, Collingwood is often credited with pointing

Arthur Ransome in the right direction, a mentor in fact. Certainly the ambience of the house in which he lived at Lanehead on Coniston was perfect for an aspiring writer.

Newly arrived in Leeds in 1878, Professor Ransome gave a lecture to the Philosophical and Literary Society in the 1879-80 session on *The Battle of Marston Moor* and a Public Saturday Afternoon Museum Lecture: *The Battle of Leeds*. (Other subjects in this series were: *Spiders and their ways; A Stick of Red Sealing Wax; Bees; Savage Art*).

In 1880 we would have found him electioneering at *The New Inn*, Otley Road. His speech on the Liberal platform was reported verbatim in the following day's papers with 'cheering, applause and laughter.'[14] Elections were not then conducted by satellite and spin-doctor.

He was at the forefront of early teacher training in Leeds. A Council Meeting of the Yorkshire College in 1884 tells us

> *the following recommendations of the Academic Board were agreed to:*
> *- 'that Professor Ransome should lecture before the Leeds Pupil Teachers' Association on the terms agreed upon.'* [15]

Professor Ransome was also instrumental in developing the University Library. Professors Rücker and Ransome along with a senior student were appointed to a library Committee in 1879. As only six students were registered as subscribers at this time, it was recommended that subscription be made compulsory. A table of books in the library showed a strong bias towards engineering and the sciences.[16]

Cyril Ransome had obtained a First at Merton College, Oxford in both Mathematics and Modern History. This breadth of knowledge led yet another Library, which he served with distinction, to describe him as 'Three professors in one'.[17] In 1888 he was Honorary Secretary of the Leeds Library, a proprietary organisation then, as now, housed in Commercial Street.

In 1890 the family moved to 2 Balmoral Terrace, off Shaw Lane (Figure 12). A lovely double fronted, stone terrace house, where the

**Figure 12.** 2 Balmoral Terrace, Arthur Ransome's home 1890-1894.

Ransomes had three servants, a cook, nurse and housemaid. Cyril's book *Short Studies of Shakespeare's Plots* was published at this time and it was here the second exotic prince came to be tutored, Tsau Chey of Burma, a nephew of King Theebaw. History shows that Theebaw was, without doubt, a villain but Tsau Chey, writing later to Professor Ransome, is most proper and well mannered though perhaps displaying an unhealthy interest in firearms!

Many years later Tsau Chey's Leeds connection surfaced again:

> *A story is told by a son of Dr. Atlay, an earlier Vicar of Leeds. He was manager of the Ruby Mines in Burmah. Mr. Frank Atlay said: 'I was sitting on the verandah of my house with a young Indian Prince who had been having lunch with me. We had spoken of many things, he having just returned from being in England. I asked him what he had liked best there? He was silent for a little while, and then said "Leeds Parish Church". I almost jumped out of my chair, as he added, "Oh, how that Choir sings." He had lived for three months in Leeds with a Professor of the Yorkshire College, and attended the Parish Church Sunday Evening Service.*[18]

Joyce Ransome, the youngest of the four children was born in 1892. Joyce went on to read French, History and Philosophy at Leeds University and later at University College, London. A writer herself, she published her own trilogy of children's stories, loosely based on the Arthurian legend in which she was particularly interested.[19]

Yet another of Professor Ransome's activities was his monthly Conversation Club meeting; gatherings at Members' houses:

**Figure 13.** 3 St Chad's Villas (on the right). Arthur Ransome's home 1894-1897. *Courtesy: Ian Ballantine*

*...the essentials being that the meetings were for the purposes of Conversation, held once a month at the houses of members, of whom there were to be twelve, and that the supper was to be simple...the sobriety of discussion was vigorously guarded because no salt of "Controversial Politics and Religion" was admitted.*

Thus in 1849. Later however:

*...the dinner grew into a gentlemanly banquet, for champagne became popular, while an expert knowledge of port was duly appreciated.*[20]

In 1894 with Arthur aged ten, the family moved to what is now the *Ascot Grange Hotel*, No. 126 Otley Road, then known as 3 St Chad's Villas. Shortly after the Ransomes left in 1897, Nos. 126 and 128 became Moorlands School (Figure 13). There the Ransome trail in Leeds pauses when Cyril with his family,

**Figure 14.** Cyril Ransome, Arthur Ransome's father.
*Courtesy: the Lupton family*

moved to a new career in Rugby where he sadly died almost immediately at the age of forty-six (Figure 14).

The Leeds pull was strong and Arthur, at the age of seventeen, returned to the Yorkshire College in 1901 as a student reading what was for him the entirely unsuitable subject of chemistry. However, this period was not entirely wasted. Ransome tells us that one day he discovered J W Machail's *The Life of William Morris* in the University Library and read:

*...of lives in which nothing seemed to matter except the making of lovely things and the making of a world to match them. I took the books home with me, walking on air, across Woodhouse Moor in a thick Leeds fog...From that moment my fate was decided...*

The Lake District and Norfolk Broads were ultimately to become his principal literary focus but Leeds continued to play an important rôle.

The widowed Edith Ransome was also drawn back to Leeds and lived from 1912-20 at Casetta, 116 Harrogate Road, Chapel Allerton (Figure 15). Arthur by this time had contracted a most unsuitable marriage from which he fled to Russia. Constance Ivy Walker met Arthur Ransome during his 'Bohemian' period in London, swept him off his feet and they

**Figure 15.** Casetta, 116 Harrogate Road. Edith Ransome's home where Arthur Ransome wrote *Six Weeks in Russia*, 1919. *Author's collection*

were married in 1909. Temperamentally incompatible, the marriage was troubled from the beginning and though a daughter, Tabitha, was born in 1911, Arthur left the country in 1913. The shock of a failing marriage was compounded by genuine surprise when he was sued for libel by Lord Alfred Douglas following the publication of his biography of Oscar Wilde.

After a protracted case, in which he personally played a minor role, he was found innocent but the trial (which Ivy enjoyed) was the last straw and war torn Russia on the brink of revolution seemed to offer the solace he needed.

Ransome witnessed and reported on the Revolution at first hand and, in 1919 he came to 116 Harrogate Road searching for momentary peace and quiet to write his book *Six Weeks in Russia*. Ransome was impressed and said in a letter to his mother:

> *My stenographer has done brilliantly and if ever I have another thing to do in such a hurry, I shall come here and use her again. She's cheap at the price.*[21]

He was clearly significantly homesick for much of his time in Russia and at least half of the 303 surviving letters to his mother were addressed to 116 Harrogate Road.

One thread running through the generations of Ransomes in Leeds was the family Lupton. There was a Lupton on the Literature Committee of the Yorkshire College which appointed Professor

**Figure 16.** Wedding of Marjorie Edith Joyce Ransome and Hugh Ralph Lupton, Kemsing, Kent, 1920. *Courtesy: the Lupton family*

Ransome in 1878. Indeed there appeared to be at least one Lupton on *every* important Committee of the day. Prominent in public life, the ubiquitous Luptons were leading lights of the Leeds élite. Dibb Lupton & Co, Solicitors of Leeds acted for the Ransomes and the families were joined when Joyce Ransome married Hugh Ralph Lupton in 1920 (Figure 16).

Joyce and Hugh settled in Leeds and, in 1919, Edith Ransome moved north again to Rupert Lodge, 28 Grove Road (Figure 17).

By now, Arthur Ransome had married again. While in Russia he had met and fallen for Trotsky's secretary, Evgenia Shelapina, and in 1924 they were married and eventually settled in this country.

Edith Ransome's Visitors' Book records Arthur's stays at Rupert Lodge with Evgenia and these entries, along with Arthur's own diaries, are primary records of a crucial time in Arthur Ransome's literary development.[22]

**Figure 17.** 28 Grove Road – Edith Ransome's home in the 1920s and '30s. *Author's collection*

On 22 March 1929, Evgenia and Arthur were in Leeds for his mother's birthday and two days later his diary records 'Began Swallows & Amazons.'[23]

In January 1931 Arthur and Evgenia walked from Rupert Lodge to Adel Church, along the route of Arthur's childhood escapades with Ric Eddison. Before he set off that day, Arthur's diary recorded 'Did complete contents list of "Swallowdale"' and on their return he wrote '6 pages. A most satisfactory day all round.'[24]

An author and journalist all his life, it is undoubtedly the *Swallows & Amazons* series which brought Arthur Ransome fame and for which he is remembered.

In 1937 *Pigeon Post* was awarded the Carnegie Medal for Best Children's Book of the Year, the first winner of an award which remains much coveted today. The Spa Hall, Scarborough was the venue for the presentation on 1 June.

Scarborough was familiar to Ransome. As a child he had holidayed in the town at the home of his godfather, the future Privy Councillor, A H D Acland, a co-author of Professor Ransome. Temple, the Archbishop of York, presented the Medal on behalf of the Library Association. Contemporaries at Rugby School, their shared youth was remembered.

Also in 1937, Ransome was asked to contribute a piece to *The*

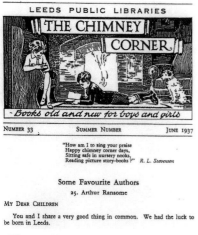

**Figure 18.** *Courtesy: Leeds City Libraries*

*Chimney Corner*, a Leeds Public Libraries publication for children (Figure 18). (These were the days of Story Half-hours held at 6.30 o'clock in the Junior Libraries, for girls and boys between 8 & 14 at the Armley, Bramley, Burley, Compton Road, Dewsbury Road, Holbeck, Hunslet and York Road Libraries).

Ransome begins:

*My Dear Children*

*    You and I share a very good thing in common. We had the luck to be born in Leeds. Now, for all kinds of reasons, Leeds is one of the best places in the world in which to be born. Let me tell you a few of them...*

*    ...Being born in a romantic town like Leeds, a town that is full of present day life, and ancient life as well, with the country, as it were, only half an hour away, you are born to get the best out of both country and town, out of past and present, and you will be the right readers for all kinds of books, town books, and country books, even country books like mine, most of which are about lakes and hills.*[25]

Ransome's Leeds connection was 'formalised' by the Honorary Doctor of Letters award by Leeds University in November 1951 of which he was immensely proud and in his diary he quoted Dr Samuel Johnson 'Every man has a lurking wish to be thought considerable in his native place'.[26] At the ceremony in 1952 he shared the platform with Wyndham Lewis. Thenceforth it was always 'Dr Ransome' both in correspondence and on introduction to strangers.

Now the Ransome papers are held safely in Special Collections at the Brotherton Library in the University of Leeds, the site of which is, almost exactly, Arthur's childhood home, 4 de Grey Road. We can safely say the spirit of Ransome has come home to Leeds.

### Notes and References

1. The Yorkshire College Minute Book 1874-1878, University of Leeds Archives.
2. Brotherton Collection, Leeds University Library.
3. *Ibid.* Unpublished manuscript autobiography of Cyril Ransome.
4. *Ibid.* Letter from Geoffrey Ransome to Arthur Ransome, 27.4.16.
5. *The Autobiography of Arthur Ransome*, p.38.
6. *Ibid.* p.39.
7. *Ibid.* p.38.
8. Brotherton Collection *op.cit* Diary entry 14.6.62.
9. *Winter Holiday*, Arthur Ransome (Jonathan Cape) 1933.
10. *Tenth Annual Report of the Leeds Charity Organisation Society*, 1881.

# RANSOME

**The relations and descendants of John Atkinson Ransome [1779 – 1837] by his second wife, Susanna Hoyle [1795 – 1880]**

Susanna Hoyle, daughter of Thomas Hoyle, Brother-in-law of W Ecroyd, one of the founders of the art of calico printing in Lancashire. His works were at Mayfield and he lived at Spring Cottage, Little Marsden, between Nelson and Brierfield in Lancashire.

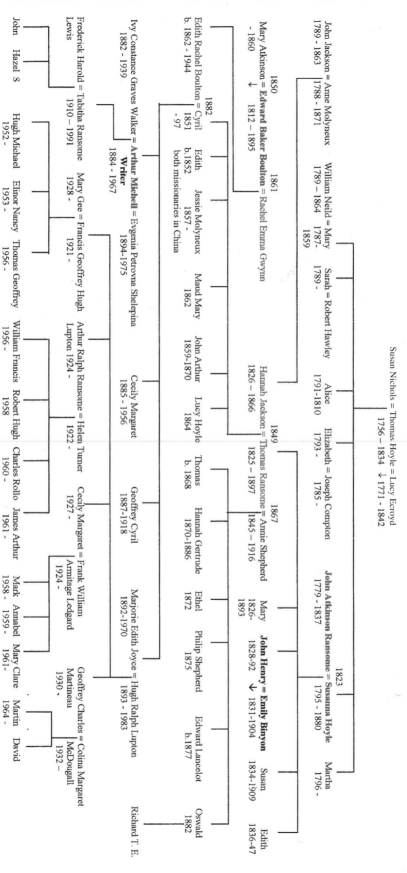

11. *Ibid.*
12. *Ibid.*
13. *Ibid.*
14. *Leeds Mercury,* 23 March 1880.
15. The Yorkshire College Council Minute Book 2. 1878-1888, University of Leeds Archive.
16. *The early years of the Yorkshire College.* Thoresby Society. Misc. Vol. 16.
17. *The Leeds Library,* Lee 1768-1968.
18. *Recollections: 60 years ago & onwards'* H. & J. & B. M. Walker, 1934.
19. *The Seeker, the Great Elm, The Hill of the Ring.* Joyce Lupton.
20. *Conversation Club, Leeds 'a memoir conceived at the 1,000 meeting...'*
21. Brotherton Collection, op.cit Letter dated 28.4.19.
22. *Ibid.* Edith Ransome's Visitors' Book.
23. *Ibid.* Diary entry 25.3.29.
24. *Ibid.* Diary entry 21.1.31.
25. Leeds Public Libraries *The Chimney Corner* Number 33, Summer Number, June 1937.
26. Brotherton Collection op.cit. Diary entry 12.11.52.

## Acknowledgements

My grateful thanks are due especially to the following: Arthur Ransome's literary executor, John Bell, for permission to quote from unpublished material. Ann Farr, on behalf of the Brotherton Collection, Leeds University Library, for permissions and her valuable support. Dr Mark Shipway, Leeds University Archive, Leeds University Library for permissions. Katherine Blanchard of Leeds City Libraries for her permissions andhelpful co-operation. Ian Ballantine for permission to reproduce the postcards from his extensive collection. A special word of thanks to the present owners of all the former Ransome homes in Leeds for their enduring courtesy. The Lupton family for their-patient and helpful contributions. Joan Newiss of Leeds for drawing my attention to the reference to Dr Atlay and Prince Tsau Chey. Judy Andrews of Windermere for the extract from her Ransome Family Tree.

## Appendix

Brief bibliography of books by Arthur Ransome with publisher and year of original publication
*The Souls of the Streets* Brown Langham 1904
*The Stone Lady* Brown Langham 1905
*Pond and Stream* Anthony Treherne & Co. 1906
*Things in Our Garden* Anthony Treherne & Co. 1906
*Highways and Byways in Fairyland* Alston Rivers Ltd. 1906
*Bohemia in London* Chapman & Hall 1907
*A History of Story-Telling* T C and E C Jack 1909
*The Book of Friendship* T C and E C Jack 1909
*Edgar Allan Poe* Martin Secker 1910
*The Hoofmarks of the Faun* Martin Secker 1911
*The Book of Love* T C and E C Jack 1911
*Oscar Wilde* Martin Secker 1912
*Portraits and Speculations* Macmillan & Co. 1913
*The Elixir of Life* Methuen 1915
*Old Peter's Russian Tales* T C and E C Jack 1916
*Aladdin and his Wonderful Lamp* Nisbet & Co. 1919
*Six Weeks in Russia in 1919* George Allen & Unwin 1919
*The Soldier and Death* J G Wilson 1920
*The Crisis in Russia* George Allen & Unwin 1921
*Racundra's First Cruise* George Allen & Unwin 1923
*The Chinese Puzzle* George Allen & Unwin 1927
*Rod and Line* Jonathan Cape 1929
*Swallows and Amazons* Jonathan Cape 1930
*Swallowdale* Jonathan Cape 1931
*Peter Duck* Jonathan Cape 1932
*Winter Holiday* Jonathan Cape 1933
*Coot Club* Jonathan Cape 1934
*Pigeon Post* Jonathan Cape 1936
*We Didn't Mean to go to Sea* Jonathan Cape 1937
*Secret Water* Jonathan Cape 1939
*The Big Six* Jonathan Cape 1940
*Missee Lee* Jonathan Cape 1941
*The Picts and the Martyrs* Jonathan Cape 1943
*Great Northern?* Jonathan Cape 1947
*Mainly about Fishing* A & C Black 1959
*Autobiography* edited by Rupert Hart-Davis – Jonathan Cape published posthumously 1976.

# 10. A Citizen of Whom Any City Might be Proud: Arthur Greenhow Lupton 1850-1930

*by Joan Newiss*

SUCH WAS THE TRIBUTE paid by the local press on the death of Arthur Greenhow Lupton, one of the four brothers popularly known as the 'Lupton Brotherhood' in their lifetimes (Figure 1).[1] This public respect was first established in the seventeenth century. The family dynasty was founded by Francis Lupton who married into the well-connected Midgeley family in 1688 and was appointed as Parish Clerk in 1694. Francis' third son William assumed the dynastic mantle and prospered in the town's principal industry as chief cloth dresser to Sir Henry Ibbetson, while establishing two of his sons as cloth merchants. The cloth dresser was the highest paid and most skilled artisan in the woollen industry whose expertise in dressing or 'finishing' cloth substantially increased its value. William's youngest son Arthur, the first to bear that name, benefited most from his father's position. It was deemed essential at that time for a

Figure 1. Arthur Greenhow Lupton c1900. *Author's Collection*

woollen merchant with international interests to speak German, so the teenage Arthur was despatched to Frankfurt. While there he became acquainted with the young Goethe and his sister, who practised their spoken English by copying his broad Yorkshire accent!

The cloth trade was the staple industry in Leeds and the population relied on it for employment. The town was run by gentlemen merchants and Arthur consolidated his position in this group when in 1773 he married an heiress, Olive Rider. In 1788, his father-in-law expressed further confidence in him by purchasing property at North Town End, including land on which to build a new

AN ANCIENT TRADE MARK.

**Figure 2.** Old trade mark of Wm Lupton & Co. Believed to show the original mill overlooking the tenter fields. *Lupton family archive.*

woollen cloth works (Figure 2). There was also a handsome mansion, which became the family home for some fifty years. It was one of a group of three built earlier in the century by the wealthy Denison family, themselves merchants of considerable substance who went on to become landed gentry. Arthur died in 1807 and the running of the Company was then shouldered by his sons William and Arthur junior.

The Lupton family's Unitarian connection begun by the heiress

**Figure 3.**

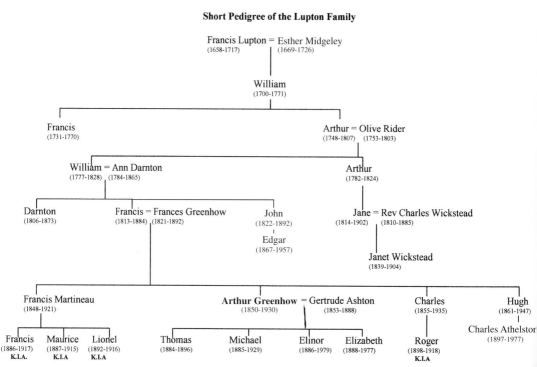

**Short Pedigree of the Lupton Family**

Olive Rider was strengthened by the marriage of one of Arthur junior's four daughters to the Reverend Charles Wicksteed, the minister at Mill Hill Chapel. By the nineteenth century, the Unitarian community was well respected in Leeds and the chapel was jocularly, but accurately referred to as 'the Mayor-making Parlour'. The Lupton family enhanced this assessment, as three of them were to occupy the mayoral chair over time (Figure 3). However, Olive's son William, had little time to spare for civic duties. The early part of the century had been a difficult period for international trade. The Napoleonic wars and the conflict with America had created havoc for business and William died, worn out, in 1828 aged only fifty. It was left to his redoubtable widow Ann, the daughter of an eminent tobacco merchant called Darnton, and her eldest son aged only twenty-two, to redeem the firm's fortunes in part by laying out Merrion Street in 1830 as a residential development adjacent to the cloth works. The area was bisected by New Briggate in 1868 (Figure 4). The son was called Darnton after his mother's family and, once the business was secured, it was he who developed the family tradition of civic service that his nephews, the 'Lupton Brotherhood' inherited so ably. Indeed, Darnton and his brothers had been the founding brotherhood; all of them involved with the community and highly respected for their charitable works.

Darnton stood above all, for his kindness was so evident and genuine that it was noted by a visitor made welcome in his home 'A rare man, so liberal, doing work and kindness in many ways', and as a host 'the embodiment of happiness and cordiality'.[3] Darnton's home was then The Harehills. The grounds of this eighteenth century mansion once extended along Harehills Lane, being in part opposite the location of the new mosque on the old Kershaw's factory site.

If Darnton was the most respected male Lupton of the mid nineteenth century, it was his brother Francis' wife, Frances Elizabeth Greenhow, who was to establish the distaff side in the public eye, a role later sustained by her grandchildren, including the two well-known daughters of Arthur Greenhow Lupton. Frances Elizabeth was married in 1847 and the family home was established at Potternewton Hall, a mansion site of some antiquity, demolished in the 1930s. Its two hundred and fifty yards long, arrow straight drive, then bordered with great elm trees, is now the location of Riviera Gardens. It was in this Hall that Arthur Greenhow Lupton was born in 1850.

Ann Lupton, the redoubtable widow who had helped save the family business lived nearby at Newton Green Hall, another lovely

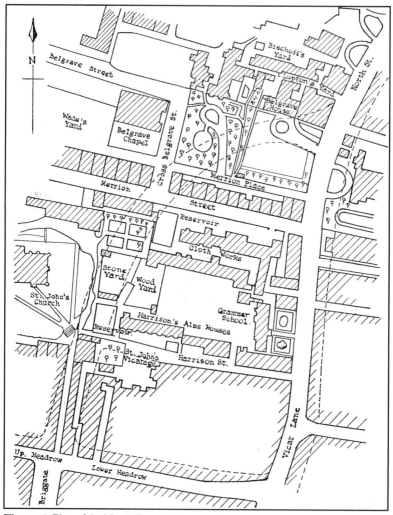

**Figure 4.** Plan of the North Town End area. *Ordnance Survey of 1847 amended by C A Lupton.*

old home, which fell victim to late twentieth century hospital development. All private transport was horse-drawn, so most mansions had an associated farm or field to provide hay. Haymaking parties were a delightful summer treat for children and in the 1850s the Reverend Wicksteed's eldest daughter Janet was invited to join Arthur and his elder brother Frankie at Newton Green. She remembered

*When the hay was about half in cocks, we and many other cousins*

*were invited to come and tumble it about as we liked, make big nests in the cocks, sit on the top and then roll down, rush up them and fall mid-way or on the top, and then jump off them, race wildly about, in fact make ourselves limitlessly and perfectly happy.*[4]

When Arthur was ten years old, his parents decided to remove to Beechwood at Roundhay. This was a larger estate and also very privately situated on Elmete Lane as it still is, though recently handsomely redeveloped as offices. This became the family's most memorable home, remaining in their ownership for over a century. Arthur lived there initially until his marriage in 1882. At the age of eleven in June 1861 he joined Frankie at Leeds Grammar School, which was still located next to the Lupton cloth works at North Town End, on

**Wellington Chambers, City Square,**
LEEDS.
SHOPS AND OFFICES TO LET.

For Particulars and to View, apply
to the Lift Attendant.

**Figure 5.** Wellington Chambers, 1903 advert. Architect: Geo Corson, 1851. *Lupton Family Archives*

what is now the site of the Grand Theatre. So Arthur and Frankie took lunch at the firm's warehouse at the junction of Wellington Street and Aire Street. This was handsomely designed by George Corson and formed a unified frontage with adjacent warehouses. It too fell prey to development in the late twentieth century (Figure 5).

Arthur and Frankie were destined to take over the family firm. Their parents though notable supporters of higher education, feared that if both boys went to university, both might become disinclined towards business. Frankie was therefore permitted to attend Trinity College, Cambridge. Arthur was taken out of school at sixteen in 1866 and was immediately apprenticed to the firm. Arthur's view of this discrimination between siblings is not recorded. He was subsequently to work tirelessly to gain funding for the infant Leeds University, a service which was acknowledged by his appointment as its first Pro-Chancellor in 1904.

He settled well, however, into the business and in 1928 wrote an account of the firm entitled *Recollections and Traditions of William Lupton & Co., Leeds* from 1773.[5] The book incorporates the history of both family and firm at home and abroad; the take-over of other business houses over the years and, the most fascinating of all, the roll call of woollen cloths whose names have passed into textile history since the development of synthetic fibres. In this book we read of Blue Uniform cloths and Piece-dyed Pilots for the railway companies liveries, Blue Superfines, Wool-dyed Drab Doeskins, Cassimeres, White Plain Superfines, Fancy Tweeds and Livery Tweeds, Stable Tweeds in dark Greys and Drabs for Undress Liveries; White Diagonals, Wool-dyed Meltons and Beavers; Aberdeen mixture with Mohair scribbled in, Tweeds of black shoddy and wool twisted with white and gold and many more. Arthur's knowledge of cloth was extensive and each 'piece' (a standard length of woven cloth) offered to him by its makers was judged initially by sight and touch, then examined over a strong light, to assess its content, quality or evidence of damage in the making.

Naturally the industry had modernised over time. Whereas at one time small clothiers had woven the 'piece' on their own handlooms in their cottages, this had been superseded in the nineteenth century by mill complexes and power looms (Figure 6). Arthur's father Francis had supported this development whilst others felt that power looms were all very well for cotton, but could never replace hand looms for the softer thread of woollen cloth which required to be 'humoured'. Francis asserted that the cloth produced on power looms was so superior that he could tell, simply by touch, which pieces had been produced on which type of loom.

Other changes that were recorded by Arthur had occurred in the important dyeing processes. Initially all wool was dyed before weaving. This is where the phrase 'dyed in the wool' came from.

**Figure 6.** Taking a 'piece' to market. *Lupton Family Archives*

Technological advances permitted the introduction of 'piece dyeing', where the whole woven piece was dyed. This new process however had its drawbacks, particularly with thick cloth which the dye did not always penetrate satisfactorily. By the mid-nineteenth century custom required every working man to have a black suit for Sundays, and the cloth used was first a Superfine and later a Faced Venetian or Diagonal. These were dyed in the piece and then 'finished'. The surface fibres of the cloths were raised, trimmed smooth across the surface, then dyed in indigo vats. After roller boiling they were 'filled up' black with Copperas and Logwood, the final result being the 'Woaded Blacks' for which Leeds was famed. If the cloths were especially heavy, the maximum penetration was difficult to achieve. The process often needed to be done six or more times to give the required finish, and required two or three months to go through, reflecting the firm's commitment to a quality product.

In his early days with the family business, Arthur had travelled widely around the country as a salesman for Wm Lupton & Co. He kept a diary of his business meetings.[6] His closest brother Charles had become friends at Rugby School with Tom Ashton of Hyde, near Didsbury. The Ashton family was wealthy and influential in business, university education and politics. Tom's sisters were young ladies of charm and achievement. Arthur was introduced and, no doubt, stayed at Hyde on some of his travels, taking especial note of one sister, Gertrude. In February 1882, Arthur's mother recorded the outcome in her diary:

> *On Tuesday 21st February, Shrove Tuesday. Gertrude Ashton left us to return to 'Ford Bank', Arthur going with her, on his way to London. On Tuesday morning we received letters from Arthur and from Gertrude telling us the most happy news of their engagement.[7]*

The wedding took place on 4 May recorded by the North Cheshire Herald:

> *Although there was not the slightest display of ostentation, the event being conducted with the utmost privacy, Mr Ashton's widespread influence did not fail to gather together a large number of spectators who thronged the church and approaches...Hundreds had to remain outside. The bride was attired in a handsome damask travelling costume, with bonnet to match.[8]*

For the honeymoon, the couple toured Wales in Arthur's dogcart, drawn by his new grey mare, which had cost him £35. Driving was his favourite pastime.

Back in Leeds it was not long before the couple moved into their chosen home, Springwood, near Oakwood, a short distance from Arthur's parents. This mansion still stands and is now converted into flats called Fraser House. It was an attractive residence, built in 1826-7 by Stephen Nicholson, for his sisters-in-law. Nicholson inherited Roundhay Park in 1833. Gertrude quickly bore four children in her new home, so Arthur extended the property. Several bills remain of the furnishings bought especially from the prestigious Leeds firm of Marsh, Jones & Cribb, Cabinet Manufacturers and Upholsterers. Room by room, they supplied bespoke furniture, carpets, curtains and fittings, beds, mattresses and bed linen to a total cost of £566 (Figure 7). The furnishings included those in the servants quarters, for example a servants' bedroom was fitted with two iron bedsteads, palliasses, wool mattresses, bolsters and pillows, two chests of drawers, two dressing glasses, one washstand, a double set of ware, a towel horse, two cane chairs and a bedside carpet. Every comfort indeed, for two young maidservants at a cost of £16.19s.0d.[9]

Gertrude came from and into families with strongly developed social conscience. Annual childbearing was no excuse for avoiding social responsibility. A new charitable organisation, the Leeds Ladies Association for the Care and Protection of Friendless Girls, had Gertrude's mother-in-law as one of its founder members in 1884. Gertrude became a subscriber in 1886 and accepted the role of Honorary Secretary a year later. Her fourth child was due early in 1888. Visitors were received as usual throughout January and their names carefully noted by Gertrude in her *At Home* book. A Miss Whitehead was engaged to re-trim the baby's cot. The task took one and a half days at a cost of two shillings per day. Nurse Hulme arrived on 22 February to take care of the mother and the baby girl born on the 26th.

**Figure 7.** Ebonised Cabinet displaying a Dresden fruit dish at Springwood. *Author's collection*

Over the next few days Gertrude's health fluctuated slightly, but on 4 March there was a rapid deterioration. Three doctors were called and they informed the shocked Arthur that his wife's case was hopeless and that she would not last the day. At noon, Gertrude lapsed into unconsciousness and, almost immediately, she gasped herself away. The widowed Arthur painfully recorded these last moments in his diary[10]. Gertrude's immediate family were travelling in Egypt and were unable to return home, so Arthur was supported by his brothers and mother who wrote ' Our dear one was laid to rest on 7th March, and loving hearts attempted, however vainly, to give what consolation might be possible to poor Arthur'. Meanwhile his father-in-law wrote from Cairo to a life-long friend 'Gertrude was so full of life and love - the loss to her children is dreadful and her poor husband whose whole life and happiness was singularly wrapped in her'[11]. On their return from Egypt the Ashton sisters-in-law took it in turns to stay at Beechwood to care for the children, while his brothers took Arthur away for holidays. There were painful tasks to perform, such as sorting Gertrude's clothes. A few dresses were carefully packed away, to be shown to the children when they were older. In 1971, when Gertrude's daughters moved from Beechwood to a smaller house, many souvenirs had to be parted with. The carved wood cot that had been so carefully trimmed for each child was sold at auction for £9.[12] The dresses were presented to the City Museum and one, a gown of red watered silk, which had cost £24 13s 4d. for materials and making up in 1881, was displayed at Abbey House in 1997.

In his wife's memory, Arthur continued to subscribe to the *Association for Friendless Girls* until his death.[13] He introduced his daughters aged twelve and ten to the charity in 1898, when they gave a gift of clothing. They became subscribers in 1907 and donated fresh produce regularly from Beechwod. They funded outings for the children and many other treats. The younger daughter, Bessie, served on the committee for thirty-nine years, including eighteen years as Chairman after which she became Honorary President. Their father never remarried; he absorbed himself in his children, his home, his business, public work, farm and horses. He ceased travelling as a salesman after 1888, to be

**Figure 8.** A G Lupton's children in 1889; left to right Michael, Elinor, Tom, Bessie.
*Lupton Family Archives.*

more at home with his young family (Figure 8). Fate however was not kind to him. His elder son, Tom, was sent to Lockers Park School in London, where there was an outbreak of scarlet fever in March 1896. Tom succumbed to the disease. Arthur was with his son from the 12th. On the 27th, Tom's throat was badly ulcerated and he was unable to swallow. By the 29th he was unconscious and struggling to breathe and he died the following day.[12] This was a scene frequently highlighted in Victorian school fiction, often melodramatically treated, but still a sober reflection of real life.

Arthur's family was ably cared for by Nurse Helen Burr and by Miss Catherine Corfield as housekeeper. Both ladies were much loved. Arthur spent time with the children whenever he could, indulging in riotous pillow fights on Saturday evenings, or carefully displaying the albums of wonderful watercolours their mother had painted before her marriage on a three months tour of Egypt. When his daughters visited Egypt in January 1939, they already had in their mind's eye 'Those pictures of the Nile, its low banks fringed with palm trees, the black rocky hills of Nubia pressing in on the river, and the strange temples and statues and sculptures.'[15] Arthur continued to fulfil his public and business roles. He also began to take his elder daughter Elinor with him for company when driving his dogcart around the countryside seeking contributions towards the University. Elinor went on to spend her own adult life in committed service to the University, which was founded in 1874 as the Yorkshire College. Just a year later, Arthur had become a member of the Board of Governors and in 1887 a member of the Council of which he was appointed chairman in 1899, having chaired already the Finance Committee since 1892. In 1904 the Yorkshire College became the University of Leeds and Arthur was appointed as the first Pro-Chancellor, having been largely responsible once again for the fund collecting that enabled the College to apply for its Charter. He was rewarded in 1910 by the honorary degree of Doctor of Law. The youth who had been deprived of a University education finally enjoyed academic honours. When he wished to retire in 1920, it was a year before an equally adequate successor could be found, and it was in June 1921 when he stepped down, at the age of seventy-one.[16].

In addition to his public service, one business concern was never enough for a man of Arthur's vision. He diversified into the improvement of services such as rail travel, water supply, waste heat and particularly electricity supply. His brothers Frank and the engineer Hugh were also involved in this venture. With others, The Yorkshire House-to-House Electricity Company was founded in

1892, though rather than house owners the first customers eager for the 'new light' that Christmas, were five principal shops in the town centre. The importance of this facility was so quickly apparent that the Corporation bought out the Company just six years later[17]. In 1989 the Leeds Industrial Museum at Armley also recognised this major development locally by establishing a new display gallery entitled Electrifying Leeds. Whereas today we take the 'new light' entirely for granted, in its early days it was the cause of great excitement and wonder. Arthur's sister-in-law Margaret Ashton, after attending an exhibition in London to see the illuminations in 1884, describing it as 'like a scene out of a fairy tale.'[18]

Subsequently, as chairman of the directors of The Yorkshire Electric Power Company, Arthur became one of the most important men in the electricity industry.

During the First World War Arthur's executive skills became even more publicly noticeable through his involvement with an enterprise whose name resounds among Leeds people even today: Barnbow. This huge shell-filling factory, located between Crossgates and Garforth, was built from scratch on 400 acres of farmland starting in August 1915. It had its own railway station which accepted some thirty-eight trains a day transporting the workforce. There were huge canteens that catered for up to 16,000 workers. There were medical and nursing services and a farm with a herd of cows whose milk, it was hoped, would help counter the effects of inhaling gunpowder. Barnbow also had its own fire brigade, served by a specially constructed reservoir. The whole complex was camouflaged to avoid detection from the air and any consequent bomb attack. Even then, the volatility of the gunpowder made Barnbow a very dangerous place. Ninety-three per cent of the workforce was female. Long hair had to be tucked into a cap and neither hairclips nor jewellery was permitted. The wearing of official identity bracelets was compulsory as an aid to the identification of bodies in the event of an explosion. Three explosions did occur resulting in the deaths of thirty-seven young women. Their deaths could not even be reported as this might have identified Barnbow to the enemy. Arthur and his fellow directors carried a heavy responsibility in catering for every requirement and precaution in connection with the enterprise.[19]

The War of course, also brought increased business for Wm Lupton & Co. In the past, volunteer military units such as the Leeds Rifles Regiment used large quantities of Rifle Green or Empress Grey Meltons. The new requirement was Khaki serge for the British Territorials and Black Melton for the Russian army, making both heavy demands and good returns for the Company. However, this was but a temporary boom. The post-war slump combined with Super Tax crippled both the firm and its' customers. Faced with a Super Tax bill for £3,284 in 1922, Arthur sent a blunt response to the inspector:

> *Last year, my firm lost over £100,000. In the face of the above loss no Income Tax can be payable, and it is an absurd anomaly that Super Tax can be claimed for the same period. How do you propose the money should be raised?* [20]

The War also brought a family crisis, with grievous effect on the Company. All the brothers' seven sons had been called into military service. Four were killed in action. Frank lost his three sons, two of whom were partners in the firm. He died of grief in 1921. Arthur found himself, at the age of seventy, heading the firm with his unmarried cousin Edgar as partner. He went down to business every day, earning a headline in the local newspaper 'Not too old at Seventy'.[21] After the War he had decided to move house. Springwood was being encroached on by development at Oakwood. Since the death of Arthur's mother in 1892 until the War, the old family home at Beechwood had been rented out. Arthur and his family moved there in 1919. Arthur had more land to farm and Bessie was happy caring for the poultry and other animals. She eventually established a prize goatherd to provide milk for invalid children.

Arthur's younger son Michael, who had survived the war unscathed, married in 1919 and moved into a stone built end-of-terrace house in Chapel Allerton. A keen huntsman, he kept his horses at Beechwood and regularly went there in the evening from business to see to the animals and to attend to farming matters with his father. Following the deaths of his cousins in the War, Michael and his young son, born in 1920, were destined to take over the family business, then already remarkable for being the oldest surviving firm in Leeds. It was not to be. Michael suffered a serious fall while out hunting, was paralysed and died some months later in 1929. His widow and children left Leeds and his father quietly succumbed to grief a few months afterwards. The obituaries were long and thoughtful, referring to the service of the entire family:

> *Where is Leeds to find for itself another Lupton family to take up for the new generations the tools that fall from the hands of the old men? We commend the example of public service rendered by one whom we now so keenly lament and so highly honour.* [22]

The mantle of Wm Lupton & Co thus fell on Elinor, with her father's retired cousin Edgar then aged sixty-three once again returned in a supporting role. Despite an upsurge of business in the Second World War, the firm never recovered satisfactorily from the aftermath of the First. Like her father Elinor bore the burden into her seventies, but finally closed down the Company in 1959. It had survived for 185 years. Yet the name of Lupton has not disappeared from public memory. In 1924 Alderman Charles Lupton was the Chairman of the Improvement Committee and proposed the redevelopment of the old Head Rows as a wide boulevard through the city centre. The newspapers jocularly called the thoroughfare 'Lupton Lane', but the historic title was retained. It is another broad highway that commemorates the family: Lupton Avenue in east Leeds. In addition, a modern block of University flats at Headingley, which replaced the 'Lupton Hall of Residence' retains the name. A prestigious firm of solicitors, once headed by Charles, still commemorates him in the title Dibb Lupton Alsop. The Honour Boards in Leeds Civic Hall record those who have sat in the Lord Mayor's Chair, including Charles and Hugh. Leeds Girls High School acknowledges Elinor's service by the Elinor Lupton Centre.

Yet the family's most famous enterprises are anonymous. On the old North Town End site, some years after it was bisected by New Briggate in 1868, the brothers created two handsome developments. One was a row of black and white 'Tudor' style shops, which took its name from the main occupant: a furniture company called Rothwell's (Figure 9). This shopping parade, as attractive as its counterparts in Chester, fell victim to the development of the inner ring road, where it runs beneath North Street. The other enterprise has more fortunately survived. This is the Grand Arcade, built in 1897 on the site of the original Lupton mill. Initially it consisted of two parallel and interconnecting rows of shops but the northernmost one was converted into the Tower Cinema in 1920. The Arcade is most renowned for its automaton clock, made

**Figure 9.** Rothwell's Parade, New Briggate, demolished in the 1960s.
*Yorkshire Post Newspaper*

by the famous local firm of Wm. Potts and described by them as 'the greatest horological feat of that century'.[23] It is a Lupton family tradition that the design of the clock was based on one seen by Arthur on a business trip to Nuremberg.

In 1923, the University honoured Arthur Greenhow Lupton by engaging Stuart Hill to paint his portrait. The artist has memorably captured the sitter's eyes that pierce the viewer with their keen observation. This was not a man to suffer fools gladly; yet he was noted for his patience and flawless temper, his unvarying courtesy and consideration towards those who differed from him, for 'he liked to speak the appreciative word'.[24] The same obituary details his fine public service, his keen sense of duty and the loss to Leeds of a life devoted to the welfare of its people, under the headline tribute 'A Citizen of whom any City might be proud'.

## Acknowledgements

I am indebted to members of the Lupton family for their generosity in permitting access to personal archives and to two privately published family histories, *The Lupton Family in Leeds* by Charles Athelstane Lupton published in 1965 and *Recollections and Traditions of William Lupton & Co* by Arthur Greenhow Lupton, published in 1928.

## Notes and References

1. *Leeds Mercury* 12.2.1930. *The Times* 11.2.1930; *Yorkshire Evening News* 8.2.1930; *Yorkshire Evening Post* 8.12.1930; *Yorkshire Post* 10.2.1930 and 12.2.1930.
2. Goethe. W. *Von Dichtung und Wahaheit* April 1764-Oct 1765.
3. Herford C H *J Estlin Carpenter - A Memorial Volume* 1929.
4. Wicksteed Janet. Recollections mss compiled 1892.
5. Lupton Arthur Greenhow. *Recollections and Traditions* privately published 1928.
6. Lupton Arthur Greenhow. Diary mss 1872-1891.
7. Lupton Frances Elizabeth. Daybook mss 1847-1892.
8. North Cheshire Herald 6.5.1882.
9. Marsh, Jones & Cribb Accounts to A G Lupton mss 1882-1883.
10. *Ibid* Diary mss Feb 22 - March 7 1888.
11. Ashton Thomas to Rathbone William correspondence mss March 16 1888.
12. Renton & Renton Auctioneers Sale of residual furnishings 'Beechwood' catalogue Nov 25 1971.
13. Leeds Ladies Association for the Care and Protection of Friendless Girls (renamed Spring House Home from 1945) Annual Reports 1884-1974 (Note: The Archives of the Society are incomplete, lacking the Annual Reports from 1968-1974 and the Minute Books from 1949-1974. The author would appreciate help in locating the above.)
14. *Ibid* Diary mss March 8-April 1 1896.
15. Lupton Elinor. Accounts of Visits to Egypt from 1939 mss compiled 1965.
16. Shimmin A N. The University of Leeds - The First Half Century Cambridge University Press 1954.
17. Hirst J D. Editor *Leeds Tercentenary Official Handbook* 1926.
Poulter J D. An Early History of Electricity Supply: *The Story of Electric light in Victorian Leeds* IEE History of Technology series vol 5 1986 p137-143.
*Leeds Mercury* 16.2.1898.
18. Ashton Margaret. Account of the illumination at the Health Exhibition, London Diary mss July 2 1884.
19. Scott W H *Leeds in the Great War* 1914-1918 Leeds Librariesand Arts Committee 1923 pp182-188.
20. Lupton A G to Oliver A A Letter mss March 9 1922.
21. *Yorkshire Evening Post* 6.9.1922.
22. *Yorkshire Post* Leader article 10.2.1930.
23. Potts Private communication courtesy of Michael Potts mss July 20 1995.
24. Schroeder Rev W L. *Tribute, Yorkshire Post* 12.2.1930.

## 11. SECONDS OUT: BOXING IN LEEDS

*by Isadore Pear*

BOXING AS A SPORT IN ITSELF, has always aroused man's primitive instincts and, since well before the First World War, has attracted popular support in Leeds. Boys and youths of every denomination and especially those from deprived areas, were lured by the idea of finding fame and fortune through mastering the noble art. So it was in the Leylands district of Leeds, which was a predominantly Jewish area in the early years of the twentieth century.

In Bridge Street there existed a room located above a general warehouse which during the day masqueraded as a small gymnasium and, in the evening, was an illicit gambling club. Any comparison between the old gyms and the modern health club with its sophisticated fixtures, fittings and equipment is purely accidental. There was no entry fee for the gym (or one penny in old money if you could afford it) and for this members were permitted the use of a punch bag, boxing gloves, skipping ropes and, for those individuals displaying talent, free tuition. However, these spartan facilities did little to dampen the enthusiasm of the boys and a steady stream of hopefuls continued to come to the gym to keep fit and, if nothing else, it gave them something to do, keeping them off the streets. Access to the Bridge Street gym was by means of a rickety wooden stairway and at the end of the room was a fire escape which provided for a quick getaway whenever the club was raided by the police, which happened as gambling was an illegal activity in those days. However, whenever a raid was imminent the organisers of the gambling were invariably forewarned by the efficient bush-telegraph that worked in the area. Several token arrests were made; the law applied; fines imposed; public interest satisfied and matters continued as before.

From these humble beginning, through the acumen of various entrepreneurs, Leeds developed into a recognised boxing centre in the north, with several well patronised stadiums sited not far from the city centre. One of the first was the National Sporting Club (no connection with the one in London) housed in an old church on Bridge Street, behind what is now the Job Centre. It was owned by a colourful character, Albert Heslop. He ran this hall for a number of years before retiring. He opened another stadium at the top of Samuel Street before selling it to a bookmaker, Georgie Barrett, who turned it into the Beaufort Club.

Another venue, was situated in Crimbles Street, Sheepscar and was managed by Simy Hart, an ex pro. This later became a billiard hall called Pemberton's, universally known as 'Pem's' and frequented by young working lads whose sole interests in life seemed to be connected with both gambling and backing horses. A third and very favourable hall was located at Cross Harrison Street, off Vicar Lane. Archie Stone opened yet another stadium, seating about 200, at the top of Skinner Lane in premises previously occupied by the British Legion. A feature of this stadium was unlicensed boxing every Saturday night which, whilst not illegal, was not subject to the rigorous rules of the British Boxing Board of Control.

Then finally there was perhaps the doyen of them all, the Brunswick Stadium in the street of that name, providing regular boxing bills every Sunday afternoon. Initially it was a concern promoted by Percy Fox, then sometime later by 'Barber' Ben Green and his brother Jack in a

**Figure 1.** Joe Fox.
*Reproduced by kind permission of Mr Gordon Fox*

**Figure 2.** Harry Mason .
*Reproduced by kind permission of Mr Danny Green.*

**Figure 3.** Alf Mansfield.
*Reproduced by kind permission of Mr Gordon Fox.*

joint promotion. The price of admission in the early days was one shilling (5p) and one and six (7½p). After the Second World War the price of admission rose to two and six (12½p). For this, fans were treated to a wealth of boxing talent, both home-grown and international. Not only was the quality of the fare offered first rate, but generally speaking the conduct of the spectators was perhaps raucous, but good natured and beyond reproach. The Green family started a dynasty which for years became synonymous with boxing in Leeds. They introduced at that time leading figures in the world of international boxing such as Jimmy Wilde, the world flyweight champion, Gumboot Smith and Harry McDermott. Also connected with the sport was Jim Windsor. He was a well-known promoter and bookmaker. He owned the Commercial Club in Vicar Lane which was not only a very popular watering hole for the boxing fraternity, but for all sportsmen in general, as was the Lonsdale in Brunswick Terrace, owned by Dave Goodman. All these halls and clubs were, within a stone's throw from each other and were the foundations of the world of professional boxing in Leeds in the early 1920s.

Given the area most of these clubs were situated in, it should come as no surprise to find that a large number of these early boxers were Jewish. Tolly and Rufky Solomon, Louis Ruddick, Joe Fox, Cockney Samuels, Cockney Buxton, Harry Mason, Tom Sharkey, Cockney Cohen, Myers Stringer, Alf Mansfield and Lew Taylor were all Jewish boys (Figures 1-3). Samuels, Buxton and Cohen were fully accredited Loiners but, because some of their forebears came from London, they were given the nickname 'Cockney'. Non-Jewish boys like Jimmy Goulding, Little Minor, Benny Thackray and Len Hampston all came from Leeds whilst Stanley Booth came from

**Figure 4.** Little Minor *Reproduced by kind permission of Mr Gordon Fox*

**Figure 5.** Jimmy Learoyd, Ben Green and Len Hampston
*Reproduced by kind permission of Mr Danny Green*

Huddersfield (Figures 4-7). Johnny Britton, Young Jim Learoyd, Jack Kirk and Harry Leach came from other parts of Yorkshire, but all were Tykes and proud of it (Figure 8). All were accomplished performers and most trained at Professor Marks' gym

**Figure 7.** Stanley Booth
*Reproduced by kind permission of Mr Gordon Fox*

**Figure 6.** Benny Thackray
*Reproduced by kind permission of Mr Danny Green*

which was situated opposite Dyson's corner off Boar Lane. Although called Louis, everyone called him Professor because of his inordinate skills as a trainer.

Cockney Samuels was a bantamweight, Cockney Buxton was a welterweight. Both these boys were managed by Jack Board and they both became Yorkshire champions in their divisions (Figure 9). Unfortunately, in later life Cockney Samuels suffered from the ill effects of a long and punishing career. Louis Ruddick never reached championship status but he fought some memorable contests albeit unsuccessfully against Tolly Solomon, Cockney Cohen. Louis Ruddick lived at Cross Stamford Street. Alf Mansfield was another top class fighter and although he tangled with the world's best, he never became a champion.

But it was the Solomon boys who really carved a name for themselves in the annals of Leeds boxing history. Tolly is the more

**Figure 8.** Jim Learoyd.       **Figure 9.** Jack Board.
*Reproduced by kind permission of Mr Danny Green*    *Reproduced by kind permission of Mr Mott Green*

famous of the two (Figure 10). He never had a manager
as such, but was encouraged and handled by his three
principle backers, Harry Dorsey, Wilf Priceman, and
Dave Goodman who were all bookmakers. The hall
at Cross Harrison Street witnessed some of Tolly's
most thrilling bouts. He possessed stamina, and
fought champions such as Spike Robson, Pedlar
Palmer, Digger Stanley, Johnny Summers and an
American champion, George Dixon. Perhaps
Tolly's most memorable fight was against Jimmy
Goulding, also of Leeds. The match was twenty
rounds for a side stake of £25 a side, plus the
purse money. It was to be 'winner take all'. Tolly
stood five foot five and a half inches and weighed
eight stone six pounds. From the start it was a
terrific bout. In the second round Tolly was almost
blinded by a heavy punch which necessitated him
having his eye lanced at the interval. He had men in
his corner, Georgie Barrett, Sam Parker and Harry
Thompson, who knew their job. Jimmy Goulding

also suffered heavy punishment. He sustained a       **Figure 10.** Tolly Soloman
broken rib and his jaw was damaged. The fight went   *Reproduced by kind permission of*
on until the sixteenth round when Tolly was          *Mr Harry Soloman*
declared the winner. Despite it being agreed the winner would take
all, Tolly handed a share of the spoils to his plucky rival. On another
occasion at one of the midnight shows that were a feature of Cross
Harrison Street, Luke Dillon, a much heavier man, was beaten by
Tolly in two rounds. Dillon's party were dissatisfied with the result
and re-matched their man a few weeks later; but he was knocked out
again in the third round. These midnight shows were very popular
with a section of the theatre going public.

   Following a recurrent hand injury Tolly was forced to retire at the
age of thirty-eight, much to the disappointment of his many fans. As
a trainer and sparring partner he assisted many up and coming
fighters such as Jack Sims, Wolfe Brosgill and Young Kavell who was
thought by many to have a great future ahead of him before he was
tragically killed in a car accident. One of Tolly's best prospects with
definite championship prospects was a lad named Solly Dover.
Solly's mother had other ideas for her son and begged Tolly to leave
him alone as she did not want to see him get hurt. Instead Solly
became a much sought after high class tailor. Tolly died in 1953 at
the age of sixty-nine leaving two children, a son and a daughter. His

son also boxed under the name of Tolly but his career was cut short by the war when he was conscripted into the mines.

Of all the lads to come out of Leeds Joe Fox topped them all (Figure 11). He became the British bantam and featherweight champion of Great Britain. Born on 8 February 1894 he began fighting in the fairground booths in 1908. He started his professional boxing career at the age of sixteen on 21 November 1910. He lived with his parents at 2 Valley Street, Newtown in the Leylands area and although somewhat bewildered by it all, his mother proudly acknowledged to everyone in her fractured English that 'Mine Joe is a boxfighter!' In only his second year as a 'pro' Joe was fighting twenty rounders. In 1914, at the age of twenty, with not even enough money to pay for a return ticket, he travelled with his brothers Percy and Nipper to gain experience in America (Figure 12). Nipper's real name was George, but nobody ever used it.

**Figure 11.** Joe Fox
*Reproduced by kind permission of Ms Pauline Crystal*

**Figure 12.** Joe Fox and brothers
*Reproduced by kind permission of Ms Anita Bransby*

Percy acted as Joe's manager and promoted all his fights while
Nipper helped to train Joe and also did a bit of boxing himself. They
successfully toured American and Australia. As a comparative
unknown Joe earned rapturous applause by his masterful displays in
Madison Square Garden, New York. Joe was not only a skilful fighter
but was also a great crowd pleaser. Fans liked his intelligent style of
boxing. At the sound of the bell he would burst out from his corner,
study his opponent and then attack him with blows from all
directions, overwhelming fighters with his superior speed and agility.
He combined an ability to stay out of the other boxers reach whilst
throwing out left jabs punctuated with an occasional right.

On his return to Britain he was joined by his youngest brother
Benny who acted as his second. Benny too boxed for a short time but
he eventually found his true mètier as a trainer and manager and was
rarely out of Joe's corner (Figure 13). In a bantamweight eliminator,
Joe out-pointed Alex Lafferty and, on 22 November 1915, Joe won
the title by stopping Jimmy Berry in sixteen
rounds. Defending his title on 17 April 1916 he
out-pointed Tommy Harrison and in a further
defence he defeated Joe Symond in the
eighteenth round when the referee stopped the
fight. This win earned Joe the outright ownership
of a Lonsdale Belt. Joe is wearing the Lonsdale
belt in Figure 2.

Joe voluntarily relinquished his crown soon
after and began to fight among the featherweights
where he eventually won the British title from
Mike Honeyman on a points verdict on 31
October 1921. However, one vital contest that he
lost was for the European title when he was
matched against Eugene Criquie in 1922.
Although Joe won every one of the first twelve
rounds on points, a momentary lapse of
concentration on his part resulted in him being
knocked out by a lucky sucker punch. It was
totally unexpected and all the Leeds punters lost
a fortune. Dave Goodman alone had a side bet of
£500 running on Joe! Joe retired with full
honours when he was thirty and went to live in
Birmingham. In his long and distinguished boxing
career he suffered only four defeats. So great was
his prestige and standing within the Leeds Jewish

**Figure 13.** Benny Fox.
*Reproduced by kind permission
of Mr Gordon Fox*

Community that when Oswald Mosley planned to hold a rally at Sheepscar, Joe was invited back to lead a counter demonstration along with his brother Percy. Mosley called off his demonstration. Joe died at the age of seventy-three. Of his brothers, Percy became a successful bookmaker and Nipper emigrated to Australia where he owned a pub in Melbourne. Also among the champions was Harry Mason. Born and bred in Leeds, although he later lived in London, Mason won the British and European Lightweight Championship when he defeated Seaman James Hall on 17 May 1923. Mason boxed with astonishing confidence and aggression throughout. He suffered a knockdown in the ninth round that was allowed by the referee, but was unanimously and vociferously condemned by the crowd as a foul blow. Hall was eventually disqualified in the twelfth round for persistent illegal tactics. On 21 November in the same year Harry successfully defended his title over twenty rounds against Ernie Rice. He decided to hang up his gloves, but then changed his mind and regained the title on 22 June 1925 by defeating Ernie Izzard; the referee stopped the match in the ninth round. A further successful defence followed on 11 February 1926 with Ernie Rice as his opponent once more. Family pressure prevailed and Harry retired for good.

Another boxing legend in the City was Little Minor (Figure 14). Although never a qualified champion in the records books he was a

**Figure 14.** Little Minor. Referee Ben Green. *Reproduced by kind permission of Mr Danny Green.*

human dynamo; a powerhouse. At the relatively young age of eighteen he won nine consecutive fight by knockouts and all well within the distance. The record speaks for itself; Bud Wally in the fourth round, Billy Hazel in the first, Tommy Kirk in the sixth, Martin Gallagher in the second, Tommy Cowley in the fourth, Terence Morgan in the seventh, Francis Biron in the sixth, Billy Yates in the fourth and Billy James in the eighth. As a fighting machine Little Minor was always impressive and he fought several exciting and thrilling contests with Benny Thackray who was also a Leeds lad. Benny was a protege of, and was trained by Professor Louis Marks. Undoubtedly, their most scintillating encounter took place at the Leeds Town Hall on 30 November 1931, which fired the imagination of all Yorkshire boxing fans. Ben Green, the well known and popular referee, described Leeds as a divided city with two distinct camps embroiled in the fierce heat of sporting controversy. The match was arranged for a purse of £200 and a £100 a side, a fortune in those days. Little Minor spent the afternoon of the fight shedding surplus ounces in the Turkish baths in Cookridge Street, whilst Benny relaxed at home in Goodman Street, Hunslet. They cancelled each other out. Benny was the boxer, the ballet dancer of the ring. Little Minor was the slugger. Benny won a round with straight lefts and boxing skill, then Little Minor drew level with a round of windmill punches. Benny Thackray eventually drew ahead by two rounds and secured the verdict. In later life they often met and remenisced about what was billed at the time as the fight of the century . They remained firm friends. It is fair comment to say that in these contests they shared the honours.

Len Hampston, was very able technician, bobbing and weaving whilst interspersing smashing rights into his opponent's body. He fought twice, albeit unsuccessfully, for the British bantamweight crown, both times against Johnny King. The first fight was held in Manchester in 1935 and the re-match in Leeds three years later.

Boxing continued at all venues in the city. A special testimonial was held for the benefit of Ben Green at the Leeds National Sporting Club, more commonly know as Heslop's. Heslop's fighters were always popular with the crowd. At the top of the bill were those boxers with an attractive track record whilst the bottom was made up of those local boys wanting to have a go. At this end of the fixture list it was more brawling rather than fighting finesse. Many of the fighters that appeared at the bottom of Heslop's bill received little or no pay. They generally fought for 'nobbins' which was the colloquial term for the coins that were thrown into the ring by the spectators at the end of a bout. The amount received was shared between the contestants and was a reflection of the appreciation or otherwise of the spectators to the bout they had just witnessed. Heslop discovered Joey Lee who did some boxing at the Judean Youth Club. Joe reported that on a good night he could earn as much as fifteen shillings (75p). Mick Homburg, unusually for a Jewish boy at this time, stood at six foot and was heavily built. He was a barber by profession but tried his skill in the ring, unfortunately with little success. Because of his size he was described as the 'Battling Dreadnought' though few of his opponents treated him with any real respect. He eventually found his niche in the fight game as a highly competent second, partnering Benny Fox at most of the fights in the Brunswick Stadium. After giving up the fight game Homburg became a highly successful travel agent.

Brunswick Stadium was well organised with regular honorary doctors in attendance of whom Dr Samuel Samuel was one (Figure 15). The permanent Master of Ceremonies was Mott Green and each contest was refereed by Ben Green, who also officiated at the National. Ben was generally and affectionately known as Barber Green. He carried out his duties with authority and without fear or favour. In the course of time he qualified as a Grade A

**Figure 15.** Dr Samuel Samuel.
*Reproduced by kind permission of Mr Edward Baker*

referee of international repute. All the champions listed in the record books between 1943-4 had been refereed by Ben at one time. He also refereed many distinguished fighters such as Benny Lynch, Kid Berg and Bruce Woodcock (Figure 16). Lynch and Berg were both world champions and our own Yorkshire-born Woodcock, came from Doncaster (Figure 17). Ben Green also had the distinction of

**Figure 16.** Kid Berg.
*Reproduced by kind permission of Mr Mott Green*

**Figure 17.** Bruce Woodcock.

being the very first radio commentator on a match that was being broadcast from Leeds Town Hall.

There was however one controversial decision in Green's otherwise unblemished career. It concerned a contest where, in addition to the purse, £30 a side was to go to each contestants. This was a high money contest in the early 1930s. The contestants were Young Mosley of Bradford and Jimmy Alderson of Brighouse; the venue was Brunswick Stadium and the fight was scheduled for fifteen rounds. Mosley was well ahead on points when he received a severe right hander on the side of the face and, although he went down, he was by no means really knocked out. By the time the referee had counted to four Mosley seemed to have sufficiently recovered his wits enough to get to his feet but, as was his prerogative, he preferred to remain down and take full advantage of the count. He let the count get to nine before he started to rise, and although he was certainly on

**Figure 18.** A boxing bill from a programme held at Leeds Town Hall on the 3 December 1956. *Reproduced by kind permission of Mr Danny Green*

his feet when the final count was called, appearing to be still straightening himself out. Now the boxing rule book explicitly states that a man is to be considered down whilst still in the act of rising. The point as to when he is completely risen and in a position to resume fighting is left to the referee to decide. Ben declared Mosley out. The ensuing debate concerning this decision went on for years. In 1965, Ben was president of the Leeds District Ex-boxers Association and on his eightieth birthday he was presented with a silver salver. He died in 1973 at the age of eighty-eight.

Boxing is a skill acquired through rigorous training but a case could be made for a genetic trait as Ben's eldest son Mott was a Boys'Yorkshire Area champion. He boxed as a paperweight at seven stone six pounds. He defeated Young Ingham and Bumper Callaghan who both became creditable professional fighters. During the war Ben's youngest son Danny boxed for his battalion, the 2nd/5th West Yorkshire Regiment, and became Brigade flyweight champion. Unfortunately, whilst on active service he was wounded in action and invalided out of the army in 1944. Unable to take up boxing professionally due to his injuries he returned to hairdressing.

After the war boxing suffered a decline in Leeds and lost a good deal of its appeal. There were only two viable stadiums left in the city, the Brunswick and the National. Ben Green had retired and his brother and partner Jack were joined by Ben's son Arthur. They continued to promote boxing but primarily at the Town Hall, and they were mostly charitable bills (Figure 18). About this time, prominent for their keen interest and love of the sport Dr Sydney Baker and Dr Clive Samuel, son-in-law and son respectively of Dr Samuel Samuel were appointed honorary official resident medical officers (Figures 19&20). They were in attendence at all major

**Figure 19.** Lt Col Dr Clive Samuel MBE. TD. BS. DPH. DIH.
*Reproduced by kind permission of Mr Edward Baker*

**Figure 20.** Dr A S Baker BSc. MB. B. CH. BAO
*Reproduced by kind permission of Mr Edward Baker*

boxing tournaments. Arthur Green went into partnership with George Relwyskow and the Brunswick promoted all-in wrestling which had begun to capture the imagination of the public. Thus ended a colourful chapter of Leeds history. The Fox and Green families were forever linked with it.

## Author's note

The following scoring rules for boxing referees was drawn up by Mr E Waltham, at that time General Secretary of the British Boxing Board of Control. They were reproduced in the Leeds Jewish Sportsman brochure for their seventeenth Annual Charity Boxing Tournament in Leeds Town Hall on 29 September, 1966 (Figure 21).

## Acknowledgements

A warm and sincere thank you to all who have so generously helped with this article, shared their reminiscences and loaned their precious photographs. It would not be what it is without their help: Edward Baker, John Boyd of Radio Leeds, Anita Bransby, Pauline Crystal, Hymy Cohen, Yoshky Etties, Gordon Fox, Mott Green, Danny Green, Harvey Gothelf, His Honour Vivian Hurwitz, Solly Jackson, Joey Lee, Leeds Local History Library, Arnold Morris, Harry Soloman, Lionel Sacofsky and Len Taylor. Last, and by no means least, a special thank you to my editor, Lynne Stevenson Tate for her benevolent but nevertheless eagle-eyed supervision. Sadly Mr Mott Green passed away during the compilation of this article. I would like to dedicate it to his memory.

**Figure 21.** The Score Card c1966.

# ANNOUNCING THE SCORE CARD

This method of scoring is different from amateur boxing as between a maximum of 5 and a minimum of 4. (This particular method has worked well, but why the minimum of four?)

The following article has been written by Mr. E. Waltham, the General Secretary of the British Boxing Board of Control.

The B.B.B. of C. have now introduced a new rule, which reads:—
"At the end of each contest, which lasts the scheduled number of rounds, the M.C. shall announce the Referee's final Score."

No doubt many patrons of Boxing Tournaments will wish to test their opinion against that of the Referee, and in order to help, I feel it may be of some assistance to give some of the basic methods of scoring.

The guiding principle in deciding which Boxer has had the better of the round is the QUANTITY and QUALITY of correctly delivered blows which land on the target.

Other factors to be considered are EFFECTIVE AGGRESSION, (leading, etc.) DEFENCE (Guarding, slipping, ducking, etc.).

SCORING PUNCHES are direct, clean blows, with the knuckle part of the closed glove of either hand.

A maximum number of 5 marks (points) is awarded, at the end of a round, to the Boxer assessed to have won the round and a proportionate number to the other contestant; if the round is considered even, both Boxers are awarded 5 marks.

The method of recording is in quarter marks. Thus, if Boxer "A" is slightly superior to Boxer "B" the round would be scored 5 — $4\frac{3}{4}$ in favour of "A". In the event of "A" being substantially superior to "B" the round would be scored 5 — $4\frac{1}{2}$.

To justify scoring 5 — $4\frac{1}{4}$ would imply that the winner was vastly superior to his opponent and possibly sent him down for a long count.

At the conclusion of the contest the Boxer securing the greater number of marks is declared the winner, if the Referee's Score Card records both Boxers as having equal marks, the contest is a draw.

Finally, please keep in mind that the Referee is closer to the Boxers than the spectators, also his judgment is based on experience.

# 12. LEEDS UNITED FOOTBALL CLUB: THE FORMATIVE YEARS 1919-1938

## *by David Saffer*

THE BIRTH OF LEEDS UNITED FOOTBALL CLUB followed the demise of Leeds City on 13 October 1919. City's extinction came about when the Football Association expelled them from the Football League for 'allegedly' making improper payments to players during World War One, and their subsequent refusal to offer accounts for inspection.

Sir Frederick Wall, secretary of the Football Association from 1895 to 1934, later wrote of the affair:

*The books were never placed on the table…It was felt that improper payments had been made and that the books would prove this. The Football Association decided to suspend the club, the directors and the official's forever.*

The Lord Mayor of Leeds, Mr Joseph Henry, pleaded for a reversal of the decision, he even offered to take control of the club, but City's refusal to hand over any documentation proved decisive.

The only person to gain re-instatement was club secretary Herbert Chapman after evidence proved he had been working at a munitions factory at the time of the 'alleged' illegal payments. He went on to become one of the greatest managers of all time during spells at Huddersfield Town and Arsenal. Auctioneers, S Whittham & Sons, were instructed to sell the goalposts, nets, boots, strips, medical equipment, even the shower baths! The players were auctioned off at the *Metropole Hotel* on the afternoon of 17 October 1919. The event was advertised as 'A Sale of Effects', and some thirty clubs turned up. Leeds City's squad was eventually sold for £10,150, Billy McLeod (171 goals from 289 games) generating the greatest fee of £1,250 from Notts County. Within hours of the auction at the *Metropole Hotel* one thousand devastated supporters gathered at Salem Central Hall for a meeting chaired by Leeds solicitor Alf Masser. The renaissance began.

A proposal that a new professional club be formed was carried unanimously; a supporters club was formed in addition to a seven-man committee who would run the club. The aim was simple,

Football League status for the City of Leeds. Joe Henry jun. was appointed the club's first chairman within twenty-four hours as the difficult path to formation began.

The first step back into football was to place adverts in the *Athletic News* and local press for players. United then joined the Midland League on 31 October 1919 after an invitation by its secretary, Mr J Nicholson, to replace Leeds City reserves. The club then moved back into Elland Road after Yorkshire Amateurs, who had been renting the ground, agreed to leave. The key to eventual success however was the financial support and dedication given by Mr J Hilton Crowther, then chairman of Huddersfield Town!

Disillusioned at a lack of local support for his own club, Crowther proposed to move Huddersfield 'lock, stock and barrel' to Elland Road. Many of the players were happy with this proposal and the majority of United's board agreed. The Football League received Crowther's proposal and gave Huddersfield till 31 December 1919 to pay off Crowther. However, in a bizarre twist Huddersfield supporters, appalled at losing their home team, demanded a right to buy Crowther out and set about raising the necessary £25,000. Meanwhile, Crowther, now United's chairman, loaned £35,000 to be repaid when Leeds reached the First Division, and began to develop a club he was convinced had more potential long term. His fellow directors were Masser, Barker, Kaye Aspinall and William Platts. Crowther's first appointment was Arthur Fairclough as secretary-manager on 26 February 1920. This was an inspired decision. Fairclough's playing career had been cut short whilst still a junior, but he had guided Barnsley to two FA Cup finals (winning in 1912) and Huddersfield to promotion and an FA Cup final.

Leeds United's first ever match was a friendly against Yorkshire Amateurs on 15 November 1919, United winning 5-2. A week later Leeds began their one and only campaign in the Midland League. After a 0-0 draw with Barnsley they eventually finished in mid-table. As the team found their 'footballing' feet, Crowther travelled the country throughout the spring canvassing for Football League votes. On 31 May 1920 his efforts were rewarded when Leeds polled the highest number of votes for Football League status.

Throughout the summer months Fairclough added to his squad and by August 28 1920 they were ready for their first match in the Football League against Port Vale. The club colours were blue and white striped shirts. Although the team consisting of Down, Duffield, Tillotson, Musgrove, Baker (captain), Walton, Mason, Goldthorpe, Thompson, Lyon and Best, lost 2-0, a new era had dawned (Figure 1).

**Figure 1.** Leeds United's first squad 1920-21: *Back row, from left to right:* Barker, Crowther (chairman), Duffield, Cooper, Hart, Brown, Jacklin, Downs, Cooper, Walton, Jeffries, Stead (asst. manager), Fairclough (manager), Murrell (trainer). *Middle row, from left to right:* Frew, Spencer, Lyons, Elson, Thompson, Stuart, Goldthorpe, Reynolds. *Front row, from left to right:* Armitage, Mason, Baker (captain), Tillotson, Musgrove, McGee, Best. *Photograph used courtesy of Yorkshire Evening Post Newspapers*

Jim Baker was the first captain of Leeds United, a centre half of experience, intelligence and enthusiasm, he was a commanding presence in defence and would play 208 matches for the club.

Len Armitage scored the first league goal in the club's history at Elland Road in a 1-2 defeat by South Shields on 1 September 1920, the first league victory followed three days later when Port Vale were defeated 3-1 at Elland Road in front of 16,958 spectators. Leeds finished the season in fourteenth place, and with an average attendance of 16,000 the future looked promising. Top-scorer during the campaign was Bob Thompson, a pre-season signing from Durham City, with eleven league goals. In what proved to be his only season at the club Thompson also became the first United player to score a hat-trick in a 'league' match when Notts County were defeated 3-0.

In United's 1921-22 campaign Jack Swan began to make a name for himself. His ten league goals included a hat-trick against Coventry City in a 5-2 victory at Elland Road.

**Figure 2.** Leeds United's squad 1923-24: *Back row, from left to right:* Murrell (trainer), Bell, Coates, Robson, Armand, Menzies, Flood, Gordon, Noble, Duffield, Ure (asst. trainer). *Third row, from left to right:* L. Baker, Frew, Smith, Hart, Morris, Bell, Swan, A. Baker, Gascoigne, Harris. *Second row, from left to right:* Whalley, Johnson, Shirwin, Poyntz, Norman (team manager), Crowther, (chairman), Fairclough (secretary-manager), Richmond, Powell. *Front row, from left to right:* Fullam, Down, Lambert, Mason, J. Baker (captain), Allen, Whipp, Speak. *Photograph used courtesy of Yorkshire Evening Post Newspapers*

The only other hat-trick came in a 3-0 victory over Leicester City from Ivan Poyntz just hours after he had got married, and a week after becoming the first United player to be sent off in a 1-2 defeat at Bury! United finished encouragingly eighth.

During the 1922-23 season a new star settled into the side, Percy Whipp. Whipp got off to a fairytale start, scoring a hat-trick in United's 3-1 triumph over West Ham on November 4 1922; the first debutante at the club to do so. Whipp finished top-scorer in the league with fifteen goals. United improved their league position for the third season running, finishing seventh, and with the superb defensive partnership of Baker and Hart, ably supported by Whalley in goal, and full-backs Duffield and Frew, the team was ready to push for promotion the following term (Figure 2).

United's squad began the 1923-24 season in confident mood. The campaign would be underpinned by two winning streaks. Initially during the autumn months Leeds won consecutive matches against Hull City 2-1 and 5-2 (Richmond scoring a hat-trick); Clapton Orient 1-0 and 1-0; Port Vale 1-0 and 3-0; and Bradford City 1-0. Then after a brief lull in form they won a further six matches consecutively against Sheffield Wednesday 1-0; Coventry City 3-1; Bristol City 1-0; South Shields 2-1; and Southampton 1-0 and 3-0. Promotion was achieved on 21 April 1924 at home to Stockport County with a resounding 4-0 win, Swan 2, Richmond and Harris scoring.

United wrapped up the Division Two title in their penultimate match of the season at home to Nelson (Figure 3). Surprisingly neither of their leading strikers, Swan nor Whipp, struck the solitary goal of the match with just three minutes remaining; that honour fell to winger Walter Coates. A rare moment of glory for Coates, his strike was one of only 3 in 47 league appearances, but what a crucial one, guaranteeing him a unique place in the club's history. Nevertheless for the twin-strikers it had been a great campaign. Swan, who struck eighteen goals, had a venomous left-foot shot and was

**Figure 3.** The team sheet from United's historic match against Nelson, April 26 1924.

always a constant danger to defenders; he went on to score fifty goals in 116 appearances. As for Whipp, who scored fifteen goals, fans loved his inventive and skilful play, dubbing him 'the arch general'. Whipp would score a total of forty-seven goals in 154 games for Leeds.

At the end of the campaign Crowther decided to resign, though he would stay on the board till his death in 1957. Having invested £54,000 he wanted his £35,000 loan back. Major Albert Braithwaite took over and promised £5,000 to the club if the public helped raise the remaining £30,000. Many fundraising events took place including a 'Lend us a Fiver' campaign, but even after World War Two £15,000 was still outstanding!

Hilton Crowther's investment of time and money must never be forgotten, without his efforts and inspired leadership the likes of John Charles, Billy Bremner, Jack Charlton would never have been.

In their first season in top-flight football (1924-25) a record crowd of 33,722 witnessed a 1-1 draw with Sunderland. Swan scored United's goal and once again top-scored with eleven goals as the players fought a relegation battle, a task they just achieved. The best result of the season came when the team bounced back from a 1-6 mauling at Arsenal to hammer Aston Villa 6-0 (Whipp scoring a hat-trick) on Christmas Day. As the players toiled Fairclough brought in new faces, wing-half Willis Edwards, centre-forward Tom Jennings and inside-left Russell Wainscoat. All would serve United with distinction.

During pre-season 1925-26 the offside law changed (a player could not be offside if two, rather than three, opponents were closer to their own goal line when the ball was last played). The upshot was goals galore. United's players found it difficult to adapt and just avoided relegation. Safety was only confirmed in the last match at home to Tottenham when Leeds put on their best display all season, winning 4-1. For Tom Jennings (Figure 4) the rule change was fantastic, his twenty-six goals made him by far United's top-scorer. His best return of goals began in a 3-6 defeat at Burnley on Boxing Day, his strike being the first of ten in nine games. As for his best performance, that came in a home clash with title challengers Arsenal, a match Leeds won 4-2 with Jennings grabbing a hat-trick.

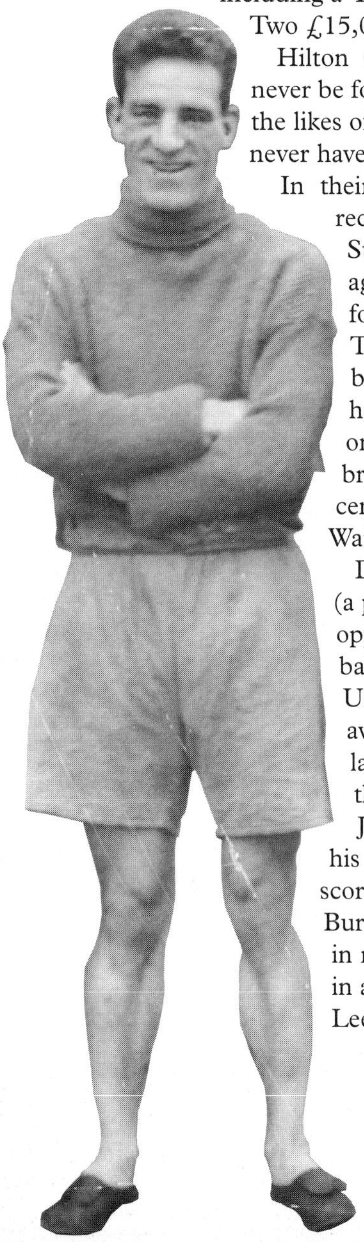

**Figure 4.** Tom Jennings was a scoring phenomenon for Leeds, netting 117 goals in 174 matches.
*Photograph used courtesy of Yorkshire Evening Post Newspapers.*

Two seasons struggling in the First Division ended with a 4-1 defeat at White Hart Lane. Sadly, inconsistency had cost them dear. On their day they could perform, as illustrated in a 6-3 win over West Ham in their final home game of the season, but overall they were unable to cope.

Although the 1926-27 campaign ended in bitter disappointment, for Jennings it had been an incredible season. Of the club's sixty-nine league goals he struck thirty-five. His tally included hat-tricks against Arsenal, Liverpool, Blackburn and Bury. In addition, he produced a scoring sequence that will probably never be bettered, striking nineteen goals in nine games, of which eleven were in consecutive matches against Arsenal (3), Liverpool (4) and Blackburn (4).

Following relegation Arthur Fairclough resigned, Leeds replaced him with Dick Ray. Strengthened by new-boys John White and Tom Mitchell, United announced their intentions in their opening match of the 1927-28 season by destroying South Shields 5-1. Their stay in Division Two would last just one season (Figure 5).

As in their previous promotion success, two winning steaks proved crucial. The first during the winter saw United win seven consecutive matches against Chelsea 5-0; Bristol City 2-1; Stoke City 5-1; Port Vale 2-1 and 3-0; South Shields 3-0 and Southampton 4-1. The second during the run-in gleaned nine more victories (in eleven

**Figure 5.** Leeds players line up prior to a fixture in 1927/28.
*Photograph used courtesy of Yorkshire Evening Post Newspapers*

games) against Fulham 2-1; Oldham Athletic 1-0; Notts County 6-0 (Keetley 3); Reading 1-0; Blackpool 4-0; West Brom 1-0; Wolves 3-0; Clapton Orient 4-0 (Keetley 3) and Chelsea 3-2. Even though Leeds lost their last two matches of the season, promotion had been achieved. Finishing on fifty-seven points, United scored ninety-eight goals, of which four or more goals were scored on ten occasions.

Top-scorers during the campaign were John White and Tom Jennings with twenty-one goals. Backing them up were Russell Wainscoat and a mid-season rookie from non-league football Charlie Keetley (eighteen goals apiece). In a marvellous achievement by the strikers it must be pointed out that Jennings total came in twenty-six starts whilst Keetley's came in just sixteen outings!

Despite some heavy defeats in 1928-29, most notably a 1-6 defeat at Huddersfield and 2-8 defeat at West Ham, Leeds had as many good days as bad as they settled for a mid-table position. Keetley with twenty goals and Wainscoat eighteen once again led the way in attack; Keetley grabbing hat-tricks against Aston Villa 4-1, Leicester City 4-1 and Everton 3-1.

Leeds introduced a number of new faces at the start of the 1929-30 season, including Jack Milburn; one of three brothers to represent the club. The changes improved results, United having their best season since formation. They even challenged for the title in the autumn, winning seven consecutive games against Everton 2-1; Sheffield Wednesday 2-1; Porstmouth 1-0; Burnley 3-0; Sunderland 4-1; Bolton 2-1 and Birmingham 1-0. Eventually though they finished fifth, a position not bettered for thirty-five years, and had the satisfaction of gaining a double over the champions-elect Sheffield Wednesday. At the heart of this success was the defensive partnership of Edwards and Hart. In attack no one person starred, though Wainscoat with fifteen league goals just shaded Jennings effort of fourteen, however Jennings achieved his figures in twenty-three games compared to Wainscoats' forty.

Willis Edwards signed for Leeds in 1925 and developed into one of the finest wing half's of his day, making 444 appearances. Edwards had everything: speed, control, strength, and stamina. He timed tackles effortlessly and to perfection, and could pass with superb timing and precision. Edwards preferred technique to brute strength. Never booked or sent off, he was a huge contrast to the stereotype 'hard' defenders of his era. Edwards was the first United player to represent England; in all winning sixteen caps. Ernie Hart signed at eighteen and proved to be an inspirational captain (Figure 6). A solid defender who dealt uncompromisingly with opposing forwards, Hart

**Figure 6.** Leeds United 1929-30. Back row, from left to right: Dick Ray (manager), George Reed, Ernie Hart, Jimmy Potts, George Milburn, Tom Jennings, A. Campbell (trainer). Front row, from left to right: Bobby Turnbull, John White, Willis Edwards, Harry Roberts, Russell Wainscoat, Tom Mitchell. *Photograph used courtesy of The Breedon Books Publishing Company Limited*

may have had a reputation for being a 'hard man', but he was sent off just once in his career. Not just a powerful centre-half, Hart had tremendous skill and tactical ability, being able to read a game brilliantly. Hart played 447 league games for Leeds and won eight England caps. Russell Wainscoat scored ninety-three times in 226 games for Leeds (Figure 6). Tall, strong, sharp and intelligent, Wainscoat not only scored his quota of goals but made far more for his colleagues. His skills deserved more than just one England cap. Tom Jennings appearances and tally of goals for Leeds would have been far greater had he not missed so many matches due to bouts of blood poisoning. Nevertheless his scoring record (117 goals) stacks up against the best anyone at the club has achieved. Top-scorer in three consecutive seasons (1926-28), Jennings chief attributes were strength and doggedness. A determined striker, he was hard to dispossess and proved a real handful for defenders when he ran at them at pace. Sadly, Jennings never really fulfilled his full potential.

There was a genuine belief that Leeds could challenge for the title in 1930-31 but unbelievably the players failed to build on the progress made the previous season and survival depended on the last match of the season at home to Derby County. A victory was essential, but Leeds were also reliant on Blackpool losing at Manchester City. Keetley saw to the first part, grabbing a brace in a 3-1 win, but a late equaliser at Maine Road by Blackpool meant relegation to Division Two again (Figure 7). The most galling aspect for the team was that they had defeated Blackpool earlier in the season 7-3, the only occasion then and now that a United eleven has scored seven away from home in a league encounter. In addition they had hammered Middlesborough 7-0 and Manchester United 5-0 (Turnbull 3). Inconsistency had cost the team dear. In

Figure 7. Charlie Keetley's career overlapped Tom Jennings, and like his teammate had an amazing strike-rate; scoring 110 goals in 169 appearances. He was spotted whilst netting 80 goals in the 1926-27 season for Alvaston and Boulton, and joined Leeds in July 1927. In his debut season he scored on his first four appearances and during his Leeds career Keetley top-scored in 1928-29, 1930-31 and 1931-32. In addition he scored three hat-tricks in consecutive seasons (1927-28, 1928-29); and is still the only player to score a hat-trick in six successive seasons (1927-28 to 1932-33).
*Photograph used courtesy of Yorkshire Evening Post Newspapers*

the depths of depression was one major plus, the budding half-back combination of Edwards-Hart-Copping. The threesome would not only all play for England, but would as a unit only be bettered at Elland Road by the Bremner-Charlton-Hunter combination of the Revie era.

Before the start of the 1931-32 season Leeds City alderman Eric Clarke took over from Braithwaite as chairman. Ray built his side around the backbone of Edwards, Hart and Copping, and added a number of fine players to his side including on the left flank Billy Furness and Tom Cochrane.

Within weeks life became sweet again as the players embarked on a club-record nine successive league victories that ultimately gain them promotion again. During this excellent run the vanquished teams were Bristol City 2-0; Oldham Athletic 5-0; Bury 4-1; Wolves 2-1; Charlton 1-0; Stoke 2-0; Manchester United 5-2; Preston North End 4-1 and Burnley 5-0. Only a late stutter towards end of the campaign denied the players a richly deserved title, but as in 1927-28 the runners-up spot was achieved. The stars of the season were undoubtedly Keetley, who once again top scored (twenty-three goals), and the ever-dependable Copping.

In 1932-33 a fourteen-match unbeaten run pushed Leeds to the edge of the title race, especially after a Boxing Day win at Herbert Chapman's Arsenal. Twenty-four hours later 56,796, the biggest crowd in the club's history at the time, crammed into Elland Road for the return. The 0-0 draw was anything but dull. Played at a relentless pace it was great entertainment. Above all, proof was there for all to see that the public of Leeds would come out in force if the team could challenge at the top of Division One. Sadly, seven defeats during February and March finished their title challenge. In addition, the big crowds quickly vanished, down to 9,000 for the final home game with Middlesborough. However, on the field Ray's team, built from limited funds, produced many fine performances, none better than their victories over Liverpool 5-0 and Newcastle United 6-1. Leeds finished eighth; Arthur Hydes top-scoring on sixteen. Off the field Alf Masser, so influential in the early days, replaced Clarke as chairman.

During the 1933-34 campaign Hydes appearances were curtailed through injury and undoubtedly his total of sixteen goals in just nineteen appearances would have been far greater had he remained fit. The highlights of his season were hat-tricks in a 5-2 win over Middlesborough and a 4-0 triumph over Blackburn. Unfortunately injury meant he missed out on United's 8-0 demolition of Leicester City in a league encounter on April 7 1934, Duggan, Mahon, Furness and Firth grabbing a brace of goals each. This club record for a win in the league still stands.

In 1934-35 Leeds began the season without Wilf Copping, a £6000 fee taking him to the defending champions Arsenal who went on to retain their title. Copping was the original 'hard man', a rock, no one frightened him, just his stare could frighten opponents (Figure 8). Copping was utterly fearless; he would shoulder charge like a bull. He never shaved on match days, which added to his 'hard man' image. However he was not just a tackler, he could pass with accuracy with the best of them. Idolised, Copping, capped twenty times by England, played 183 games for Leeds and fans would never forget this wonderful player with the bone-crunching tackle.

As for the season, Leeds fought a relegation battle throughout. There were some desperate results at Stoke 1-8 (an unwelcome club record!), West Brom 3-6, and Chelsea 1-7 (after taking an early lead).

Mid-term the team changed their club colours from blue and white stripes to blue and gold halved shirts, white shorts and blue stockings with gold tops. In addition, Ray resigned. Billy Hampson

**Figure 8.** Leeds United line up during their 1933-34 campaign: *Back row, from left to right:* Hornby, G. Milburn, Moore, Jones, J. Milburn, Copping. *Front row, from left to right:* Mahon, Roper, Hart, Keetley, Furness, Cochrane. Missing from this team group is Arthur Hydes.

*Photograph used courtesy of The Breedon Books Publishing Company Limited*

took over and guided the team to safety with two games to spare. Top-scorer was a fit-again Hydes who struck twenty-two goals in 30 games, including a hat-trick in the biggest win of the campaign at home to Blackburn 5-1.

In 1935-36 United finished eleventh; the highlights being back-to-back home wins over Sheffield Wednesday 7-2, Harry Duggan grabbing his only hat-trick for the club (forty-five goals in 187 appearances), and Bolton Wanderers 5-2. George Brown, in his only season at the club, top scored with eighteen goals.

An unusual record was created when Jack Milburn scored nine penalties during the campaign. Milburn would miss just a handful of games throughout his career at Leeds, amassing 408 appearances. Sadly the campaign would finish with stalwart defender Ernie Hart playing his last games at Elland Road after his distinguished career. Today, Hart still resides in the top-ten list for league appearances at the club. There could be no better representative from this era.

In 1936-37 Leeds gained just three points away from home all season and looked relegation certainties for long periods. Their biggest problem was key striker Arthur Hydes being injured for long spells. In desperation Hampson signed thirty-four-year old Gordon Hodgson. Signing the veteran striker may have been perceived as desperation but the South African had an impeccable pedigree, having hit 233 goals in 258 games for Liverpool. Hodgson lived up to his reputation, scoring on his debut; a 1-7 defeat at Everton, but crucially he scored in three of United's four victories during the run-in; the last a 3-0 win over Sunderland in the penultimate game of the season. Leeds defeated Portsmouth 3-1 in the last game to eventually finish nineteenth.

Top-scorer for the third consecutive campaign was Hydes with eleven in ninteen appearances, however this would be his last season at the club. Top-scorer on four occasions, he amassed eighty-two goals in 137 appearances during his time at the club.

With Hodgson in attack Leeds looked comfortable again, and with a solid defence, that included Bert Sprotson, Jack Milburn and Tom Holley, they finished the 1937-38 campaign in ninth position. It could have been higher; in November they had sat third, but a poor

**Figure 9.** Leeds United 1938-39: Back row, from left to right: Jack Hargreaves, Willis Edwards, Jim, Twomey, Tom Holley, Ken Gadsby, Bobby Browne. Front row, from left to right: Tom Cochrane, George Ainsley, Jack Milburn, Gordon Hodgson, Eric Stephenson.

*Photograph used courtesy of The Breedon Books Publishing Company Limited*

run between February and March ended that hope. Unsurprisingly Hodgson top-scored with twenty-five league goals, including four in the most entertaining match of the season at home to Everton, a thriller that ended 4-4.

The final season before the outbreak of War saw Leeds finish thirteenth, the highlight an 8-2 defeat of Leicester on October 1 1938 with Hodgson scoring a club-record five goals (Figure 9). In all Hodgson scored 53 goals for Leeds in 86 games, a wonderful strike-rate.

On 2 September 1939 Leeds lost at home to Sheffield United the following day Britain declared war on Germany. All Football League fixtures were suspended and regional tournaments began. For Leeds, like many clubs, an uncertain future lay ahead, but with an average gate of 19,300 there was plenty of scope for improvement when the professional game resumed.

Leeds United had come a long way in the twenty years since formation. Although, due to financial constraints, they had to develop talent and sell when the price was right, they had undoubtedly proved they could hold their own; spending thirteen seasons out of nineteen in the top-flight. Many fine players had represented the team, a number had won international recognition, but above all the board knew that if they produced a winning team massive crowds could be attracted. The future beckoned.

## Further Reading

1 Don Warters, *Leeds United - The Official History of the Club.* Wensum Books (Norwich) Ltd, 1979.
2 Malcolm Macdonald & Martin Jarred, *The Leeds United Cup Book 1920-1991*, The Breedon Books Publishing Company Limited, 1991.
3 Malcolm Macdonald & Martin Jarred, *The Leeds United Story*, The Breedon Books Publishing Company Limited, 1992.
4 Malcolm Macdonald & Martin Jarred, *Leeds United A Complete Record*, The Breedon Books Publishing Company Limited, 1996.
5 Andrew Mourant, *The Official Illustrated History of Leeds 1919-1996*, Reed International Books Ltd, 1996.
6 David Saffer and Howard Dapin, *Leeds United Football Club*, Tempus Publishing Ltd, 1999.
7 Andrew Mourant, *Essential History Leeds United*, Headline Book Publishing, 2000.

## Acknowledgements

My sincere thanks to the Yorkshire Evening Post Newspapers and The Breedon Books Publishing Company Limited for allowing me to use their photographs; Leeds United and Tony Lazenby for allowing me to use their match programmes.

# CONTRIBUTORS

---

## 1. THE ABERFORD FLY LINE

---

**Graham Hudson** was born and educated in Leeds, attending the Leeds Central High School and Leeds College of Art. Until retirement in 1998 he was a senior lecturer at the Kent Institute of Art & Design based in Canterbury. His interests embrace both Yorkshire and Kent local history and the history of printing and design. He is a founder member (1974) and secretary of the Ephemera Society, and has had many articles on aspects of design history published in the *Ephemerist* and other journals. His Shire Album *The Victorian Printer* was published in 1996. Graham's initial research on the Aberford Fly Line was carried out whilst studying for his Art Teacher's Diploma in 1962-3, when he made it the subject of his ATD thesis. Further research resulted in his book *The Aberford Railway & the History of the Garforth Collieries*, published by David & Charles in 1971. Having a future second edition in mind, he would welcome further information on the railway, the collieries and the Gascoigne family.

---

## 2. ROUNDHAY HALL

---

**Margaret Plows** (née Thirsk) was born in Leeds, and lived at the Lodge, Roundhay Hall until she married and moved to Bradford in 1971. Returning to Leeds in 1980 Margaret lives with her husband Trevor and their two daughters Sam and Vicky in Gledhow. After leaving Allerton Grange Comprehensive School in 1967 she completed a secretarial course at Park Lane College followed by various office jobs. Her interest in history began at school and from 1990 she studied for several GCSE's at Swarthmore including one in Local and Regional History. Since then she has studied history modules at Leeds University and Springfield Mount gaining the Certificate in Higher Education for Economic and Social History with Local Regional History. For relaxation she especially enjoys gardening, walking, reading and spending time with her family.

## 3. RISE AND FALL OF INDUSTRIALISATION IN BURLEY-IN-WHARFEDALE

**Pam Shaw** worked as a generic social worker in Leeds (principally involved with the needs of elderly people), before moving to Burley-in-Wharfedale in 1980. As a mature student she obtained O levels in English and Psychology and became fascinated by the history of Greenholme Mills whilst studying for a B A (Hons) Social Science Degree in Home and Community Studies. In addition she has a Diploma in Higher Education, certificates in Direct Training (City and Guilds), Counselling in the Development of Learning, Food Hygiene and Tai Chi. She is also an Affiliate to the Institute of Training and Development. As a result of her mature educational achievements Pam became involved in two BBC TV Programmes on age discrimination in the workplace and remains concerned about the rights of older people, feeling that age should not matter unless you are a bottle of wine or a cheese! Pam has three adult children and three grandchildren. She enjoys walking in the Yorkshire Dales and her latest interest is in researching her family history.

## 4. THE END OF THE HILL

**Maisie Morton** was born in Wortley, Leeds and attended West Leeds High School. Before her marriage in 1945 she worked for the LMS at Hunslet Lane Goods Station mostly on the switchboard. She was founder member of the Family History Section of the Yorkshire Archaeological Society and served that section as secretary, editor, chairman and president, writing many articles for the *Family Historian*. Particularly interested in children, she taught at Sunday School for many years, and was connected with other youth movements, besides being a child minder for a considerable time. She also enjoys writing children's stories and long letters. From the later 1960s she has worked for the YAS in voluntary capacity and for the West Yorkshire Archive Service at the YAS at Claremont in Leeds. She has a son and daughter and two grandsons.

## 5. THE LOST VILLAGE OF LOTHERTON

**Dave Weldrake** was born in Dewsbury and has lived most of his life in West Yorkshire. His interest in history and archaeology developed at school. Although he studied English and French at college his passion for the past eventually won out and he went into archaeology after a short spell of teaching. He is now the Education Officer for the West Yorkshire Archaeology Service and a regular panellist on the BBC Radio Leeds history phone-in *Who, What, Where*.

## 6. A BRIEF HISTORY OF THE NATIONAL INSTITUTE OF HOUSEWORKERS, LEEDS 1951-1972

**Christine Nolan** was born in Leeds. She has interests in social history; welfare rights; women's issues and education. She left school at fifteen without any qualifications but returning to education as a mature student. Christine gained a letter of distinction for her research into the Domestic Economy for a BA (Hons) Degree. Christine has contributed to *The Guardian*. She has recently finished studying for an Advanced Diploma in Person-Centred Counselling. Christine lives in Chapel Allerton. In her spare time she is doing research for a book on women who clean in private households, as she feels it is very important to record their oral history. Education, books and travel have enriched her life. The most important people in her life are her husband Trevor and her family who encouraged and supported her return to education, and not forgetting her beloved first grandson, Jack.

## 7. THE HISTORY OF THE LEEDS DENTAL INSTITUTE SCHOOL OF DENTISTRY

**Harold Saffer** was born in Leeds in 1927, and was educated at both the City of Leeds School and Roundhay School. After graduating in Dentistry at Leeds University in 1949, he then served as a Dental Officer in the Army for two years, spending the majority of the time in Egypt, followed by two years as a Dental Officer in the Territorial Army. Subsequently, he worked in general practice and the School Dental Services in Leeds and the West Riding. In 1953, he was awarded a Fellowship in Children's Dentistry to study at the Guggenheim Institute in New York. Returning to England in 1954, he settled down, having general practices in the Hyde Park, Park Row, and Park Square areas of Leeds. During that time, he also did voluntary dental work for underprivileged children in Israel until retirement in 1997. He married Valerie in 1956, and they have four children and eleven grandchildren, all living locally. Since retiring, they travel extensively, and enjoy spending time with their children and grandchildren.

## 8. DREAM BUILDERS: THE THOMPSONS OF GOLDEN ACRE

**Tony Shelton** was born in London and studied geography at Manchester University and town planning at Leeds School of Town Planning (now part of Leeds Metropolitan University). A twenty-five year stint as a town-planner, mainly with Leicester and Leeds city councils, led to project work, including the restoration of Leeds' Kirkgate Market Hall and the Leeds transport strategy, and city centre management. Early retirement in 1998 provided the opportunity to resurrect his interest in writing and for the research leading to *Dream Builders* and his book on the history of Golden Acre Park, *Leeds' Golden Acres*. He is married with two children and two grandchildren. Interests other than writing include painting, walking, music and family history. He now lives in Grange-over-Sands, Cumbria.

## 9. ARTHUR RANSOME: BORN IN A ROMANTIC TOWN LIKE LEEDS

**Margaret Ratcliffe** was born in Batley and educated at Notre Dame Grammer School in Leeds. Originally trained as a private secretary, she is now a property administrator in Boston Spa. Margaret has lived in Leeds since her marriage and has had a lifetime devotion to Yorkshire CCC, Leeds Rugby League and Leeds United. For many years she contributed regular feature articles to cricket and rugby league magazines, including Cup Final programmes and to two books: *13 Winters* and *13 Worlds*. Some years ago her husbank, Joe, introduced her to the *Swallows & Amazons* series of books by Arthur Ransome and, finding that the author was born in Leeds, she has become a keen researcher and enthusiast on all aspects of the Ransome phenomenon. Margaret contributed the section of the Leeds Homes in the Ransome Society's publication *Ransome at Home*. She has addressed the Society's regional and national gatherings, the Thoresby Society, the Friends of the Dymock Poets and the National Trust on Ransome-related topics.

## 10. A CITIZEN OF WHOM ANY CITY WOULD BE PROUD: ARTHUR GREENHOW LUPTON 1850-1930

**Joan Newiss** was educated at Harehills Primary and Roundhay High Schools and graduated from Nottingham University with an honours degree in Slavonic Studies in 1959. Subsequently, became a Chartered Librarian, employed primarily at the City of Leeds and Carnegie College of Education. Earlier experience in Leeds Reference Library engendered interest in local history, and she is a founder member of the Oakwood and District Historical Society. On a casual visit to a junkshop, she discovered a box a 100-year-old glass negatives of 'Springwood', A G Lupton's first mansion home at Roundhay. The generous loan of archives by his descendants has enabled her to compile this profile of his life and times.

## 11. SECONDS OUT: BOXING IN LEEDS

**Isadore Pear** was born in Leeds in 1920. He left school in 1934 at the age of fourteen and worked in a clothing factory until he was conscripted in May 1940. He served six years in the West Yorkshire Regiment and rose to the rank of Company Sergeant Major, Warrant Officer II. On being demobilized he went into business with his brother establishing the firm C & I Pear Ltd, Clothing Manufacturers. He retired early at the age of fifty-nine and enrolled at Park Lane College as a mature student taking A-levels. He then went on to obtain an LLB(Hons) degree at Leeds Polytechnic. He is an active and prominent member of the Leeds Jewish Community and, although no longer involved, was a founder member of AJEX, the Association of Jewish Ex-Servicemen and Women in Leeds; an organisation which was formed initially to fight anti-semitism. He recently compiled the 120 years history of his synagogue the Beth Hamerdrash Hagadol, and is a regular contributor to its fortnightly broadsheet.

## 12. LEEDS UNITED FOOTBALL CLUB: THE FORMATIVE YEARS 1919-1939

**David Saffer** is Leeds born and has followed the fortunes of Leeds United since 1968 when his father took him at the age of eight to his first match, the 1968 Fairs Cup Final against Ferencvaros. Educated at Roundhay High Grammar School, he gained an Honours Degree in Business Studies in 1985. After seven years selling computers in 'the smoke', relocation brought him back to Leeds. Today he runs his own computer consultancy, IT Support Department Ltd, and in his spare time follows United's current team from the Family Stand with his son. He met his wife Deborah while studying, they married in 1986 and have three children, Daniella, Abigail and Jake. His writing exploits began in 1997 when on the spur of the moment the idea Leeds United Cup Kings 1972 was conceived. Since its publication in March 1998, writing credits include Leeds United Football Club, Leeds Expert, Leeds In Europe, Manchester City Cup Kings 1956, Manchester City 1880-2000 and a contribution in Aspects of Leeds 2.

# INDEX OF PLACES
## (LEEDS AND YORKSHIRE)